10/14

1—

SAM HENDERSON

The Magic Whistle

BLOWS

Other Books by Sam Henderson

Humor Can Be Funny
Oh That Monroe

SAM HENDERSON

The Magic Whistle

BLOWS

St. Martin's Griffin ⚑ New York

The author can be reached at mwhistle@aol.com

Contents originally appeared in *Duplex Planet Illustrated, Flatter, Last Gasp Comics and Stories, New York Press, Pulse!, SPX97, The Stranger,* and *Zero Zero*. Comics on pages 57 and 72 are reprinted by kind permission of David Greenberger.

Introduction copyright © 1999 by Andy Richter.

Edited by Corin See & Dana Albarella

Library of Congress Cataloging-in-Publication Data

ISBN 0-312-24532-7

First Edition: November 1999

10 9 8 7 6 5 4 3 2 1

INTRODUCTION

When you live in New York City, and I mean live as opposed to reside, you end up, without even really trying, acquiring various circles of friends that you probably wouldn't have ever gotten to know if you'd stayed in Portland, or Knoxville, or in my case, Chicago. I have two such circles; my cartoonist friends, and my porno friends. The two groups actually overlap nicely, I suppose because of the combination of the cartoonist's perpetual impoverishment, and the pornographer's perpetual willingness to exploit the impoverished. And then there's also the two groups' shared love of drink.

I relate all this because it was at a cartoonist party to which I was invited by one of my porn pals that I first met Sam Henderson. It was about five years ago, and I had been on television for a year or so. I was on my way to the bathroom when a guy with glasses popped out of the crowd and called me Mr. Richter, which always throws me a little except when I'm being addressed by a hotel clerk. He hurriedly said, ``I do a comic, and I'd like you to read it, and here it is.'' He then shoved a comic in my hand and scurried off, sort of in the way someone in a Benny Hill skit would hand someone a lit bomb and scurry off before the explosion left the recipient soot-faced and blinking.

For some reason, when you're on TV, people give you their stuff all the time; bands send CDs, authors send books, inventors send inventions, and most of the time, the stuff is pretty shitty. So when I got home after the party, I read the xeroxed minicomic the shy guy had given me, and was really surprised. It wasn't shitty. In fact, it was hilarious. Inside this little book—well, pamphlet, really—called ``Magic Whistle'' was a deeply intelligent comedic art masquerading as relentless head-hammering stupidity; in other words, the kind of stuff that makes me happiest; the kind of work to which I aspire.

I've gotten to know Sam better in the years since then, both from reading "Magic Whistle," and from hanging out with him at various parties and artsy-fartsy gatherings. One night stands out in particular: There was this porno party that one of my cartoonist friends told me about, although I guess it wasn't really a porno party per se. It was some sort of fetish-themed night at a club in the meatpacking district that a friend was throwing as a money-making venture. Sam showed up with probably the same intentions that I had—to support our friend—but also to get there early and get as many drinks as we could before leaving when all the corny spanky-spanky "performances" got started. However, they had a dress code. To sport the preferred attire meant getting done up as some sort of S&M robot, or, at the least, uptight (or lazy) party-poopers like myself could get by with wearing all black. Sam, unaware of the costume requirements, came to the door wearing jeans and a blue shirt, and was promptly turned away despite his protests. Rather than giving up, he got on the subway, went all the way home to Brooklyn, changed and came back. He was now wearing the accepted black pants and a black t-shirt, but with a little added touch. A sort of protest, I suppose. Over the outside of his pants he was wearing a pair of regular old white Fruit of the Loom briefs. The velvet rope was unlatched, and Sam waltzed in.

Retarded. Brilliant. That's the Sam Henderson you'll get to know and love as you read this book. He's one of my favorite comedians, and my feelings for him are best summed up by what one of Sam's readers wrote in the letters section of a recent issue of "Magic Whistle": "Fuck those motherfuckers who say your shit's not cool!" Ah, yes. Fuck those motherfuckers, indeed.

ANDY RICHTER
New York City, 1999

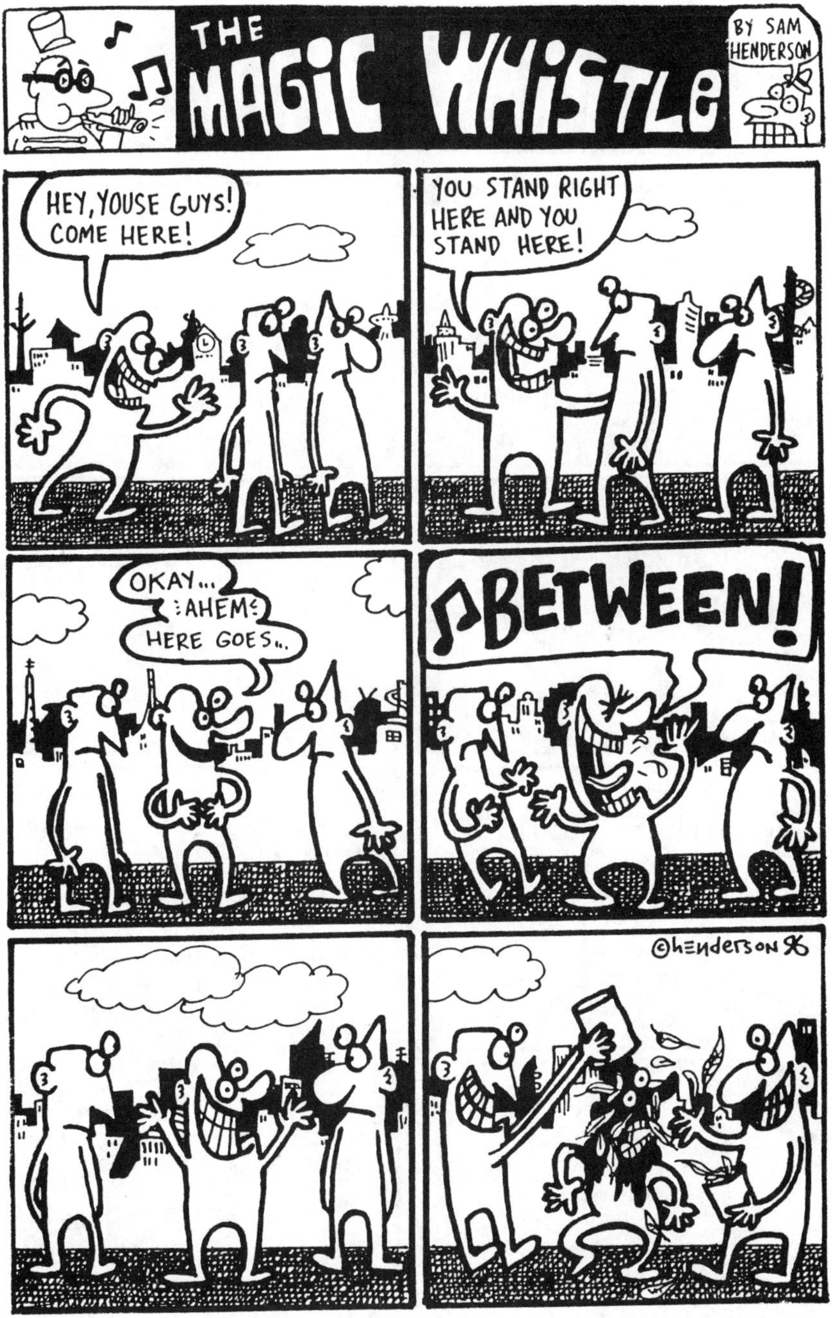
THE MAGIC WHISTLE
BY SAM HENDERSON
HEY, YOUSE GUYS! COME HERE!
YOU STAND RIGHT HERE AND YOU STAND HERE!
OKAY... AHEM HERE GOES...
BETWEEN!
©henderson 96

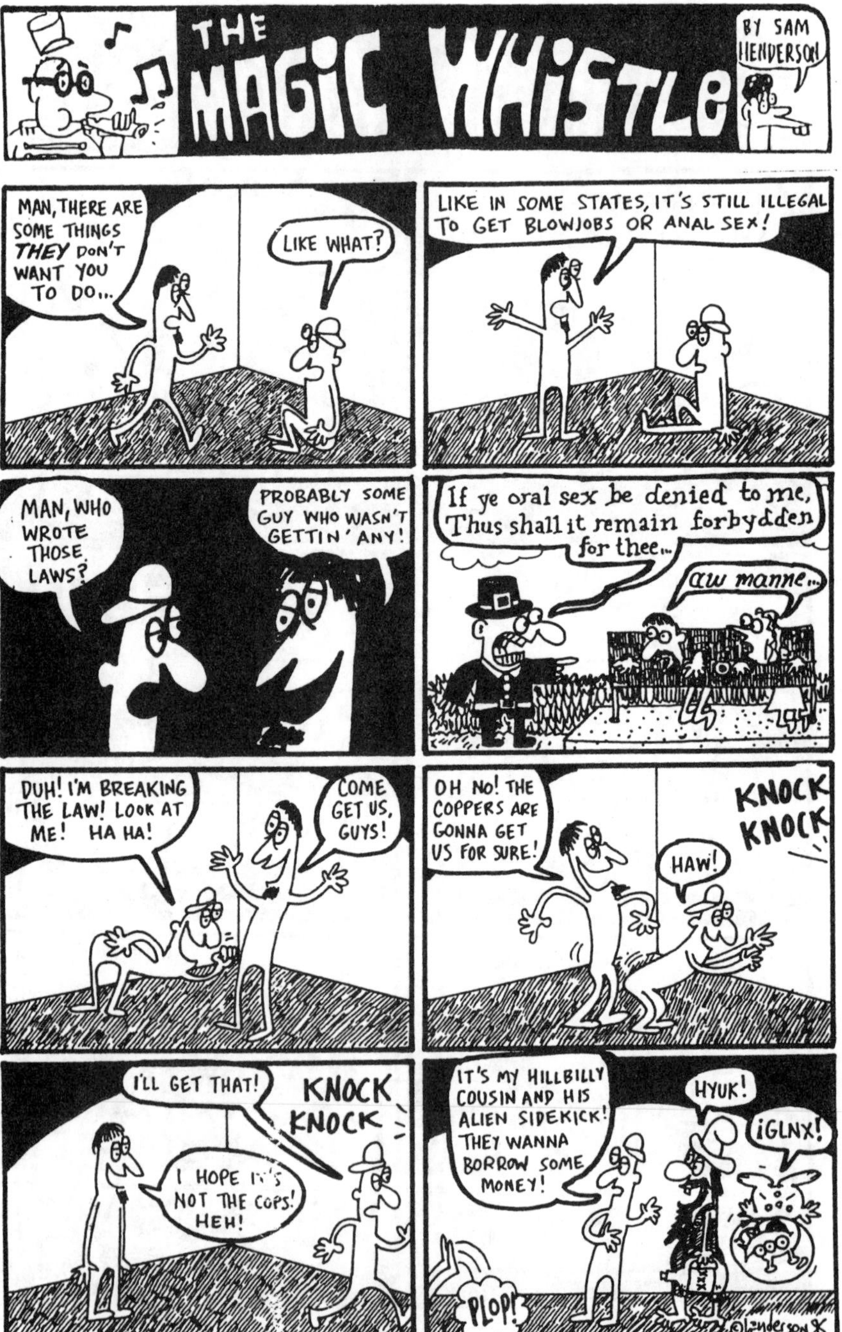
THE MAGIC WHISTLE
BY SAM HENDERSON
MAN, THERE ARE SOME THINGS THEY DON'T WANT YOU TO DO...
LIKE WHAT?
LIKE IN SOME STATES, IT'S STILL ILLEGAL TO GET BLOWJOBS OR ANAL SEX!
MAN, WHO WROTE THOSE LAWS?
PROBABLY SOME GUY WHO WASN'T GETTIN' ANY!
If ye oral sex be denied to me, Thus shall it remain forbydden for thee...
aw manne...
DUH! I'M BREAKING THE LAW! LOOK AT ME! HA HA!
COME GET US, GUYS!
OH NO! THE COPPERS ARE GONNA GET US FOR SURE!
HAW!
KNOCK KNOCK
I'LL GET THAT!
KNOCK KNOCK
I HOPE IT'S NOT THE COPS! HEH!
IT'S MY HILLBILLY COUSIN AND HIS ALIEN SIDEKICK! THEY WANNA BORROW SOME MONEY!
HYUK!
¡GLNX!
PLOP!
©Henderson 96

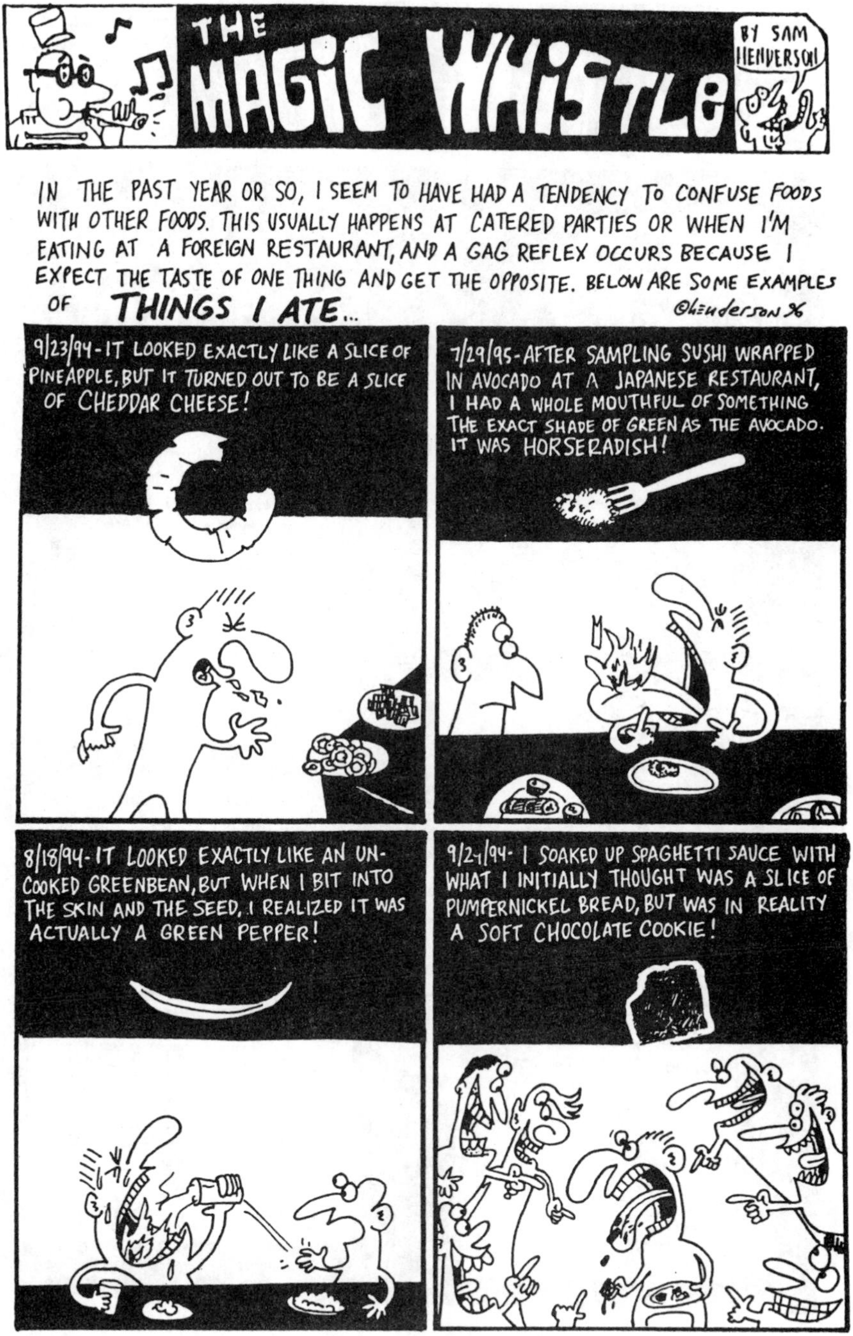
THE MAGIC WHISTLE
BY SAM HENDERSON
IN THE PAST YEAR OR SO, I SEEM TO HAVE HAD A TENDENCY TO CONFUSE FOODS WITH OTHER FOODS. THIS USUALLY HAPPENS AT CATERED PARTIES OR WHEN I'M EATING AT A FOREIGN RESTAURANT, AND A GAG REFLEX OCCURS BECAUSE I EXPECT THE TASTE OF ONE THING AND GET THE OPPOSITE. BELOW ARE SOME EXAMPLES OF
THINGS I ATE...
©henderson 96
9/23/94 - IT LOOKED EXACTLY LIKE A SLICE OF PINEAPPLE, BUT IT TURNED OUT TO BE A SLICE OF CHEDDAR CHEESE!
7/29/95 - AFTER SAMPLING SUSHI WRAPPED IN AVOCADO AT A JAPANESE RESTAURANT, I HAD A WHOLE MOUTHFUL OF SOMETHING THE EXACT SHADE OF GREEN AS THE AVOCADO. IT WAS HORSERADISH!
8/18/94 - IT LOOKED EXACTLY LIKE AN UN-COOKED GREENBEAN, BUT WHEN I BIT INTO THE SKIN AND THE SEED, I REALIZED IT WAS ACTUALLY A GREEN PEPPER!
9/24/94 - I SOAKED UP SPAGHETTI SAUCE WITH WHAT I INITIALLY THOUGHT WAS A SLICE OF PUMPERNICKEL BREAD, BUT WAS IN REALITY A SOFT CHOCOLATE COOKIE!

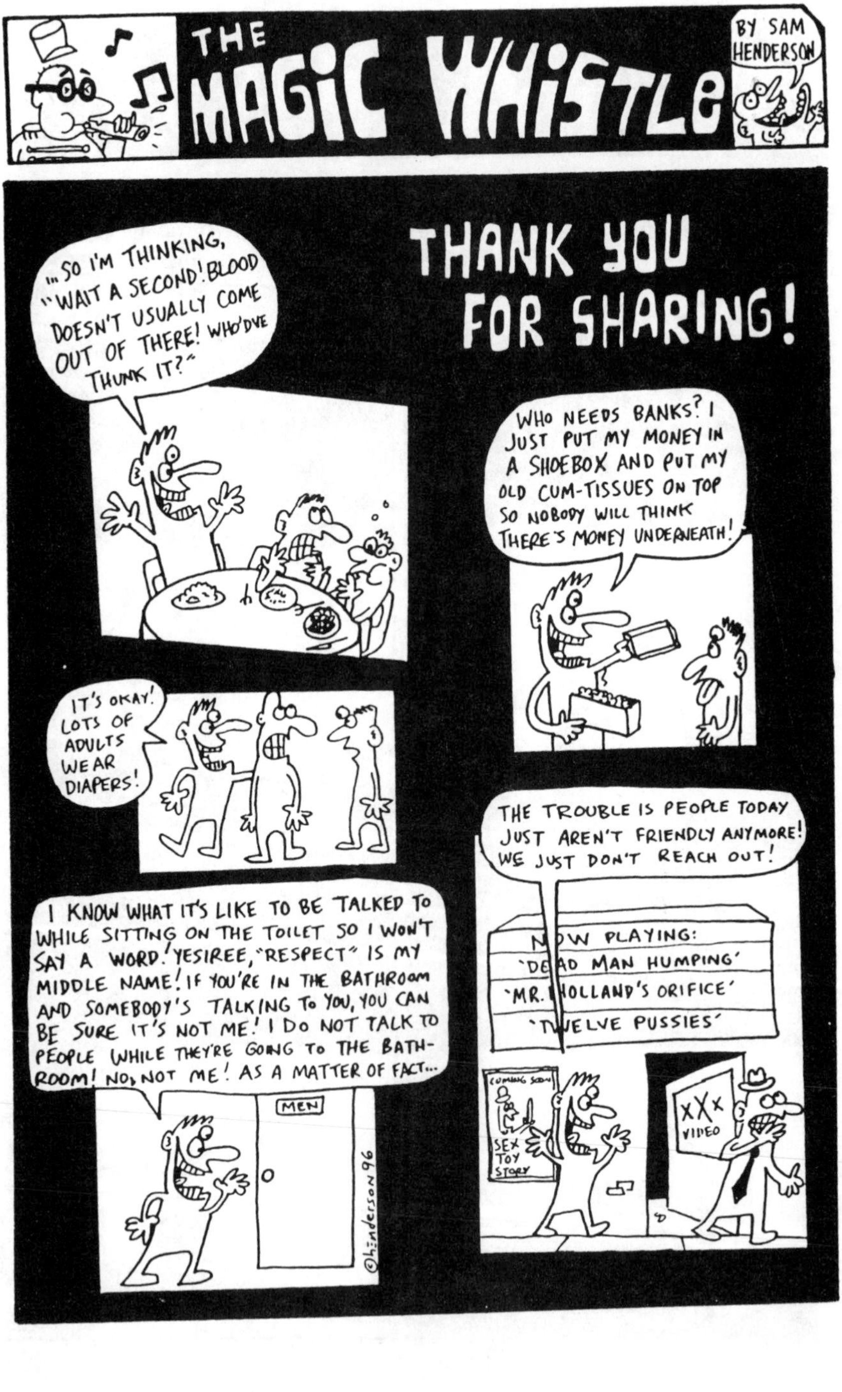
THE MAGIC WHISTLE
BY SAM HENDERSON
THANK YOU FOR SHARING!
...SO I'M THINKING, "WAIT A SECOND! BLOOD DOESN'T USUALLY COME OUT OF THERE! WHO'DVE THUNK IT?"
WHO NEEDS BANKS? I JUST PUT MY MONEY IN A SHOEBOX AND PUT MY OLD CUM-TISSUES ON TOP SO NOBODY WILL THINK THERE'S MONEY UNDERNEATH!
IT'S OKAY! LOTS OF ADULTS WEAR DIAPERS!
THE TROUBLE IS PEOPLE TODAY JUST AREN'T FRIENDLY ANYMORE! WE JUST DON'T REACH OUT!
NOW PLAYING:
'DEAD MAN HUMPING'
'MR. HOLLAND'S ORIFICE'
'TWELVE PUSSIES'
SEX TOY STORY
XXX VIDEO
I KNOW WHAT IT'S LIKE TO BE TALKED TO WHILE SITTING ON THE TOILET SO I WON'T SAY A WORD! YESIREE, "RESPECT" IS MY MIDDLE NAME! IF YOU'RE IN THE BATHROOM AND SOMEBODY'S TALKING TO YOU, YOU CAN BE SURE IT'S NOT ME! I DO NOT TALK TO PEOPLE WHILE THEY'RE GOING TO THE BATHROOM! NO, NOT ME! AS A MATTER OF FACT...
MEN
©henderson96

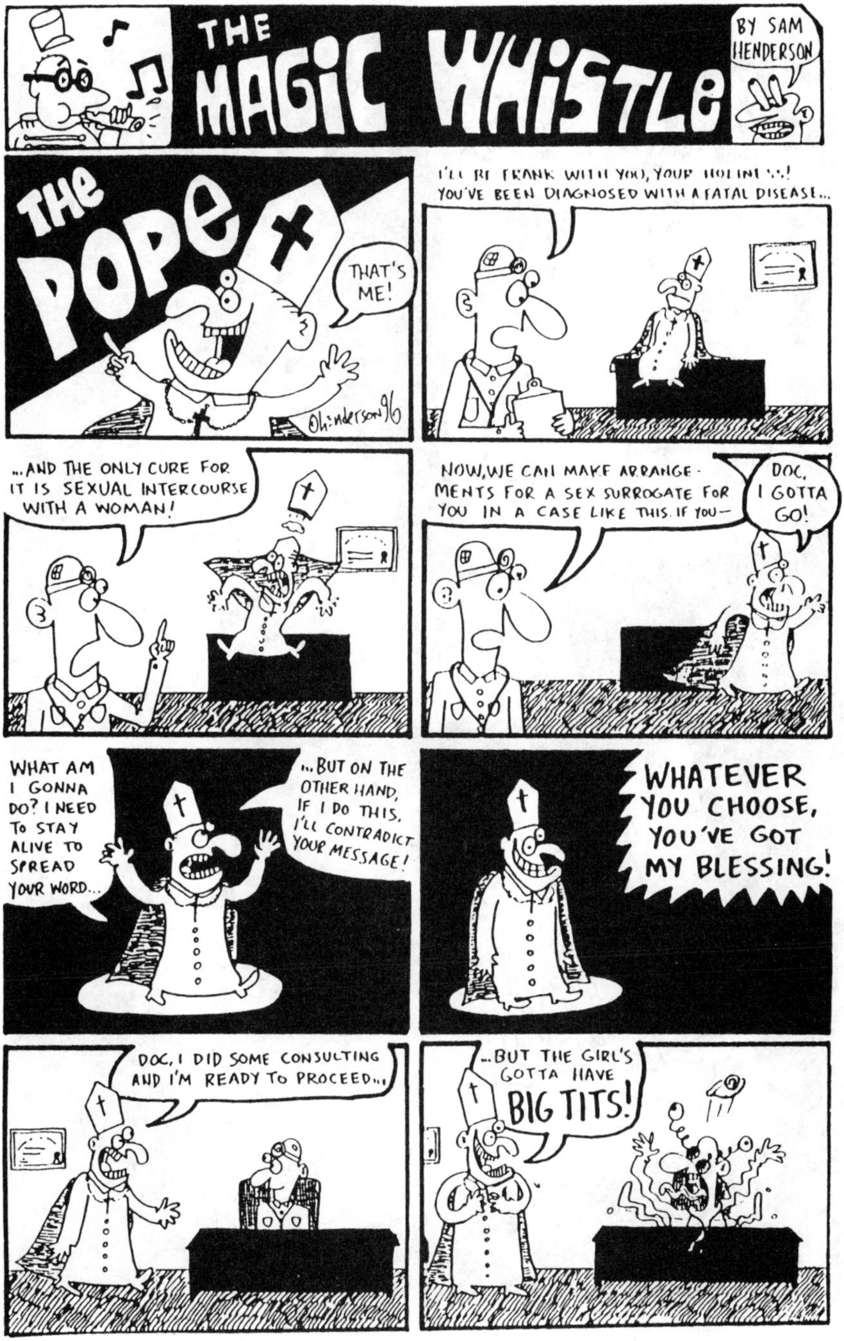
THE MAGIC WHISTLE
BY SAM HENDERSON
THE POPE
THAT'S ME!
©Henderson 96
I'LL BE FRANK WITH YOU, YOUR HOLINESS! YOU'VE BEEN DIAGNOSED WITH A FATAL DISEASE...
...AND THE ONLY CURE FOR IT IS SEXUAL INTERCOURSE WITH A WOMAN!
NOW, WE CAN MAKE ARRANGE-MENTS FOR A SEX SURROGATE FOR YOU IN A CASE LIKE THIS. IF YOU—
DOC, I GOTTA GO!
WHAT AM I GONNA DO? I NEED TO STAY ALIVE TO SPREAD YOUR WORD...
...BUT ON THE OTHER HAND, IF I DO THIS, I'LL CONTRADICT YOUR MESSAGE!
WHATEVER YOU CHOOSE, YOU'VE GOT MY BLESSING!
DOC, I DID SOME CONSULTING AND I'M READY TO PROCEED...
...BUT THE GIRL'S GOTTA HAVE BIG TITS!

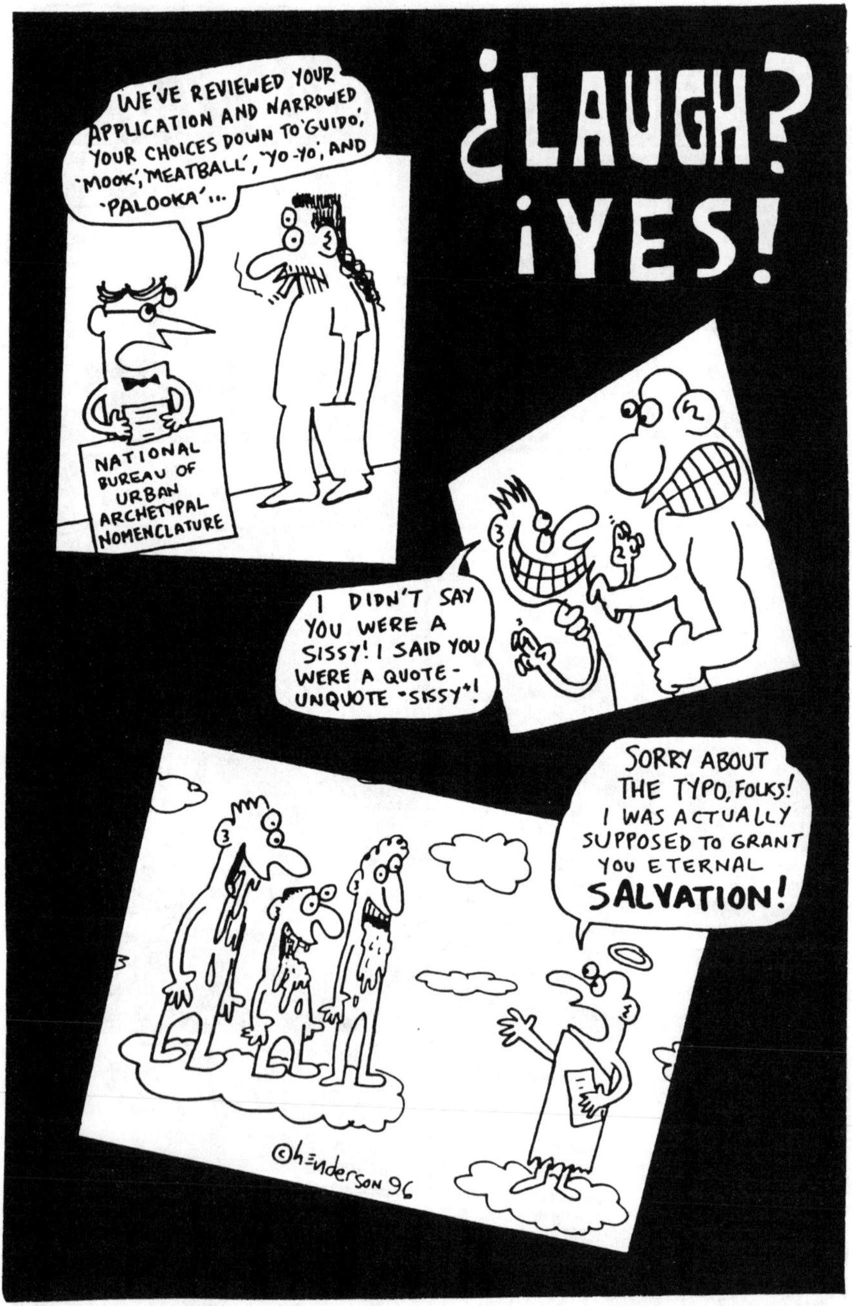

¿LAUGH? ¡YES!
WE'VE REVIEWED YOUR APPLICATION AND NARROWED YOUR CHOICES DOWN TO 'GUIDO', 'MOOK', 'MEATBALL', 'YO-YO', AND 'PALOOKA'...
NATIONAL BUREAU OF URBAN ARCHETYPAL NOMENCLATURE
I DIDN'T SAY YOU WERE A SISSY! I SAID YOU WERE A QUOTE-UNQUOTE "SISSY"!
SORRY ABOUT THE TYPO, FOLKS! I WAS ACTUALLY SUPPOSED TO GRANT YOU ETERNAL SALVATION!
©henderson 96

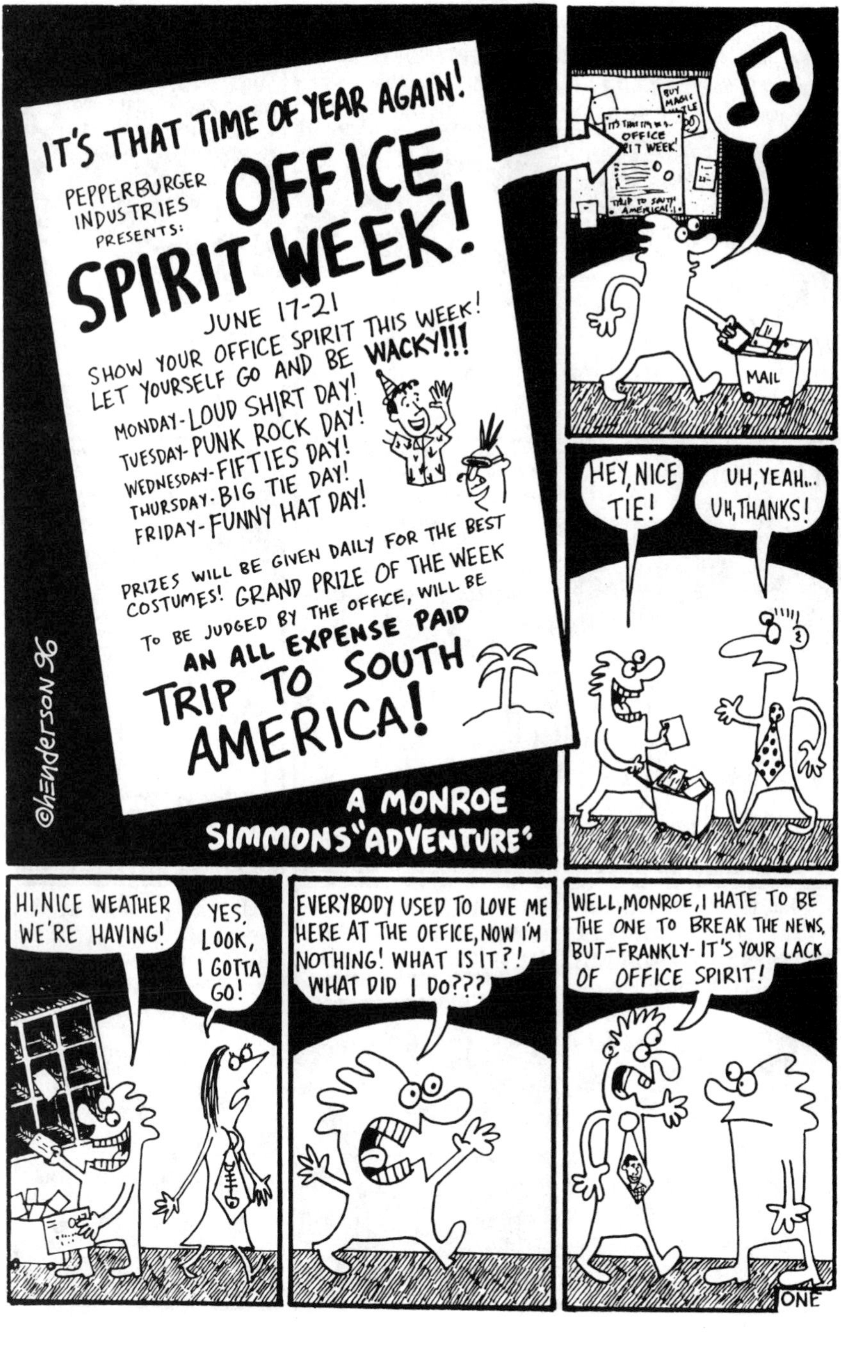
IT'S THAT TIME OF YEAR AGAIN!
PEPPERBURGER INDUSTRIES PRESENTS:
OFFICE SPIRIT WEEK!
JUNE 17-21
SHOW YOUR OFFICE SPIRIT THIS WEEK! LET YOURSELF GO AND BE WACKY!!!
MONDAY-LOUD SHIRT DAY!
TUESDAY-PUNK ROCK DAY!
WEDNESDAY-FIFTIES DAY!
THURSDAY-BIG TIE DAY!
FRIDAY-FUNNY HAT DAY!
PRIZES WILL BE GIVEN DAILY FOR THE BEST COSTUMES! GRAND PRIZE OF THE WEEK TO BE JUDGED BY THE OFFICE, WILL BE
AN ALL EXPENSE PAID
TRIP TO SOUTH AMERICA!
©henderson 96
A MONROE SIMMONS "ADVENTURE"
MAIL
HEY, NICE TIE!
UH, YEAH... UH, THANKS!
HI, NICE WEATHER WE'RE HAVING!
YES. LOOK, I GOTTA GO!
EVERYBODY USED TO LOVE ME HERE AT THE OFFICE, NOW I'M NOTHING! WHAT IS IT?! WHAT DID I DO???
WELL, MONROE, I HATE TO BE THE ONE TO BREAK THE NEWS, BUT—FRANKLY—IT'S YOUR LACK OF OFFICE SPIRIT!
ONE

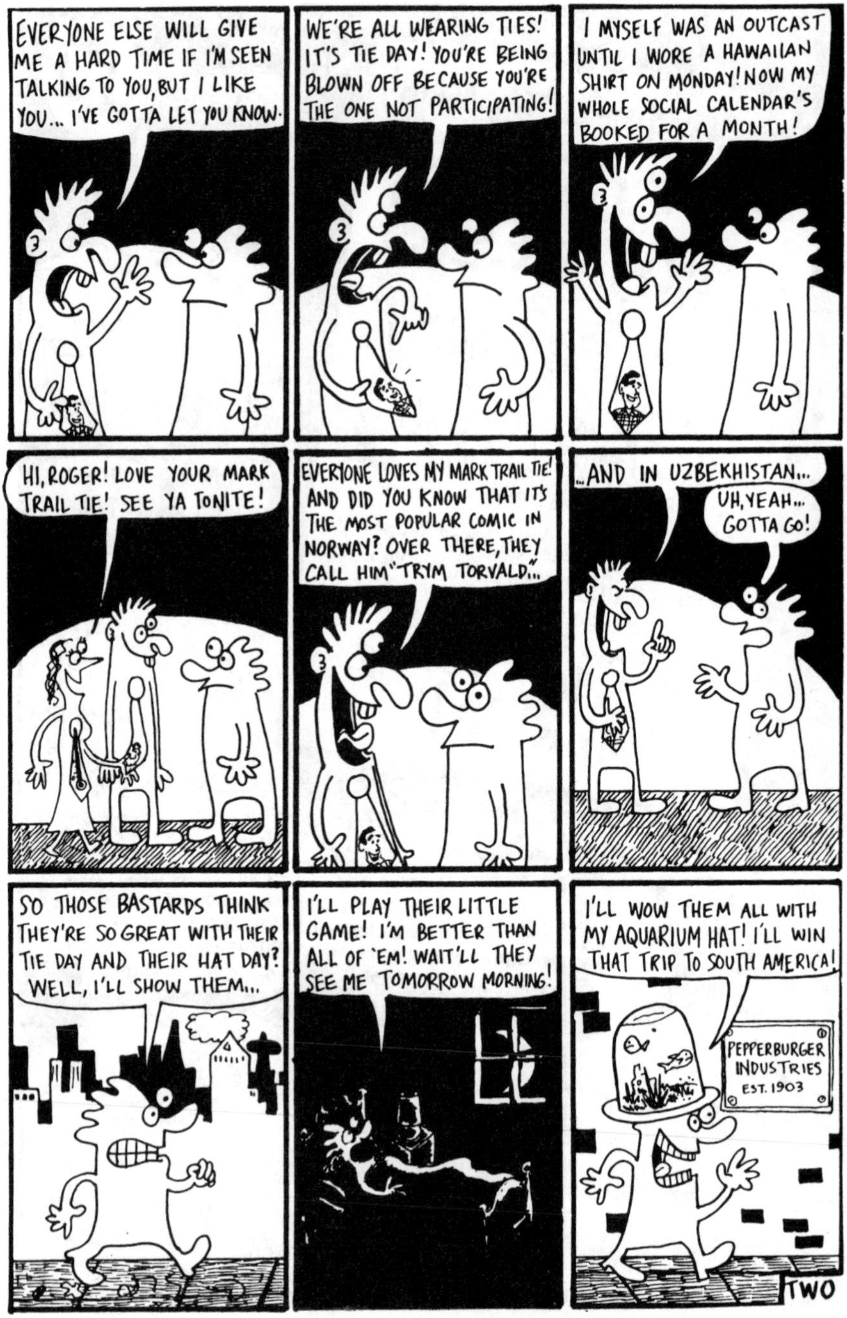
EVERYONE ELSE WILL GIVE ME A HARD TIME IF I'M SEEN TALKING TO YOU, BUT I LIKE YOU... I'VE GOTTA LET YOU KNOW.
WE'RE ALL WEARING TIES! IT'S TIE DAY! YOU'RE BEING BLOWN OFF BECAUSE YOU'RE THE ONE NOT PARTICIPATING!
I MYSELF WAS AN OUTCAST UNTIL I WORE A HAWAIIAN SHIRT ON MONDAY! NOW MY WHOLE SOCIAL CALENDAR'S BOOKED FOR A MONTH!
HI, ROGER! LOVE YOUR MARK TRAIL TIE! SEE YA TONITE!
EVERYONE LOVES MY MARK TRAIL TIE! AND DID YOU KNOW THAT IT'S THE MOST POPULAR COMIC IN NORWAY? OVER THERE, THEY CALL HIM "TRYM TORVALD"...
...AND IN UZBEKHISTAN...
UH, YEAH... GOTTA GO!
SO THOSE BASTARDS THINK THEY'RE SO GREAT WITH THEIR TIE DAY AND THEIR HAT DAY? WELL, I'LL SHOW THEM...
I'LL PLAY THEIR LITTLE GAME! I'M BETTER THAN ALL OF 'EM! WAIT'LL THEY SEE ME TOMORROW MORNING!
I'LL WOW THEM ALL WITH MY AQUARIUM HAT! I'LL WIN THAT TRIP TO SOUTH AMERICA!
PEPPERBURGER INDUSTRIES EST. 1903
TWO

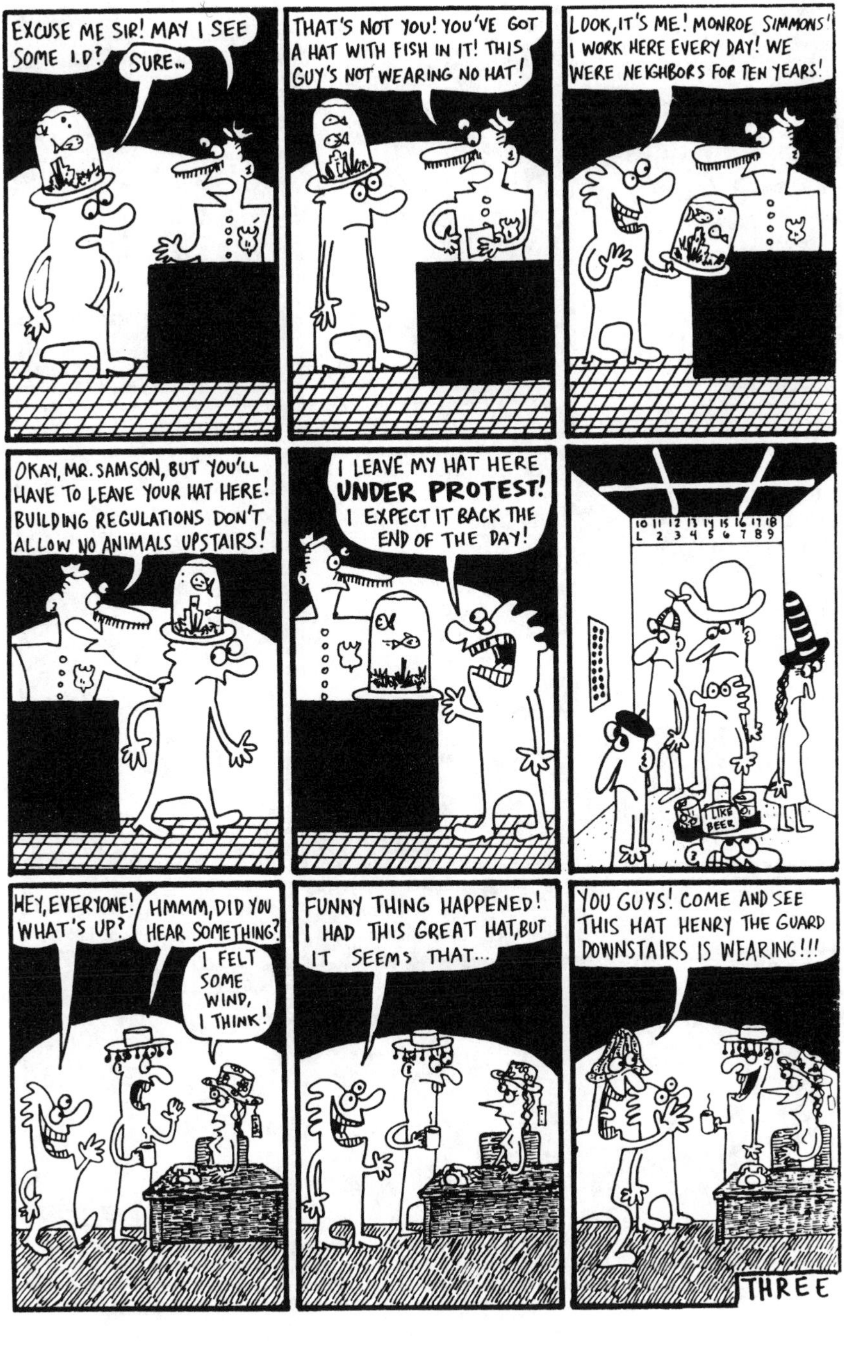
EXCUSE ME SIR! MAY I SEE SOME I.D?
SURE..
THAT'S NOT YOU! YOU'VE GOT A HAT WITH FISH IN IT! THIS GUY'S NOT WEARING NO HAT!
LOOK, IT'S ME! MONROE SIMMONS! I WORK HERE EVERY DAY! WE WERE NEIGHBORS FOR TEN YEARS!
OKAY, MR. SAMSON, BUT YOU'LL HAVE TO LEAVE YOUR HAT HERE! BUILDING REGULATIONS DON'T ALLOW NO ANIMALS UPSTAIRS!
I LEAVE MY HAT HERE UNDER PROTEST! I EXPECT IT BACK THE END OF THE DAY!
10 11 12 13 14 15 16 17 18
L 2 3 4 5 6 7 8 9
I LIKE BEER
HEY, EVERYONE! WHAT'S UP?
HMMM, DID YOU HEAR SOMETHING?
I FELT SOME WIND, I THINK!
FUNNY THING HAPPENED! I HAD THIS GREAT HAT, BUT IT SEEMS THAT...
YOU GUYS! COME AND SEE THIS HAT HENRY THE GUARD DOWNSTAIRS IS WEARING!!!
THREE

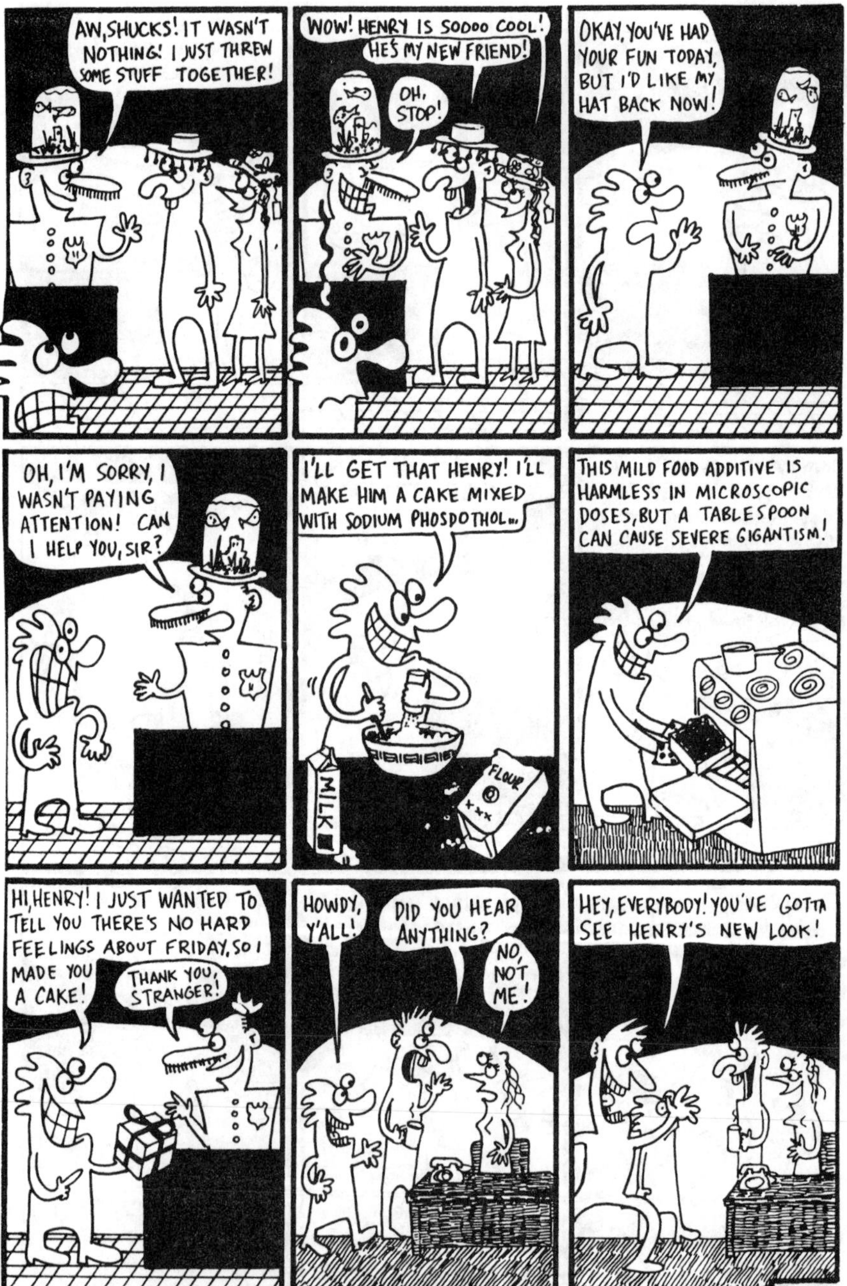

AW, SHUCKS! IT WASN'T NOTHING! I JUST THREW SOME STUFF TOGETHER!
WOW! HENRY IS SODOO COOL!
HE'S MY NEW FRIEND!
OH, STOP!
OKAY, YOU'VE HAD YOUR FUN TODAY, BUT I'D LIKE MY HAT BACK NOW!
OH, I'M SORRY, I WASN'T PAYING ATTENTION! CAN I HELP YOU, SIR?
I'LL GET THAT HENRY! I'LL MAKE HIM A CAKE MIXED WITH SODIUM PHOSDOTHOL...
MILK
FLOUR
THIS MILD FOOD ADDITIVE IS HARMLESS IN MICROSCOPIC DOSES, BUT A TABLESPOON CAN CAUSE SEVERE GIGANTISM!
HI, HENRY! I JUST WANTED TO TELL YOU THERE'S NO HARD FEELINGS ABOUT FRIDAY, SO I MADE YOU A CAKE!
THANK YOU, STRANGER!
HOWDY, Y'ALL!
DID YOU HEAR ANYTHING?
NO, NOT ME!
HEY, EVERYBODY! YOU'VE GOTTA SEE HENRY'S NEW LOOK!

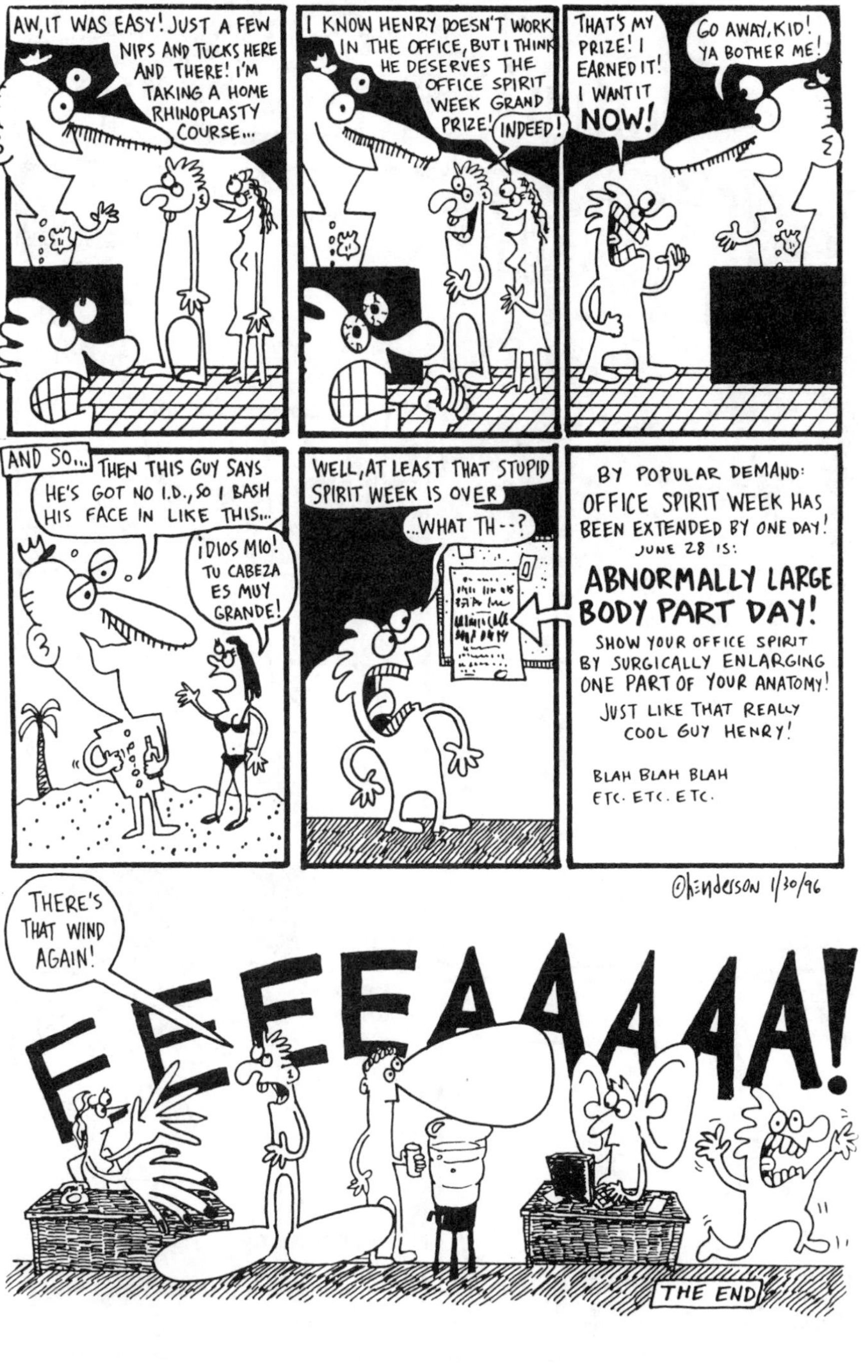
AW, IT WAS EASY! JUST A FEW NIPS AND TUCKS HERE AND THERE! I'M TAKING A HOME RHINOPLASTY COURSE...
I KNOW HENRY DOESN'T WORK IN THE OFFICE, BUT I THINK HE DESERVES THE OFFICE SPIRIT WEEK GRAND PRIZE!
INDEED!
THAT'S MY PRIZE! I EARNED IT! I WANT IT NOW!
GO AWAY, KID! YA BOTHER ME!
AND SO...
THEN THIS GUY SAYS HE'S GOT NO I.D., SO I BASH HIS FACE IN LIKE THIS...
¡DIOS MIO! TU CABEZA ES MUY GRANDE!
WELL, AT LEAST THAT STUPID SPIRIT WEEK IS OVER
...WHAT TH--?
BY POPULAR DEMAND:
OFFICE SPIRIT WEEK HAS BEEN EXTENDED BY ONE DAY!
JUNE 28 IS:
ABNORMALLY LARGE BODY PART DAY!
SHOW YOUR OFFICE SPIRIT BY SURGICALLY ENLARGING ONE PART OF YOUR ANATOMY!
JUST LIKE THAT REALLY COOL GUY HENRY!
BLAH BLAH BLAH
ETC. ETC. ETC.
©henderson 1/30/96
THERE'S THAT WIND AGAIN!
EEEEAAAAA!
THE END

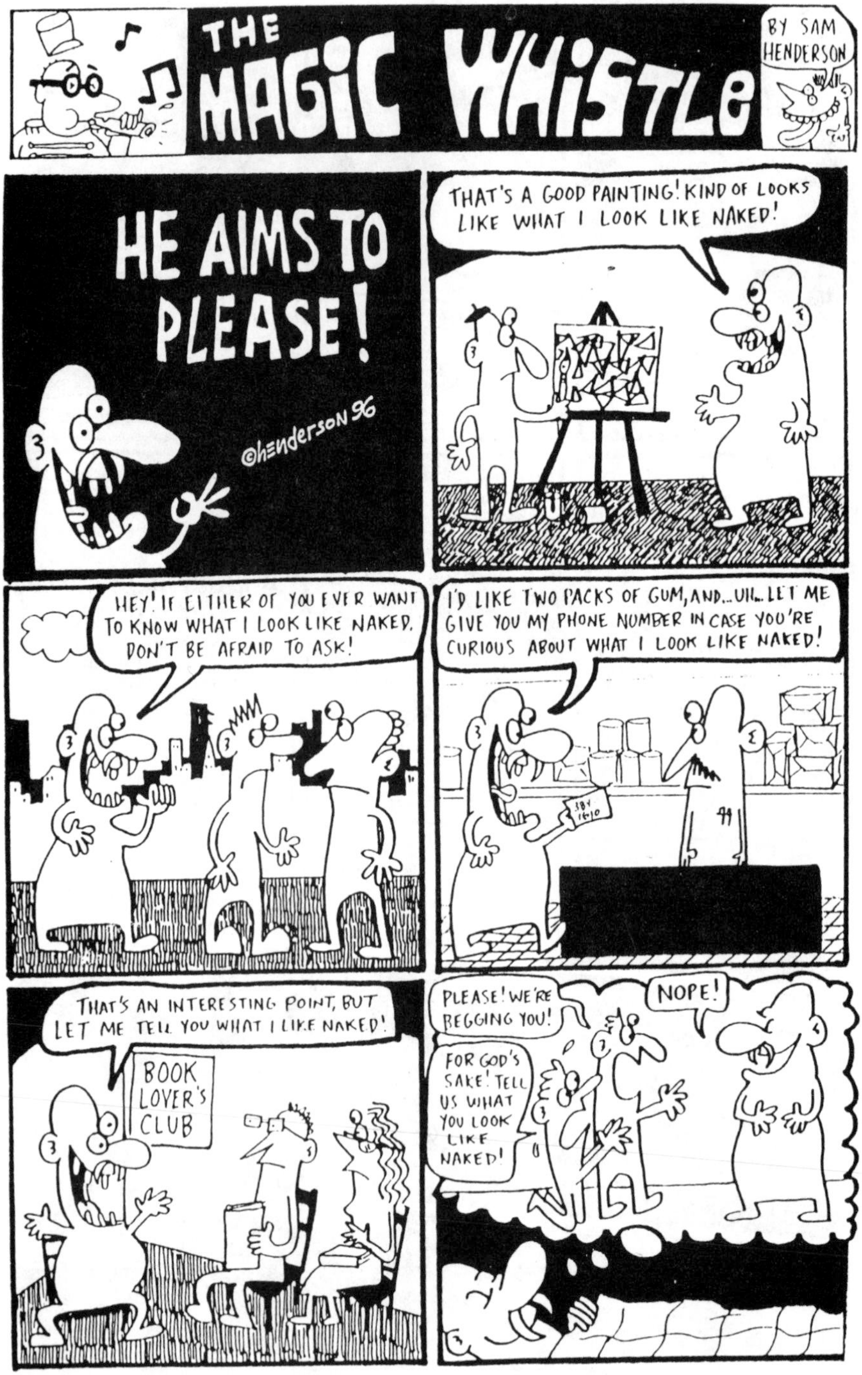
THE MAGIC WHISTLE
BY SAM HENDERSON
HE AIMS TO PLEASE!
©henderson 96
THAT'S A GOOD PAINTING! KIND OF LOOKS LIKE WHAT I LOOK LIKE NAKED!
HEY! IF EITHER OF YOU EVER WANT TO KNOW WHAT I LOOK LIKE NAKED, DON'T BE AFRAID TO ASK!
I'D LIKE TWO PACKS OF GUM, AND... UH... LET ME GIVE YOU MY PHONE NUMBER IN CASE YOU'RE CURIOUS ABOUT WHAT I LOOK LIKE NAKED!
THAT'S AN INTERESTING POINT, BUT LET ME TELL YOU WHAT I LIKE NAKED!
BOOK LOVER'S CLUB
PLEASE! WE'RE BEGGING YOU!
FOR GOD'S SAKE! TELL US WHAT YOU LOOK LIKE NAKED!
NOPE!

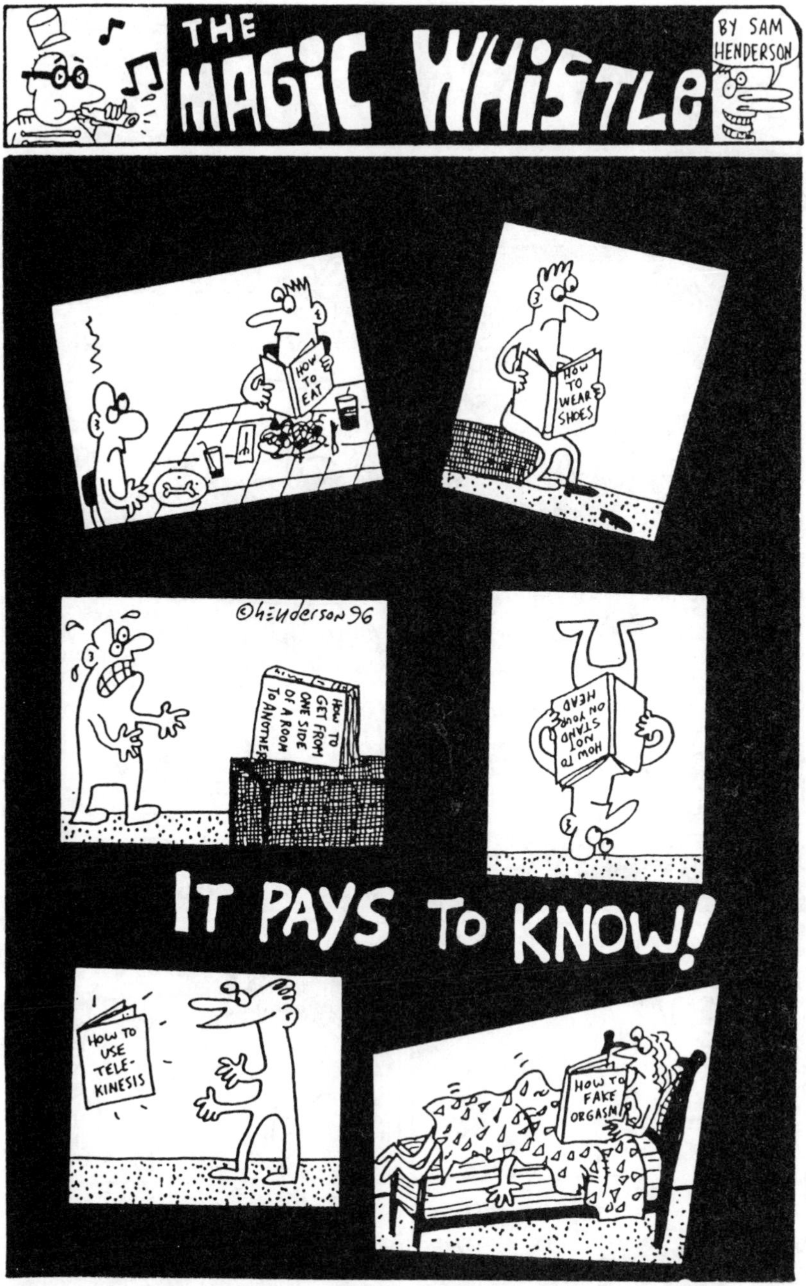
THE MAGIC WHISTLE
BY SAM HENDERSON
HOW TO EAT
HOW TO WEAR SHOES
©henderson 96
HOW TO GET FROM ONE SIDE OF A ROOM TO ANOTHER
HOW TO NOT STAND ON YOUR HEAD
IT PAYS TO KNOW!
HOW TO USE TELE-KINESIS
HOW TO FAKE ORGASM

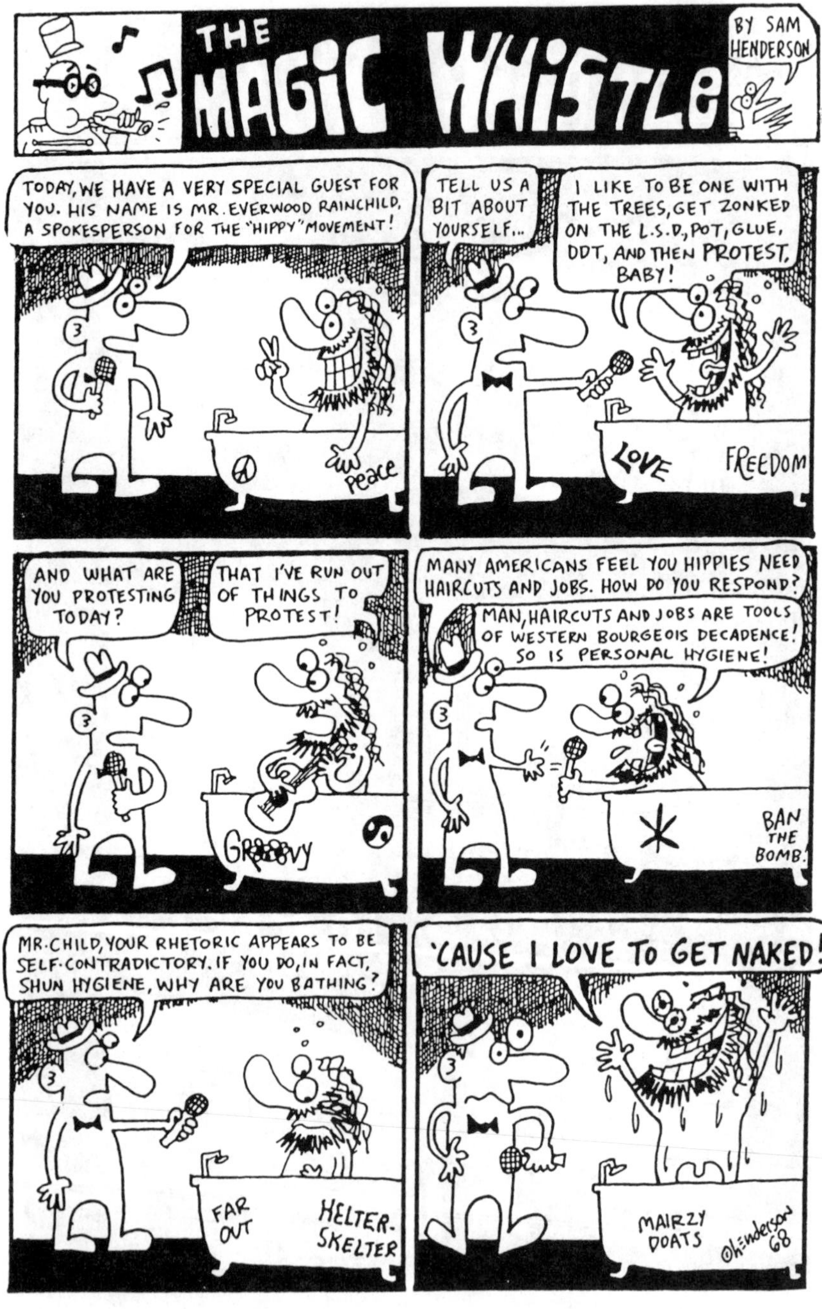
THE MAGIC WHISTLE
BY SAM HENDERSON
TODAY, WE HAVE A VERY SPECIAL GUEST FOR YOU. HIS NAME IS MR. EVERWOOD RAINCHILD, A SPOKESPERSON FOR THE "HIPPY" MOVEMENT!
PEACE
TELL US A BIT ABOUT YOURSELF...
I LIKE TO BE ONE WITH THE TREES, GET ZONKED ON THE L.S.D., POT, GLUE, DDT, AND THEN PROTEST, BABY!
LOVE
FREEDOM
AND WHAT ARE YOU PROTESTING TODAY?
THAT I'VE RUN OUT OF THINGS TO PROTEST!
GROOOVY
MANY AMERICANS FEEL YOU HIPPIES NEED HAIRCUTS AND JOBS. HOW DO YOU RESPOND?
MAN, HAIRCUTS AND JOBS ARE TOOLS OF WESTERN BOURGEOIS DECADENCE! SO IS PERSONAL HYGIENE!
BAN THE BOMB!
MR. CHILD, YOUR RHETORIC APPEARS TO BE SELF-CONTRADICTORY. IF YOU DO, IN FACT, SHUN HYGIENE, WHY ARE YOU BATHING?
FAR OUT
HELTER-SKELTER
'CAUSE I LOVE TO GET NAKED!
MAIRZY DOATS
©henderson 68

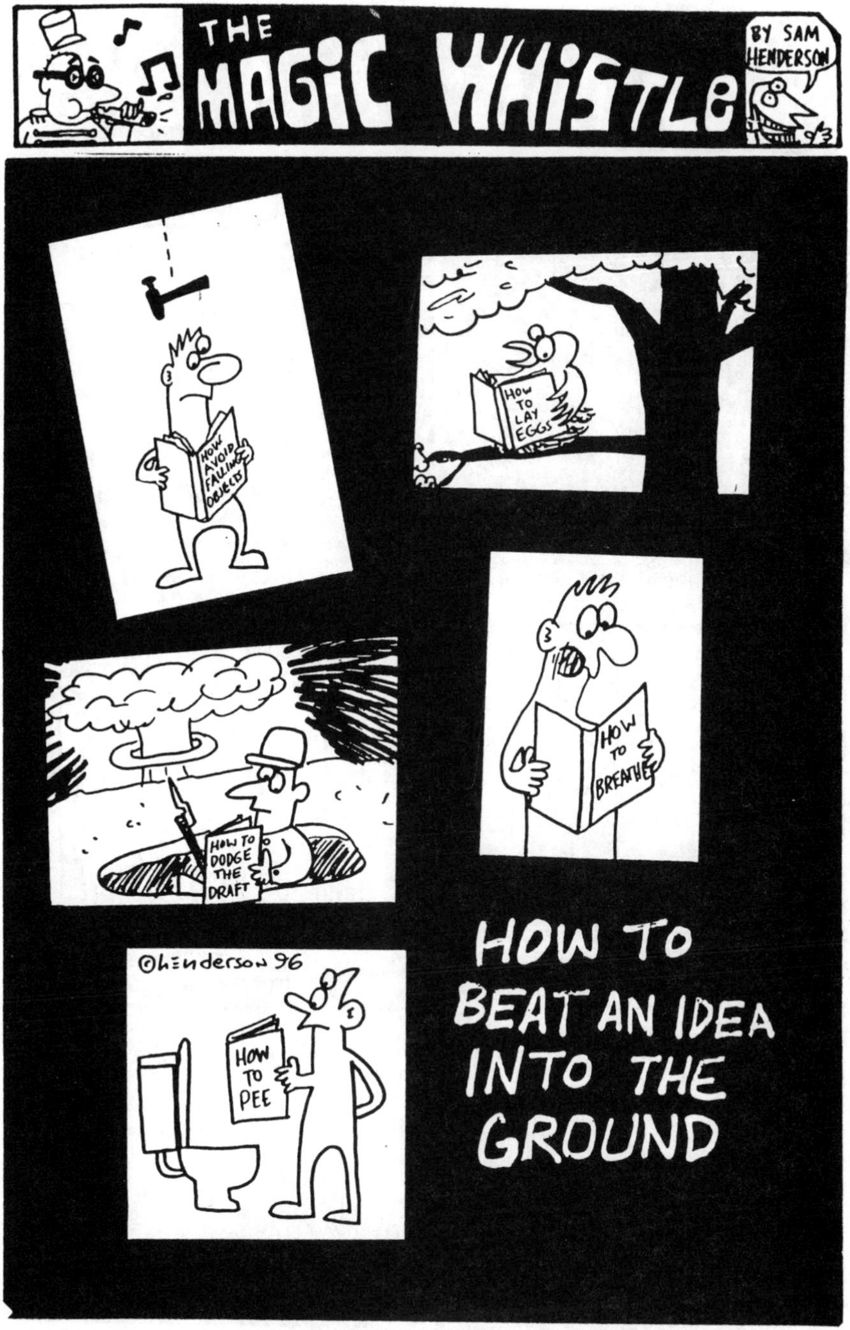
THE MAGIC WHISTLE
BY SAM HENDERSON
HOW AVOID FALLING OBJECTS
HOW TO LAY EGGS
HOW TO BREATHE
HOW TO DODGE THE DRAFT
©henderson 96
HOW TO PEE
HOW TO BEAT AN IDEA INTO THE GROUND

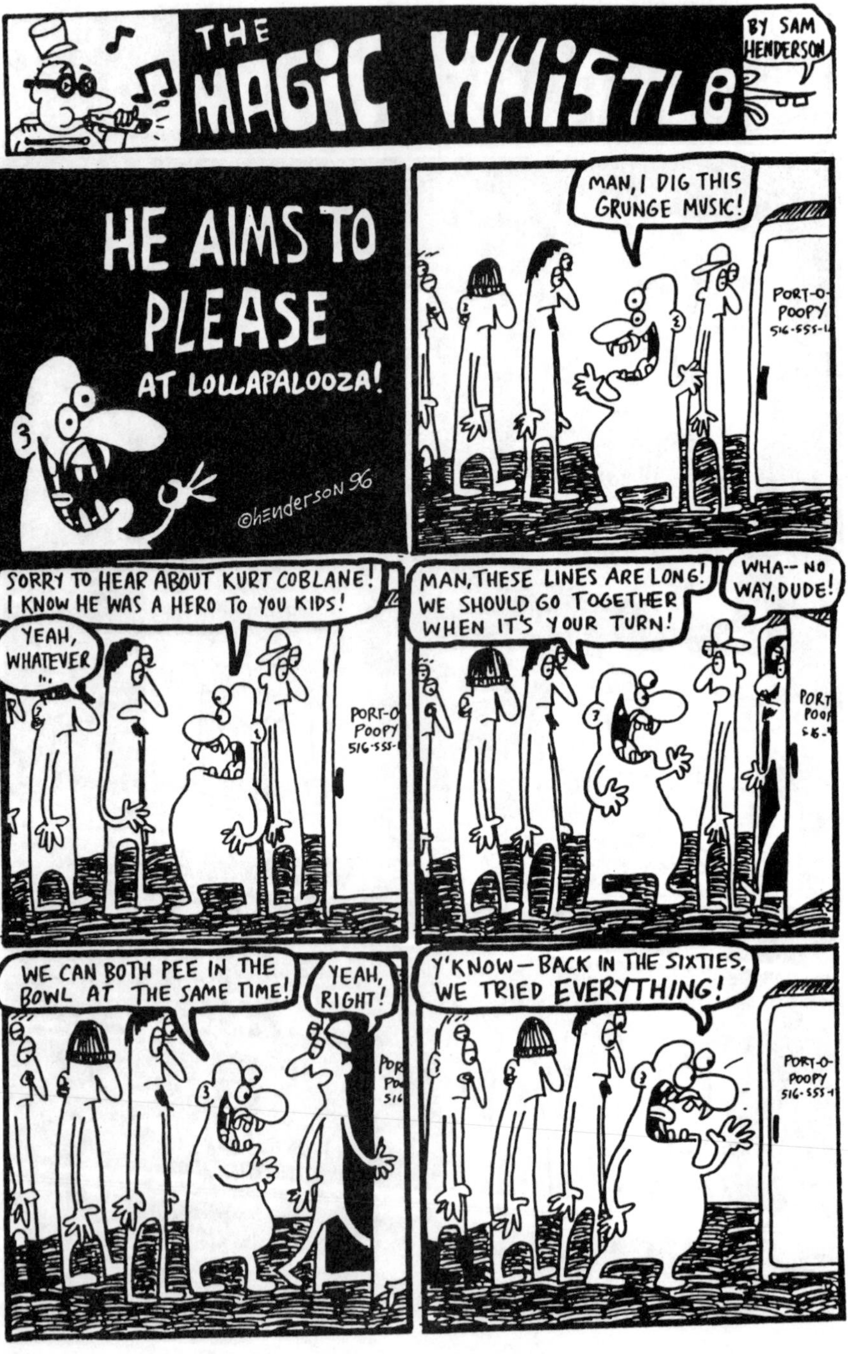
THE MAGIC WHISTLE
BY SAM HENDERSON
HE AIMS TO PLEASE AT LOLLAPALOOZA!
©henderson 96
MAN, I DIG THIS GRUNGE MUSIC!
PORT-O-POOPY
SORRY TO HEAR ABOUT KURT COBLANE! I KNOW HE WAS A HERO TO YOU KIDS!
YEAH, WHATEVER ...
PORT-O POOPY
MAN, THESE LINES ARE LONG! WE SHOULD GO TOGETHER WHEN IT'S YOUR TURN!
WHA-- NO WAY, DUDE!
WE CAN BOTH PEE IN THE BOWL AT THE SAME TIME!
YEAH, RIGHT!
Y'KNOW—BACK IN THE SIXTIES, WE TRIED EVERYTHING!
PORT-O-POOPY

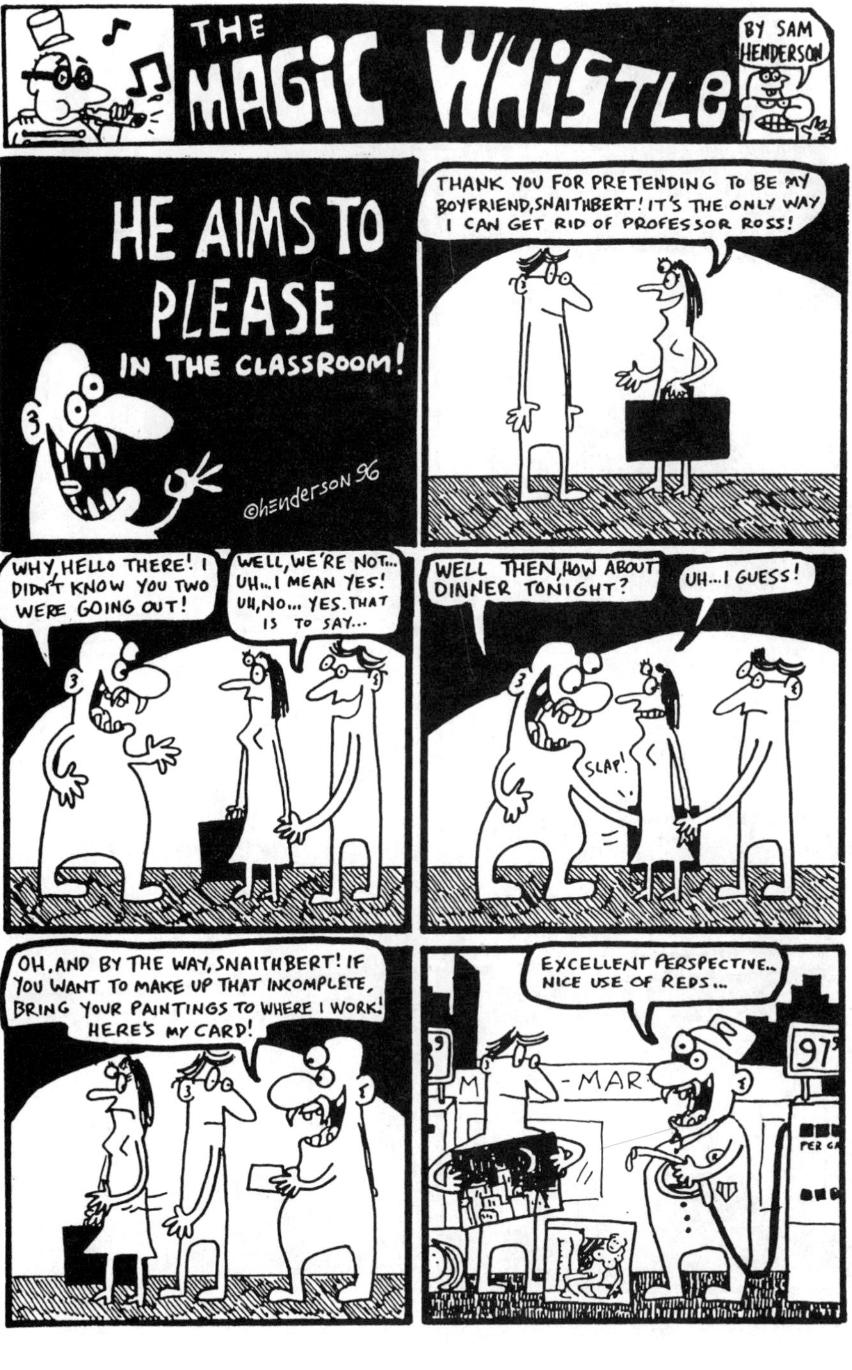
THE MAGIC WHISTLE
BY SAM HENDERSON
HE AIMS TO PLEASE IN THE CLASSROOM!
©henderson 96
THANK YOU FOR PRETENDING TO BE MY BOYFRIEND, SNAITHBERT! IT'S THE ONLY WAY I CAN GET RID OF PROFESSOR ROSS!
WHY, HELLO THERE! I DIDN'T KNOW YOU TWO WERE GOING OUT!
WELL, WE'RE NOT... UH... I MEAN YES! UH, NO... YES. THAT IS TO SAY...
WELL THEN, HOW ABOUT DINNER TONIGHT?
UH... I GUESS!
SLAP!
OH, AND BY THE WAY, SNAITHBERT! IF YOU WANT TO MAKE UP THAT INCOMPLETE, BRING YOUR PAINTINGS TO WHERE I WORK! HERE'S MY CARD!
EXCELLENT PERSPECTIVE.. NICE USE OF REDS...
-MAR
97
PER GA

GIRLY STAMP

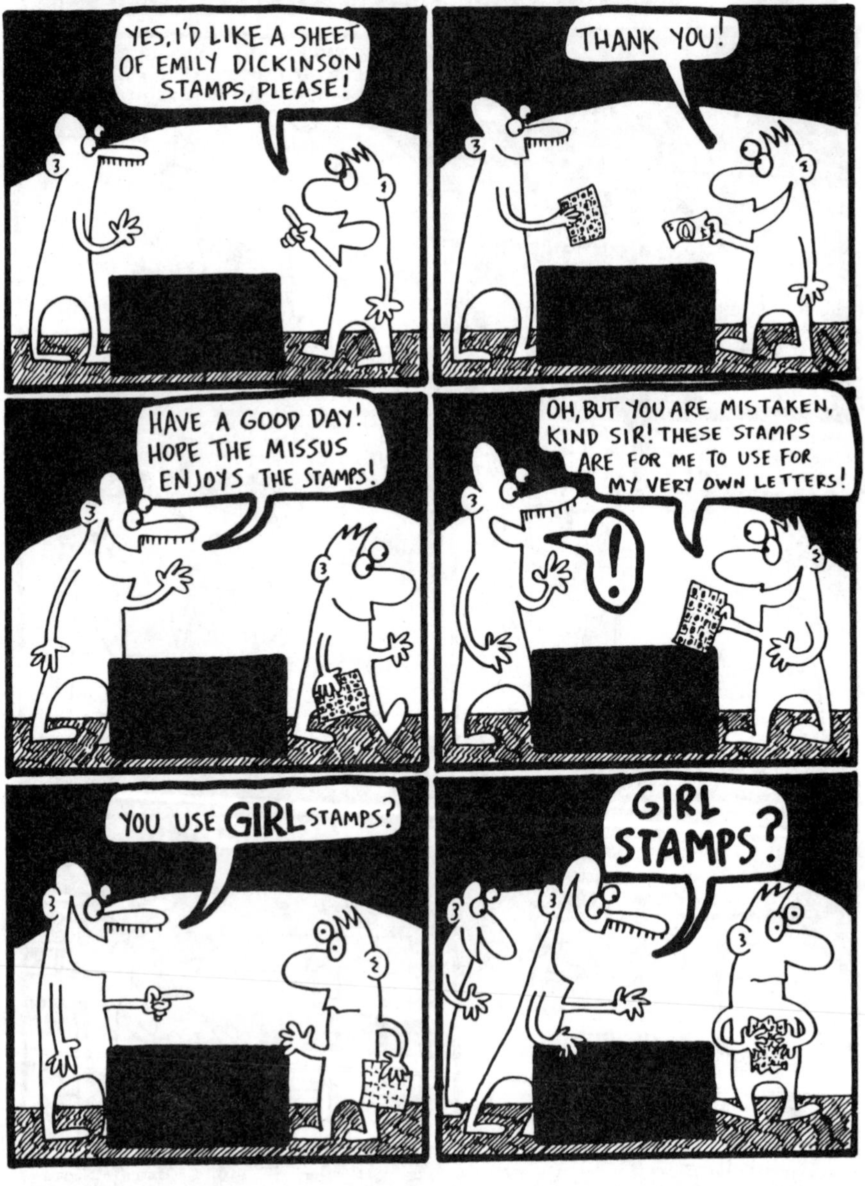
YES, I'D LIKE A SHEET OF EMILY DICKINSON STAMPS, PLEASE!
THANK YOU!
HAVE A GOOD DAY! HOPE THE MISSUS ENJOYS THE STAMPS!
OH, BUT YOU ARE MISTAKEN, KIND SIR! THESE STAMPS ARE FOR ME TO USE FOR MY VERY OWN LETTERS!
!
YOU USE GIRL STAMPS?
GIRL STAMPS?

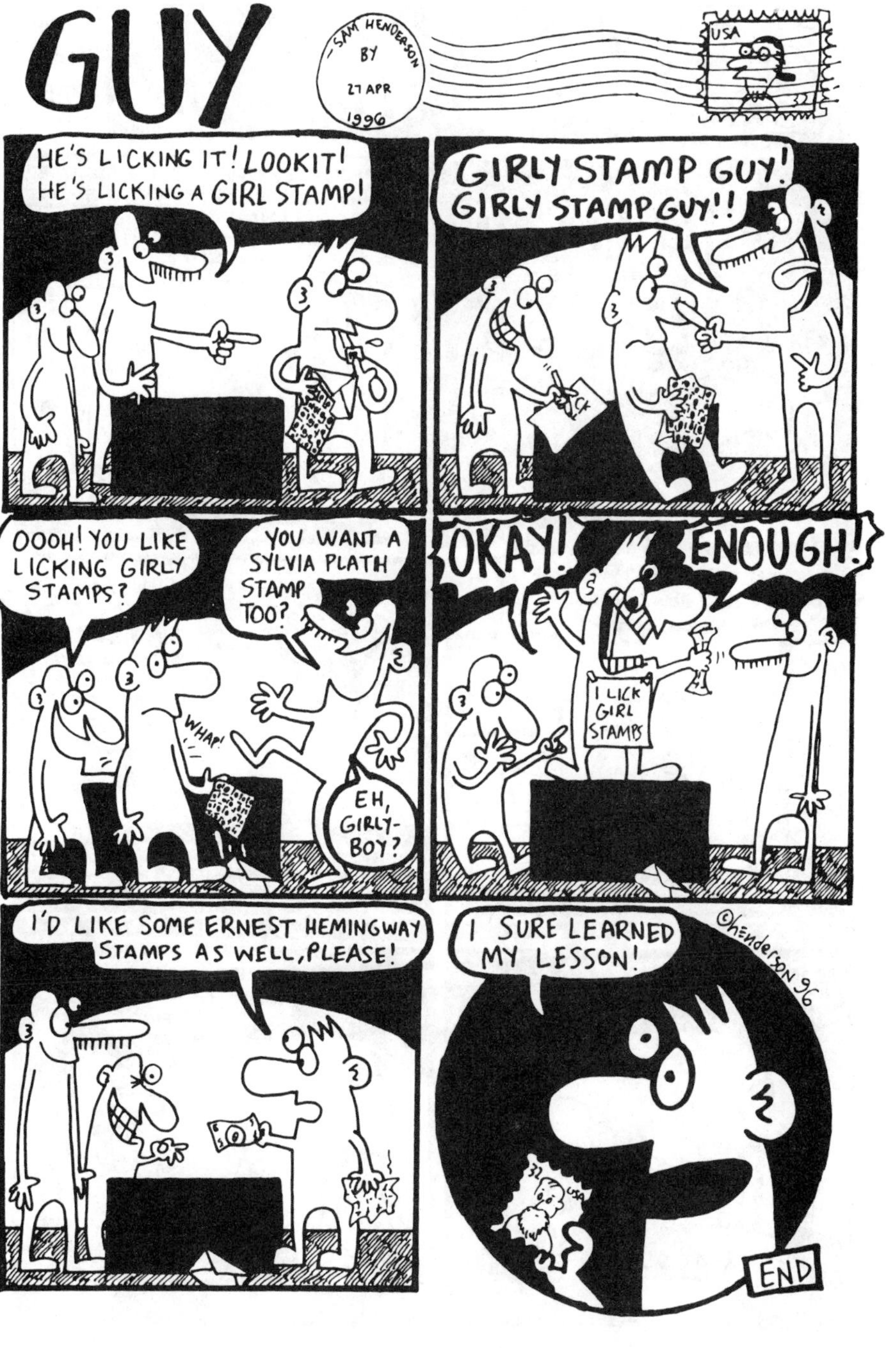
GUY
SAM HENDERSON
BY
27 APR
1996
USA
32
HE'S LICKING IT! LOOKIT! HE'S LICKING A GIRL STAMP!
GIRLY STAMP GUY! GIRLY STAMP GUY!!
OOOH! YOU LIKE LICKING GIRLY STAMPS?
YOU WANT A SYLVIA PLATH STAMP TOO?
WHAP!
EH, GIRLY-BOY?
OKAY!
ENOUGH!
I LICK GIRL STAMPS
I'D LIKE SOME ERNEST HEMINGWAY STAMPS AS WELL, PLEASE!
I SURE LEARNED MY LESSON!
©henderson 96
END

THE MAGIC WHISTLE

BY SAM HENDERSON

HE AIMS TO PLEASE

ON A DATE!

©henderson 96

I HOPE YOU DON'T FIND THIS TOO AWKWARD, US BEING TEACHER AND STUDENT. IF YOU GET A GOOD GRADE, I WANT YOU TO KNOW IT'S NOT JUST 'CAUSE WE'RE PROBABLY GONNA SLEEP TOGETHER!

UH-HUH... ER... COULD YOU EXCUSE ME FOR A MOMENT?

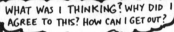

WHAT WAS I THINKING? WHY DID I AGREE TO THIS? HOW CAN I GET OUT?

OH, WHY BOTHER? I'LL HAVE TO FACE HIM IN CLASS NEXT WEEK ANYWAY! I'LL JUST TURN DOWN HIS ADVANCES POLITELY...

SORRY I TOOK SO LONG...

OH, HI...

I DIDN'T THINK YOU WERE COMING BACK SO I ATE ALL YOUR FOOD!

THE MAGIC WHISTLE
BY SAM HENDERSON
WE'RE GONNA PARTY LIKE IT'S 1999!
WE'RE GONNA PARTY LIKE IT'S 1999 B.C!
WE'RE GONNA PARTY LIKE IT'S 19,999!
WE'RE GONNA PARTY LIKE IT'S MCMXCIX!
WE'RE GONNA PARTY LIKE IT'S 1499!
WE'RE GONNA PARTY LIKE IT'S (π x 636.6221) + .006606!
©henderson 96

THE MAGIC WHISTLE

BY SAM HENDERSON

THE CARTOON BELOW SHOULD BE INTERPRETED IN THE IRONIC CONTEXT IN WHICH IT WAS INTENDED. THERE IS NO EVIDENCE WHETHER A FEMALE CHIEF EXECUTIVE WOULD BE ANY MORE OR LESS COMPETENT THAN ANY OF OUR PREVIOUS OFFICE-HOLDERS OF THE MALE PERSUASION, CONTRARY TO DEBATES PRO AND CON; WHICH HAVE BEEN ARGUED ON RELIGIOUS, RATIONAL, AND OTHER GROUNDS.

SATIRISTS HAVE USED GENDER ROLES AS TARGETS FOR DECADES, SUBJECT MATTER RUNNING THE GAMUT FROM THE SOPHOMORIC TO THE ALTRUISTIC. WRITERS AND ARTISTS HAVE USED THIS MEDIUM TO HELP COPE WITH A CHANGING WORLD, WHETHER IT BE OSTENSIBLY TO EDUCATE AND ENLIGHTEN, OR TO EXPOSE THE SUPPOSED FOLLIES AND HYPOCRISIES OF OUR SOCIETY. WITH THE GRADUAL EROSION OF AN ARCHAIC PATRIARCHY IN THE WESTERN WORLD OVER THE LATTER HALF OF THE TWENTIETH CENTURY, THOSE WHO FEAR THIS CHANGE HAVE PORTRAYED WOMEN IN POWER AS "CASTRATING MAN-HATERS". IT IS ALSO COMMON, IN A VICIOUS AS WELL AS SELF-DEPRECATING FASHION, TO DEPICT THE MALE SEX AS SLAVES TO THEIR OWN REPRODUCTIVE CELLS (REGARDLESS OF LIFESTYLE OR SOCIAL CLASS) OFTEN COMPROMISING THEIR OWN VIRTUE IN FAVOR OF THEIR LIBIDINAL DESIRES, A SUBSTANTIAL PORTION OF WHICH INCORPORATES MAMMARIAN FIXATION.

A CARTOON IS AN ASSIMILATION OF SYMBOLS WHICH IS RE-INTERPRETED TO REFLECT OUR TIMES, AND IT IS IN THIS TRADITION I CHOOSE TO PRESENT THIS CONCEPT TO ENTERTAIN YOU, THE READER. — Sam Henderson

IF A WOMAN WAS PRESIDENT

SEAL OF

SHOW US YOUR TITS!!!

NEXT WEEK: DEFENDING "IF WE HAD A PRESIDENT WHO USED HEROIN"

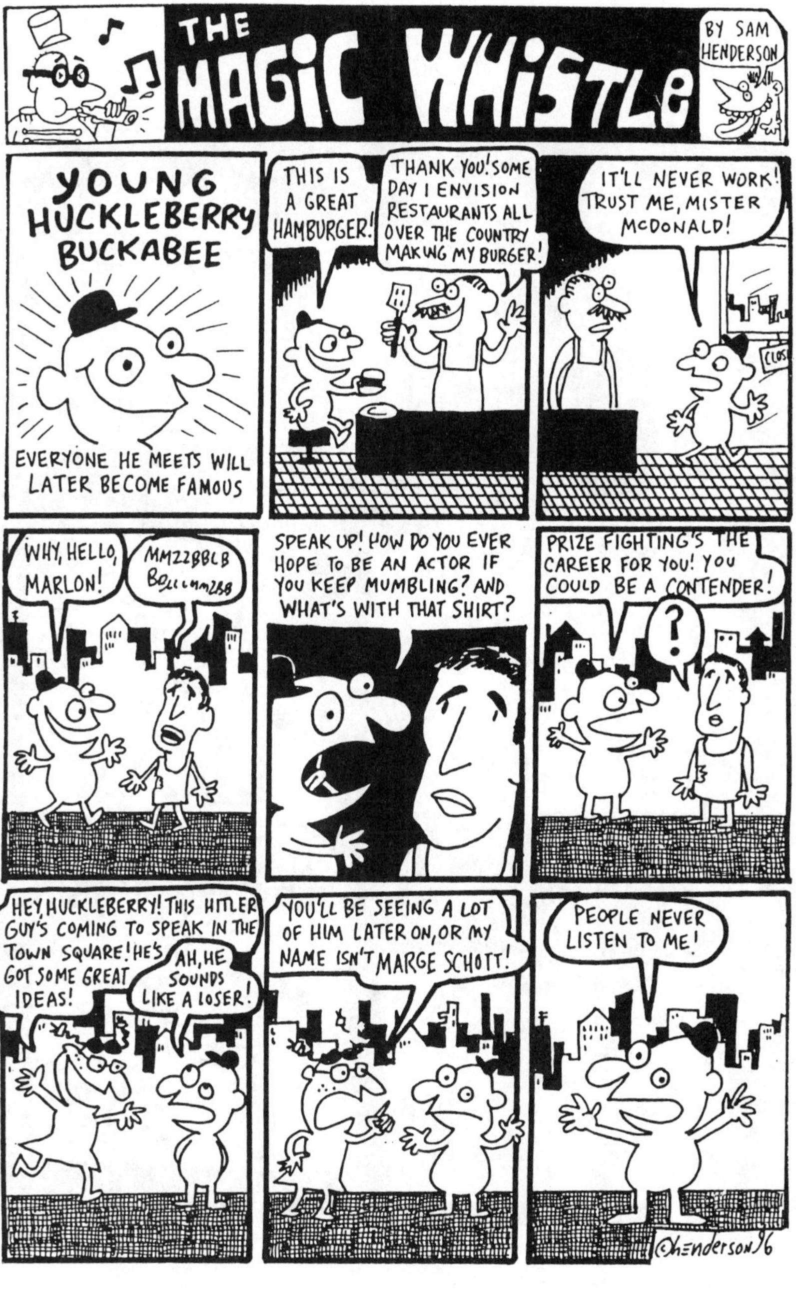
THE MAGIC WHISTLE
BY SAM HENDERSON
YOUNG HUCKLEBERRY BUCKABEE
EVERYONE HE MEETS WILL LATER BECOME FAMOUS
THIS IS A GREAT HAMBURGER!
THANK YOU! SOME DAY I ENVISION RESTAURANTS ALL OVER THE COUNTRY MAKING MY BURGER!
IT'LL NEVER WORK! TRUST ME, MISTER MCDONALD!
WHY, HELLO, MARLON!
MMZZBBLB
SPEAK UP! HOW DO YOU EVER HOPE TO BE AN ACTOR IF YOU KEEP MUMBLING? AND WHAT'S WITH THAT SHIRT?
PRIZE FIGHTING'S THE CAREER FOR YOU! YOU COULD BE A CONTENDER!
?
HEY, HUCKLEBERRY! THIS HITLER GUY'S COMING TO SPEAK IN THE TOWN SQUARE! HE'S GOT SOME GREAT IDEAS!
AH, HE SOUNDS LIKE A LOSER!
YOU'LL BE SEEING A LOT OF HIM LATER ON, OR MY NAME ISN'T MARGE SCHOTT!
PEOPLE NEVER LISTEN TO ME!
©henderson 96

YOU CAN'T GO WRONG WITH CHICKENS
YOU CALLIN' ME A LIAR?
CHICKENS FOR SALE
I DON'T LIKE YOU!
TRY IT! IT TASTES JUST LIKE ME!
©henderson97
HEY, YOU! YEAH, YOU!
YOU SUCK!
I'M TALKIN' TO YOU!
YOU CALLING ME A LIAR?
PEOPLE FOR SALE

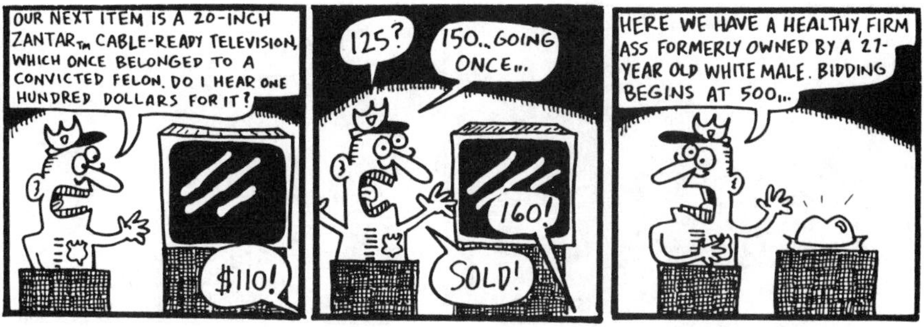
OUR NEXT ITEM IS A 20-INCH ZANTAR™ CABLE-READY TELEVISION, WHICH ONCE BELONGED TO A CONVICTED FELON. DO I HEAR ONE HUNDRED DOLLARS FOR IT?
$110!
125?
150.. GOING ONCE...
160!
SOLD!
HERE WE HAVE A HEALTHY, FIRM ASS FORMERLY OWNED BY A 27-YEAR OLD WHITE MALE. BIDDING BEGINS AT 500...

SEIZED ASSets

©henderson 96

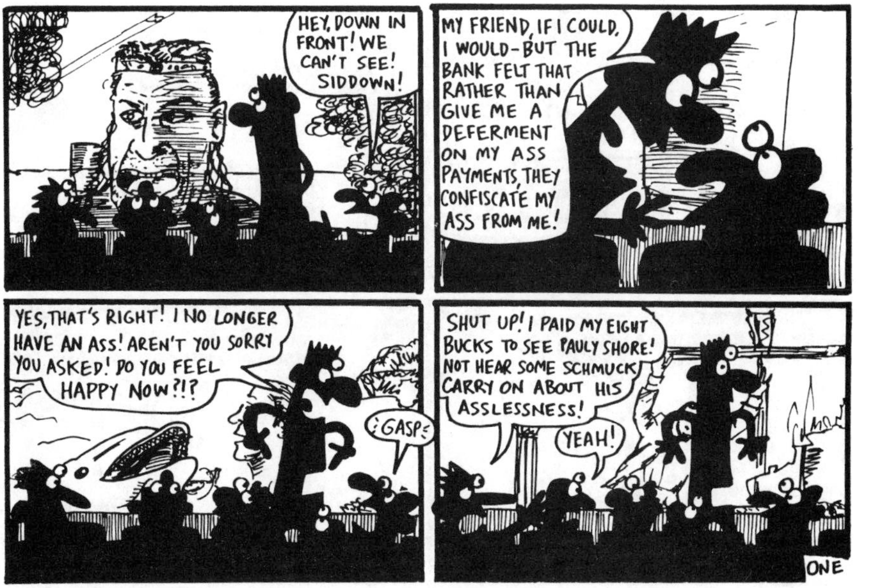
HEY, DOWN IN FRONT! WE CAN'T SEE! SIDDOWN!
MY FRIEND, IF I COULD, I WOULD-BUT THE BANK FELT THAT RATHER THAN GIVE ME A DEFERMENT ON MY ASS PAYMENTS, THEY CONFISCATE MY ASS FROM ME!
YES, THAT'S RIGHT! I NO LONGER HAVE AN ASS! AREN'T YOU SORRY YOU ASKED! DO YOU FEEL HAPPY NOW?!?
GASP
SHUT UP! I PAID MY EIGHT BUCKS TO SEE PAULY SHORE! NOT HEAR SOME SCHMUCK CARRY ON ABOUT HIS ASSLESSNESS!
YEAH!

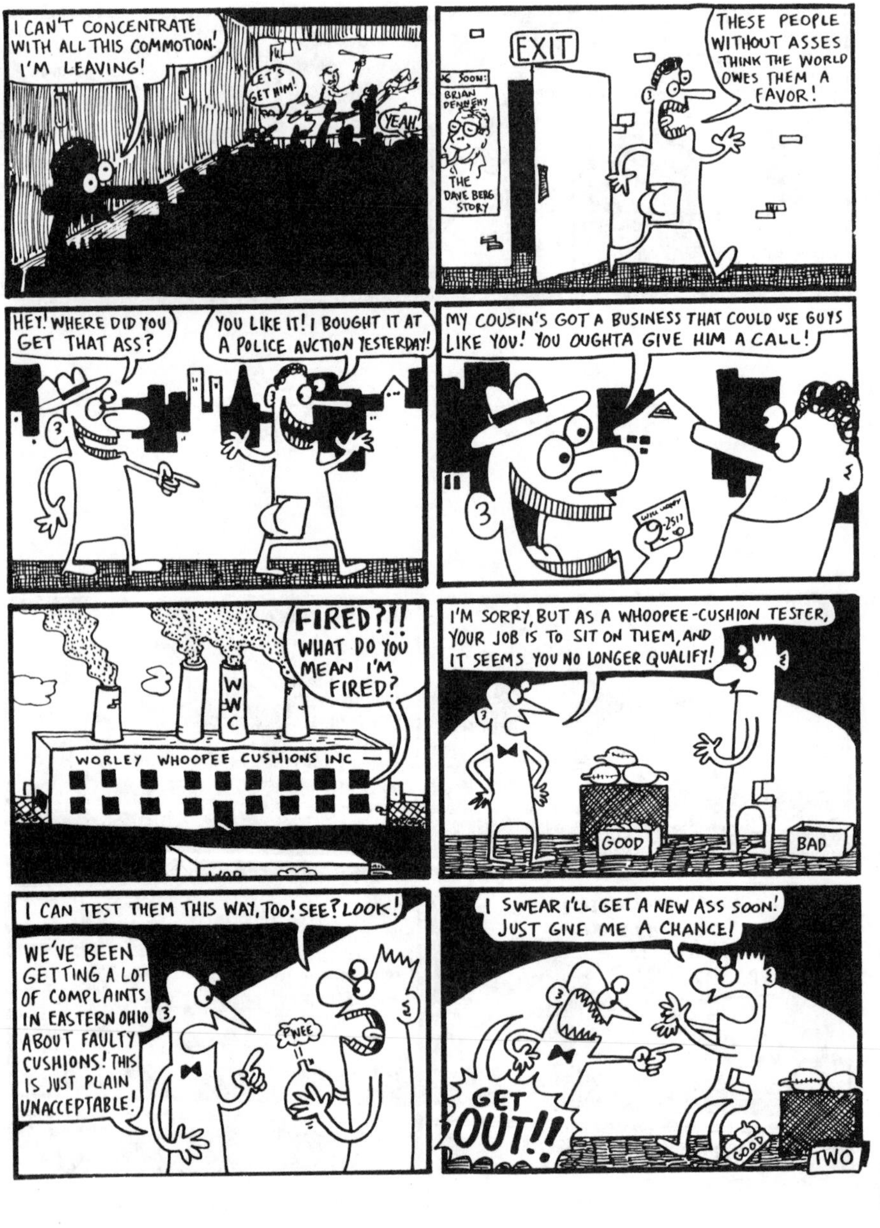
I CAN'T CONCENTRATE WITH ALL THIS COMMOTION! I'M LEAVING!
LET'S GET HIM!
YEAH!
EXIT
SOON: BRIAN DENNEHY THE DAVE BERG STORY
THESE PEOPLE WITHOUT ASSES THINK THE WORLD OWES THEM A FAVOR!
HEY! WHERE DID YOU GET THAT ASS?
YOU LIKE IT! I BOUGHT IT AT A POLICE AUCTION YESTERDAY!
MY COUSIN'S GOT A BUSINESS THAT COULD USE GUYS LIKE YOU! YOU OUGHTA GIVE HIM A CALL!
FIRED?!! WHAT DO YOU MEAN I'M FIRED?
WWC
WORLEY WHOOPEE CUSHIONS INC
I'M SORRY, BUT AS A WHOOPEE-CUSHION TESTER, YOUR JOB IS TO SIT ON THEM, AND IT SEEMS YOU NO LONGER QUALIFY!
GOOD
BAD
I CAN TEST THEM THIS WAY, TOO! SEE? LOOK!
WE'VE BEEN GETTING A LOT OF COMPLAINTS IN EASTERN OHIO ABOUT FAULTY CUSHIONS! THIS IS JUST PLAIN UNACCEPTABLE!
PWEE
I SWEAR I'LL GET A NEW ASS SOON! JUST GIVE ME A CHANCE!
GET OUT!!
GOOD
TWO

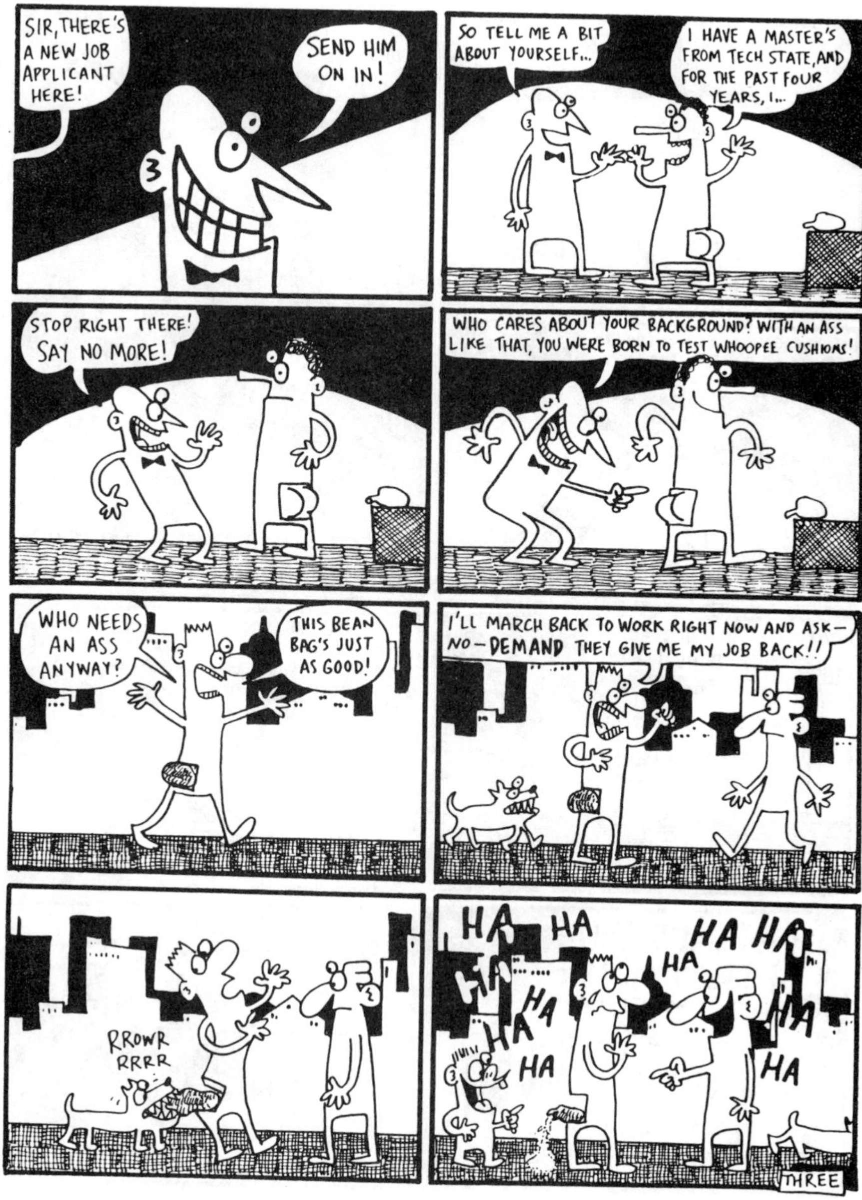
SIR, THERE'S A NEW JOB APPLICANT HERE!
SEND HIM ON IN!
SO TELL ME A BIT ABOUT YOURSELF...
I HAVE A MASTER'S FROM TECH STATE, AND FOR THE PAST FOUR YEARS, I...
STOP RIGHT THERE! SAY NO MORE!
WHO CARES ABOUT YOUR BACKGROUND? WITH AN ASS LIKE THAT, YOU WERE BORN TO TEST WHOOPEE CUSHIONS!
WHO NEEDS AN ASS ANYWAY?
THIS BEAN BAG'S JUST AS GOOD!
I'LL MARCH BACK TO WORK RIGHT NOW AND ASK— NO—DEMAND THEY GIVE ME MY JOB BACK!!
RROWR RRRR
HA HA HA HA
HA HA HA
HA HA HA
HA HA
THREE

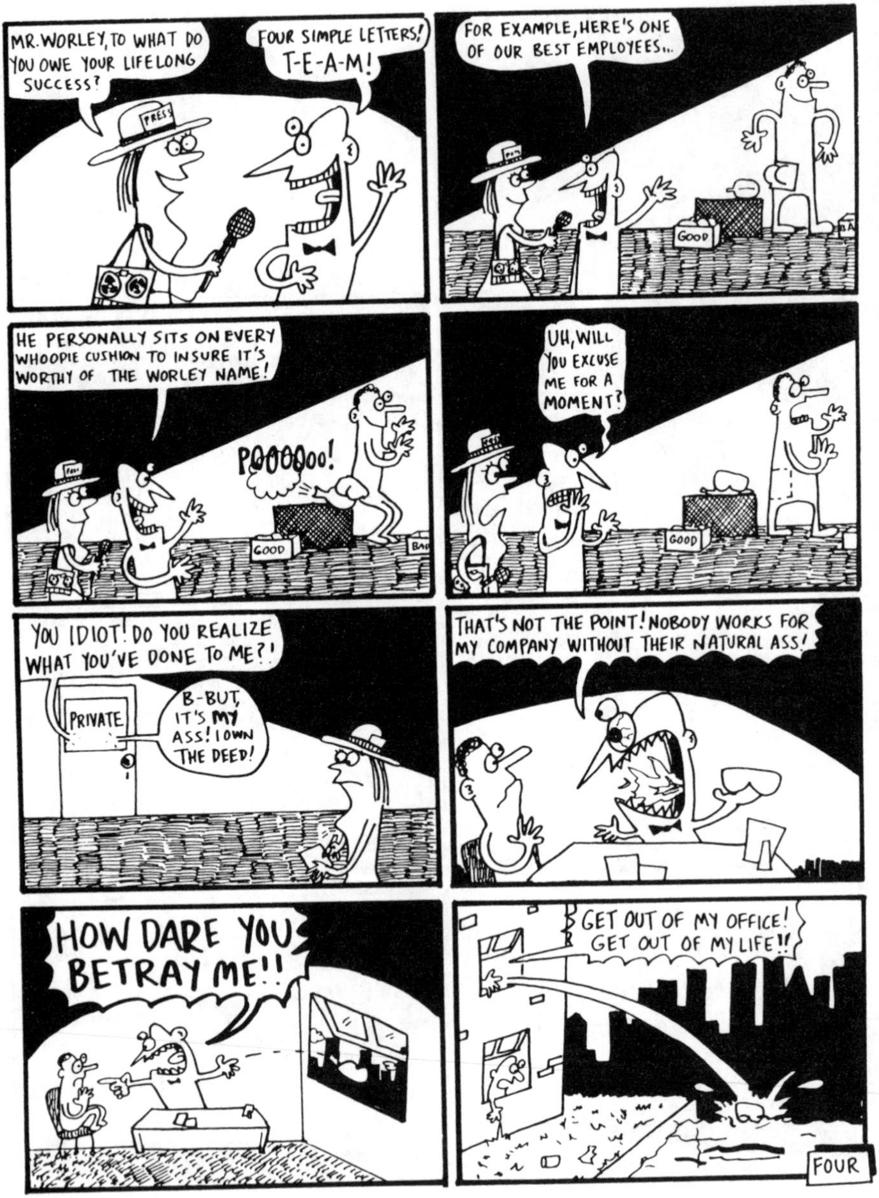
MR. WORLEY, TO WHAT DO YOU OWE YOUR LIFELONG SUCCESS?
PRESS
FOUR SIMPLE LETTERS! T-E-A-M!
FOR EXAMPLE, HERE'S ONE OF OUR BEST EMPLOYEES...
GOOD
HE PERSONALLY SITS ON EVERY WHOOPIE CUSHION TO INSURE IT'S WORTHY OF THE WORLEY NAME!
POOOOOoo!
GOOD
UH, WILL YOU EXCUSE ME FOR A MOMENT?
GOOD
YOU IDIOT! DO YOU REALIZE WHAT YOU'VE DONE TO ME?!
PRIVATE
B-BUT, IT'S MY ASS! I OWN THE DEED!
THAT'S NOT THE POINT! NOBODY WORKS FOR MY COMPANY WITHOUT THEIR NATURAL ASS!
HOW DARE YOU BETRAY ME!!
GET OUT OF MY OFFICE! GET OUT OF MY LIFE!!
FOUR

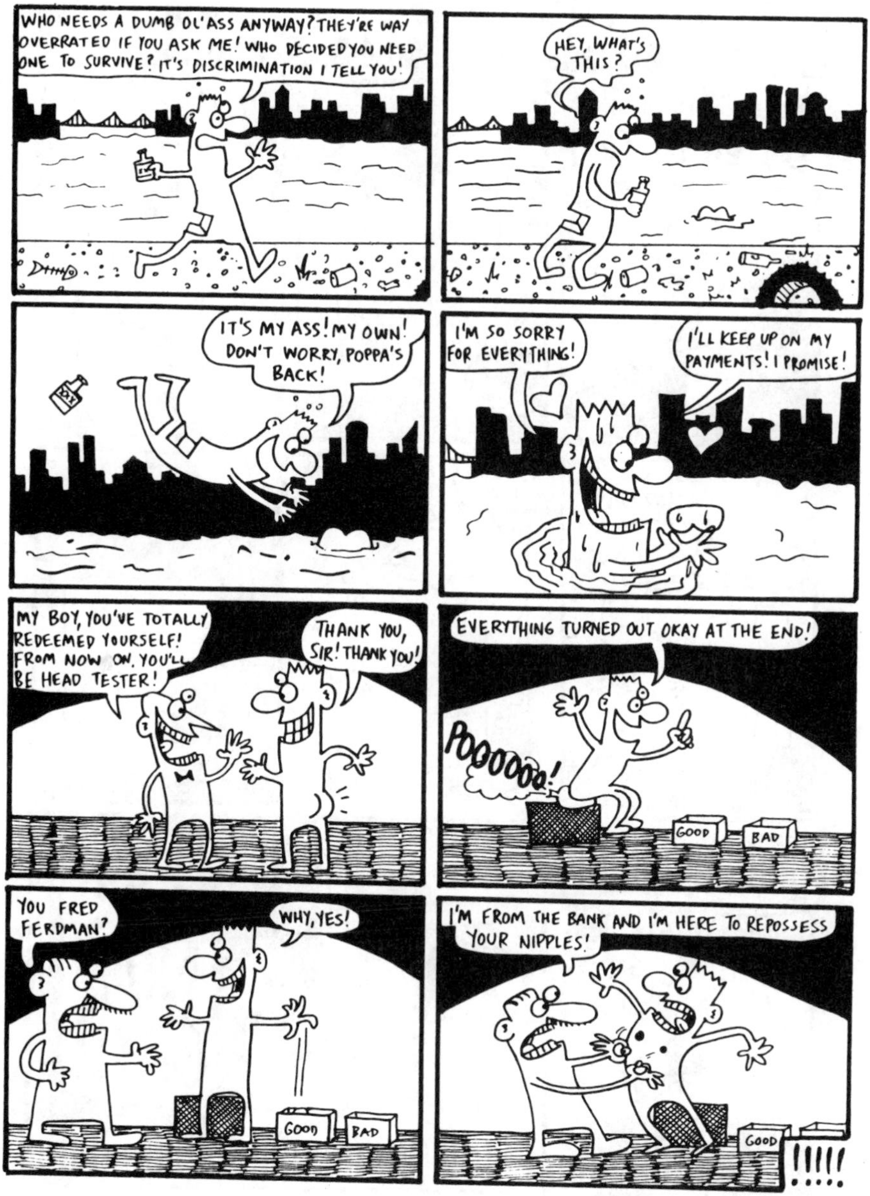
WHO NEEDS A DUMB OL' ASS ANYWAY? THEY'RE WAY OVERRATED IF YOU ASK ME! WHO DECIDED YOU NEED ONE TO SURVIVE? IT'S DISCRIMINATION I TELL YOU!
HEY, WHAT'S THIS?
IT'S MY ASS! MY OWN! DON'T WORRY, POPPA'S BACK!
I'M SO SORRY FOR EVERYTHING!
I'LL KEEP UP ON MY PAYMENTS! I PROMISE!
MY BOY, YOU'VE TOTALLY REDEEMED YOURSELF! FROM NOW ON, YOU'LL BE HEAD TESTER!
THANK YOU, SIR! THANK YOU!
EVERYTHING TURNED OUT OKAY AT THE END!
POOOOOOO!
GOOD
BAD
YOU FRED FERDMAN?
WHY, YES!
GOOD
BAD
I'M FROM THE BANK AND I'M HERE TO REPOSSESS YOUR NIPPLES!
GOOD
!!!!!

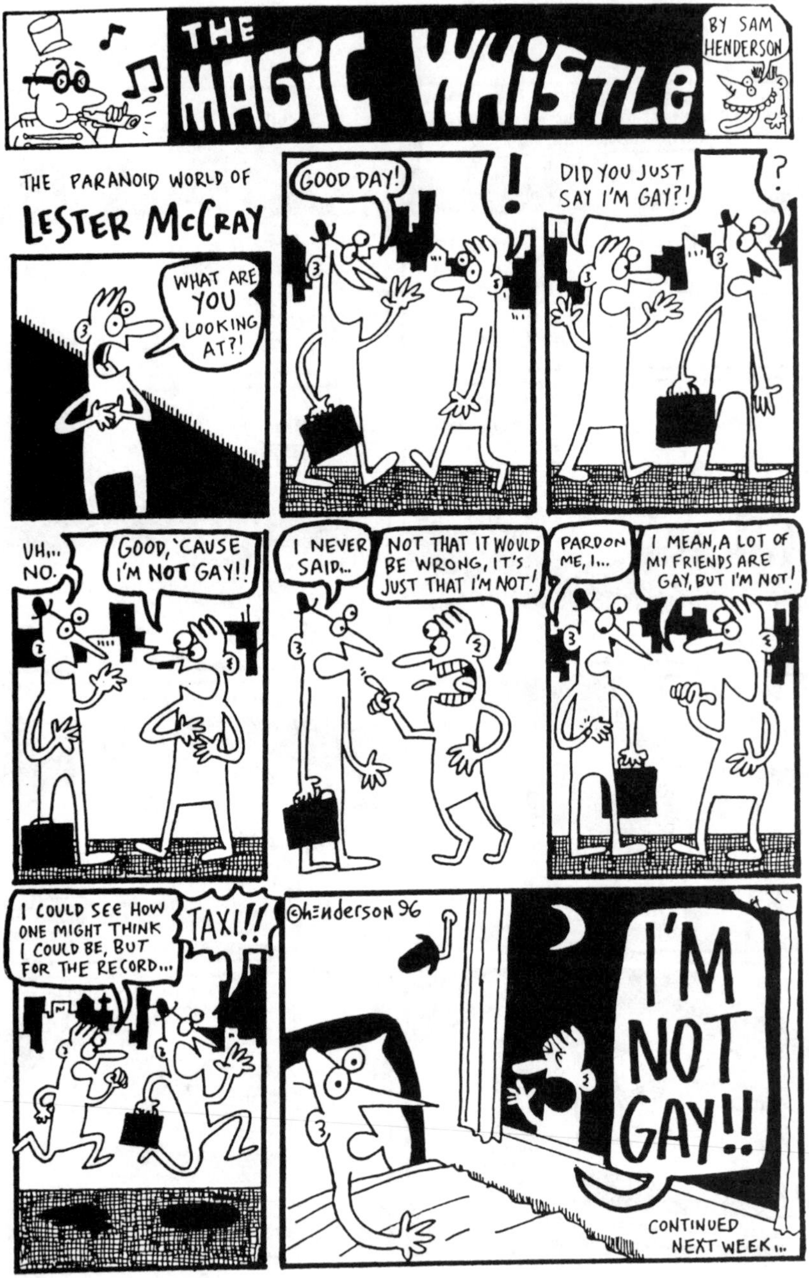

THE MAGIC WHISTLE
BY SAM HENDERSON
THE PARANOID WORLD OF
LESTER McCRAY
WHAT ARE YOU LOOKING AT?!
GOOD DAY!
!
DID YOU JUST SAY I'M GAY?!
?
UH... NO.
GOOD, 'CAUSE I'M NOT GAY!!
I NEVER SAID...
NOT THAT IT WOULD BE WRONG, IT'S JUST THAT I'M NOT!
PARDON ME, I...
I MEAN, A LOT OF MY FRIENDS ARE GAY, BUT I'M NOT!
I COULD SEE HOW ONE MIGHT THINK I COULD BE, BUT FOR THE RECORD...
TAXI!!!
©henderson 96
I'M NOT GAY!!
CONTINUED NEXT WEEK...

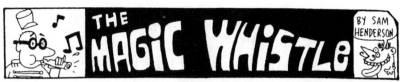

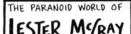

THE MAGIC WHISTLE
BY SAM HENDERSON
THE PARANOID WORLD OF
LESTER McCRAY
LAST WEEK, LESTER MCCRAY MISUNDERSTOOD SOMEBODY, AND THOUGHT THE MAN SAID HE WAS GAY. ALTHOUGH NOT HOMOPHOBIC, LESTER HAS GONE TO GREAT LENGTHS TO LET EVERYONE KNOW HE IS NOT GAY...
THAT'S 'CAUSE I'M NOT!
©henderson 96
IT'S OK IF YOU'RE GAY BUT I'M NOT!!
LESTER McCRAY IS NOT GAY
FOR THE MILLIONTH TIME, I'M NOT GAY!!
SOAP BOX
NEWS LESTER NOT GAY
MR. McCRAY, WE NEED TO HAVE A TALK...
I REPRESENT THE PEOPLE OF THIS FAIR CITY AND WE DEMAND YOU CEASE TELLING OF HOW YOU'RE NOT GAY...
...AND FURTHERMORE, NOBODY GIVES A RAT'S ASS WHETHER YOU ARE OR NOT BECAUSE YOU'RE ANNOYING TO PEOPLE OF ALL SEXUAL ORIENTATIONS!
THANK GOODNESS WE'VE CLEARED THAT ALL UP...
AND WHILE I HAVE YOU HERE, I WANT TO LET YOU KNOW I DON'T MASTURBATE!!
NOT ONLY DO I NOT DO THAT, I'VE NEVER EVEN THOUGHT ABOUT IT...
HERE WE GO AGAIN!

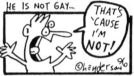

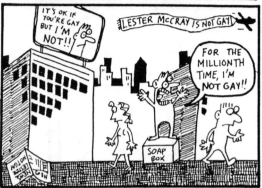

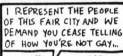

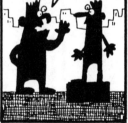

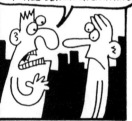

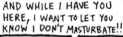

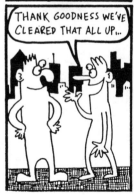

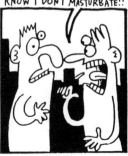

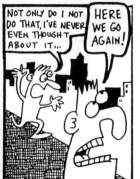

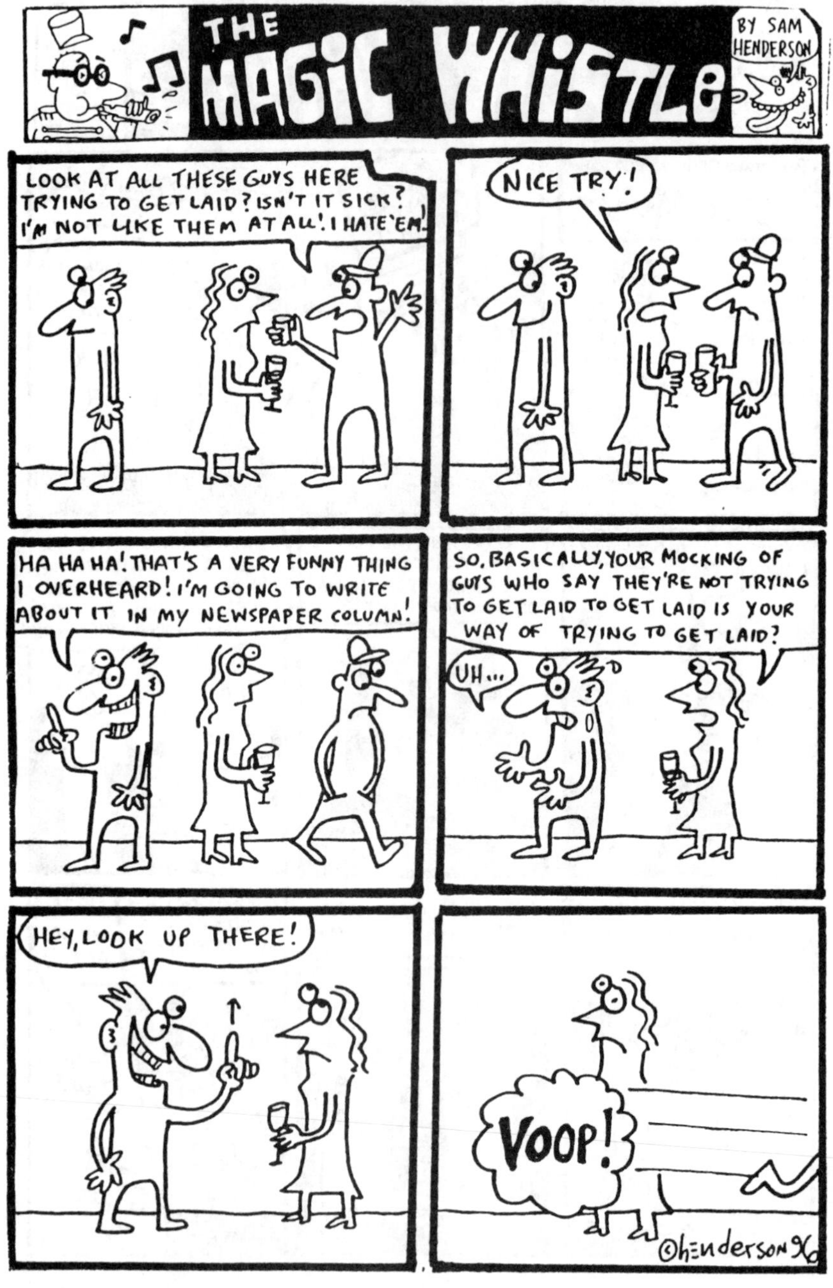
THE MAGIC WHISTLE
BY SAM HENDERSON
LOOK AT ALL THESE GUYS HERE TRYING TO GET LAID? ISN'T IT SICK? I'M NOT LIKE THEM AT ALL! I HATE 'EM!
NICE TRY!
HA HA HA! THAT'S A VERY FUNNY THING I OVERHEARD! I'M GOING TO WRITE ABOUT IT IN MY NEWSPAPER COLUMN!
SO, BASICALLY, YOUR MOCKING OF GUYS WHO SAY THEY'RE NOT TRYING TO GET LAID TO GET LAID IS YOUR WAY OF TRYING TO GET LAID?
UH...
HEY, LOOK UP THERE!
VOOP!
©henderson 96

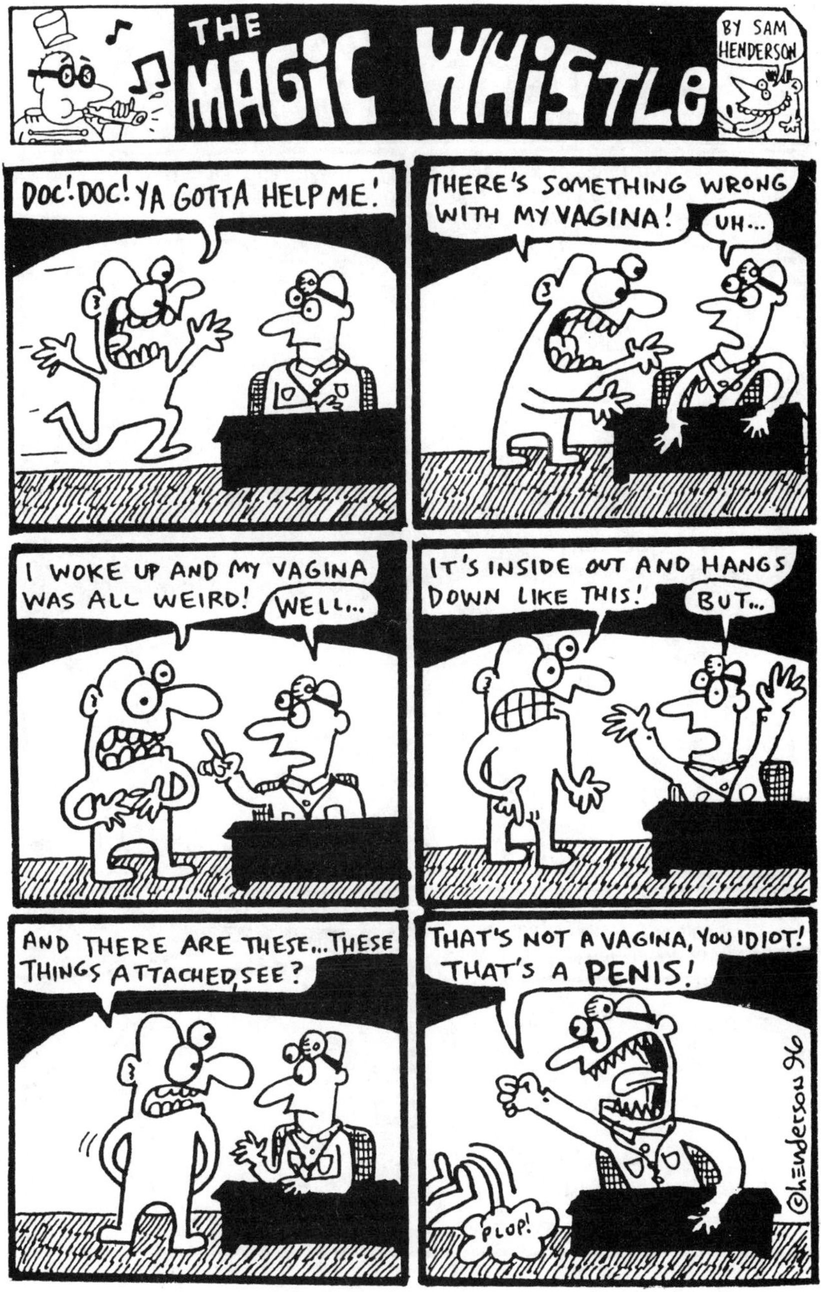
THE MAGIC WHISTLE
BY SAM HENDERSON
DOC! DOC! YA GOTTA HELP ME!
THERE'S SOMETHING WRONG WITH MY VAGINA!
UH...
I WOKE UP AND MY VAGINA WAS ALL WEIRD!
WELL...
IT'S INSIDE OUT AND HANGS DOWN LIKE THIS!
BUT...
AND THERE ARE THESE... THESE THINGS ATTACHED, SEE?
THAT'S NOT A VAGINA, YOU IDIOT! THAT'S A PENIS!
PLOP!
©henderson 96

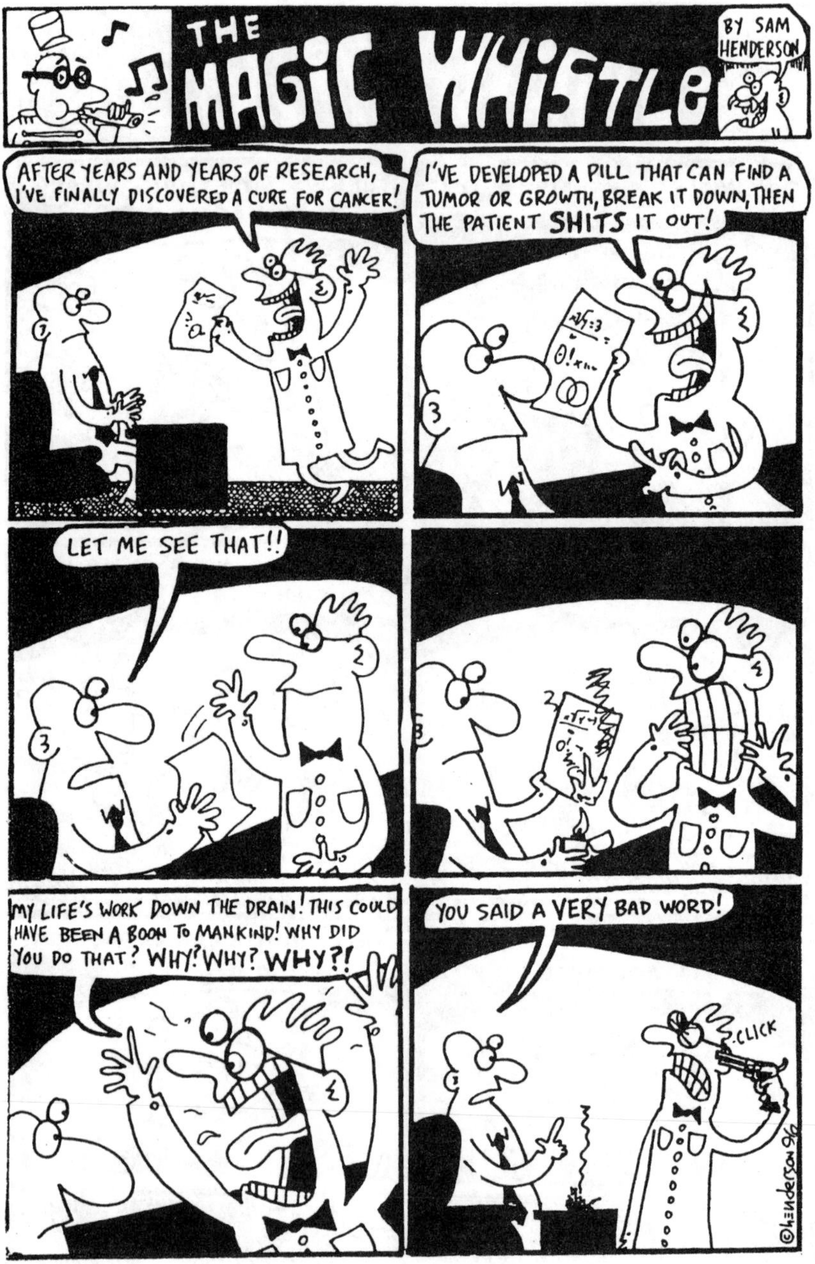
THE MAGIC WHISTLE
BY SAM HENDERSON
AFTER YEARS AND YEARS OF RESEARCH, I'VE FINALLY DISCOVERED A CURE FOR CANCER!
I'VE DEVELOPED A PILL THAT CAN FIND A TUMOR OR GROWTH, BREAK IT DOWN, THEN THE PATIENT SHITS IT OUT!
LET ME SEE THAT!!
MY LIFE'S WORK DOWN THE DRAIN! THIS COULD HAVE BEEN A BOON TO MANKIND! WHY DID YOU DO THAT? WHY? WHY? WHY?!
YOU SAID A VERY BAD WORD!
CLICK
©henderson 96

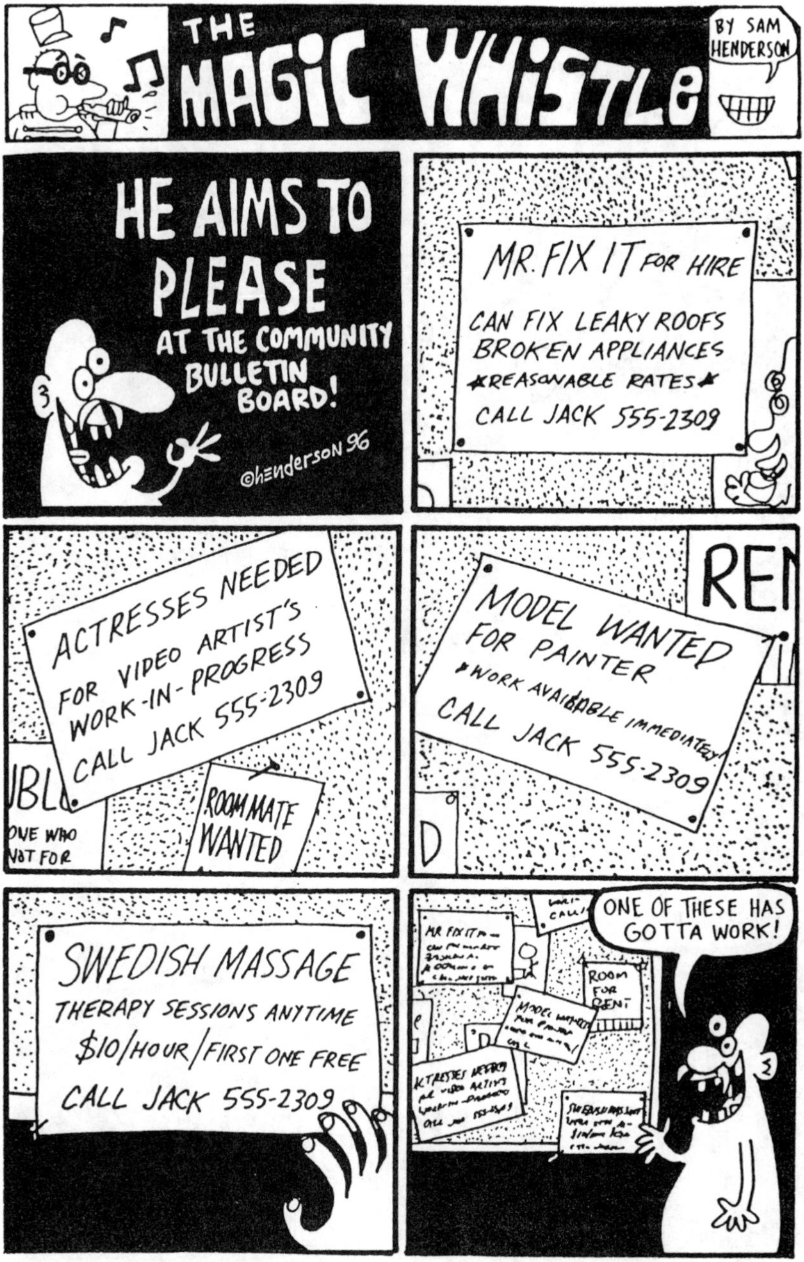
THE MAGIC WHISTLE
BY SAM HENDERSON
HE AIMS TO PLEASE AT THE COMMUNITY BULLETIN BOARD!
©henderson 96
MR. FIX IT FOR HIRE
CAN FIX LEAKY ROOFS
BROKEN APPLIANCES
★REASONABLE RATES★
CALL JACK 555-2309
ACTRESSES NEEDED
FOR VIDEO ARTIST'S
WORK-IN-PROGRESS
CALL JACK 555-2309
ROOMMATE WANTED
MODEL WANTED
FOR PAINTER
*WORK AVAILABLE IMMEDIATELY
CALL JACK 555-2309
SWEDISH MASSAGE
THERAPY SESSIONS ANYTIME
$10/HOUR/FIRST ONE FREE
CALL JACK 555-2309
ROOM FOR RENT
ONE OF THESE HAS GOTTA WORK!

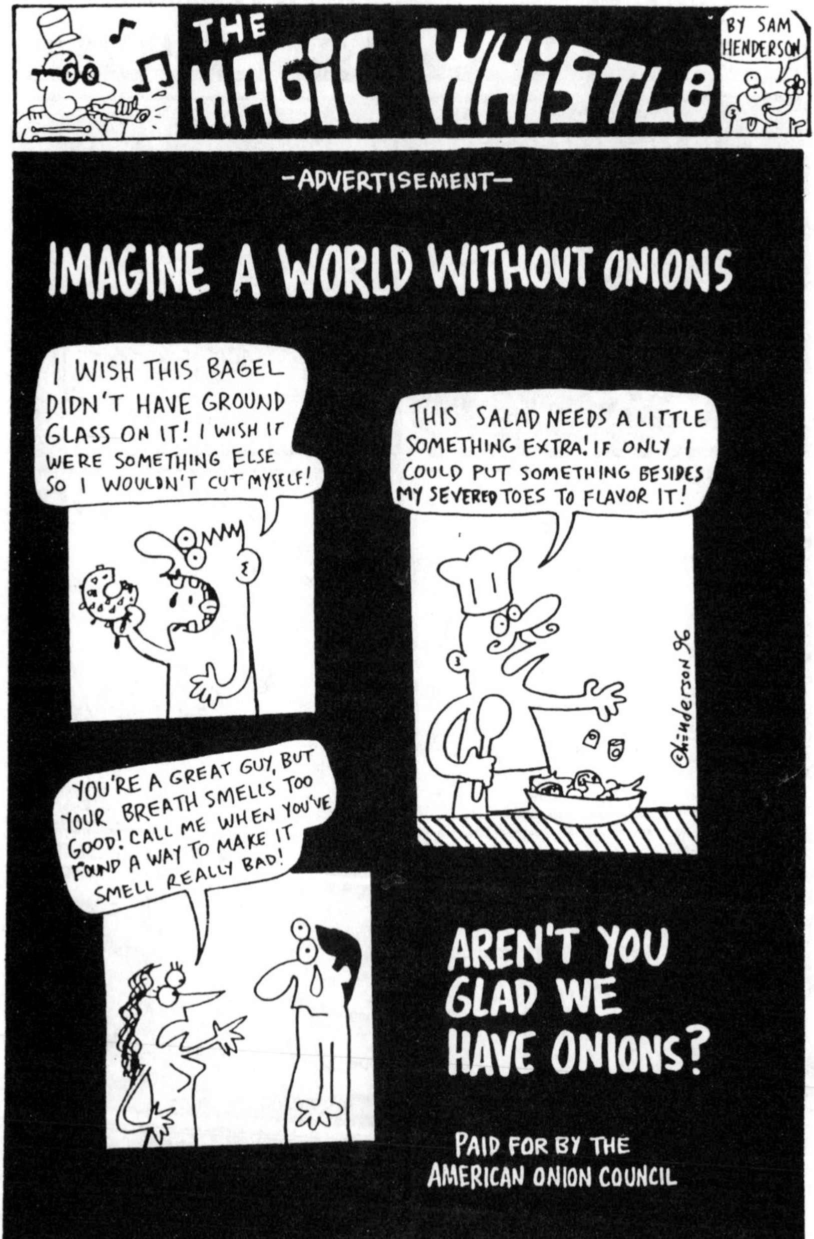
THE MAGIC WHISTLE
BY SAM HENDERSON
-ADVERTISEMENT-
IMAGINE A WORLD WITHOUT ONIONS
I WISH THIS BAGEL DIDN'T HAVE GROUND GLASS ON IT! I WISH IT WERE SOMETHING ELSE SO I WOULDN'T CUT MYSELF!
THIS SALAD NEEDS A LITTLE SOMETHING EXTRA! IF ONLY I COULD PUT SOMETHING BESIDES MY SEVERED TOES TO FLAVOR IT!
©Henderson 96
YOU'RE A GREAT GUY, BUT YOUR BREATH SMELLS TOO GOOD! CALL ME WHEN YOU'VE FOUND A WAY TO MAKE IT SMELL REALLY BAD!
AREN'T YOU GLAD WE HAVE ONIONS?
PAID FOR BY THE AMERICAN ONION COUNCIL

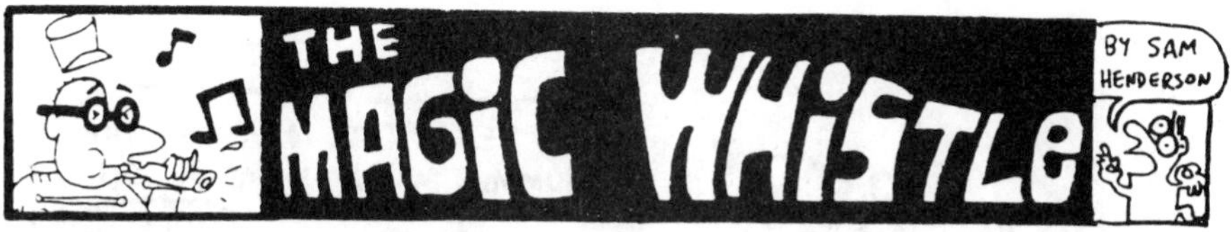
THE MAGIC WHISTLE
BY SAM HENDERSON

SORRY, MY PARENTS MADE ME DRAW THESE...

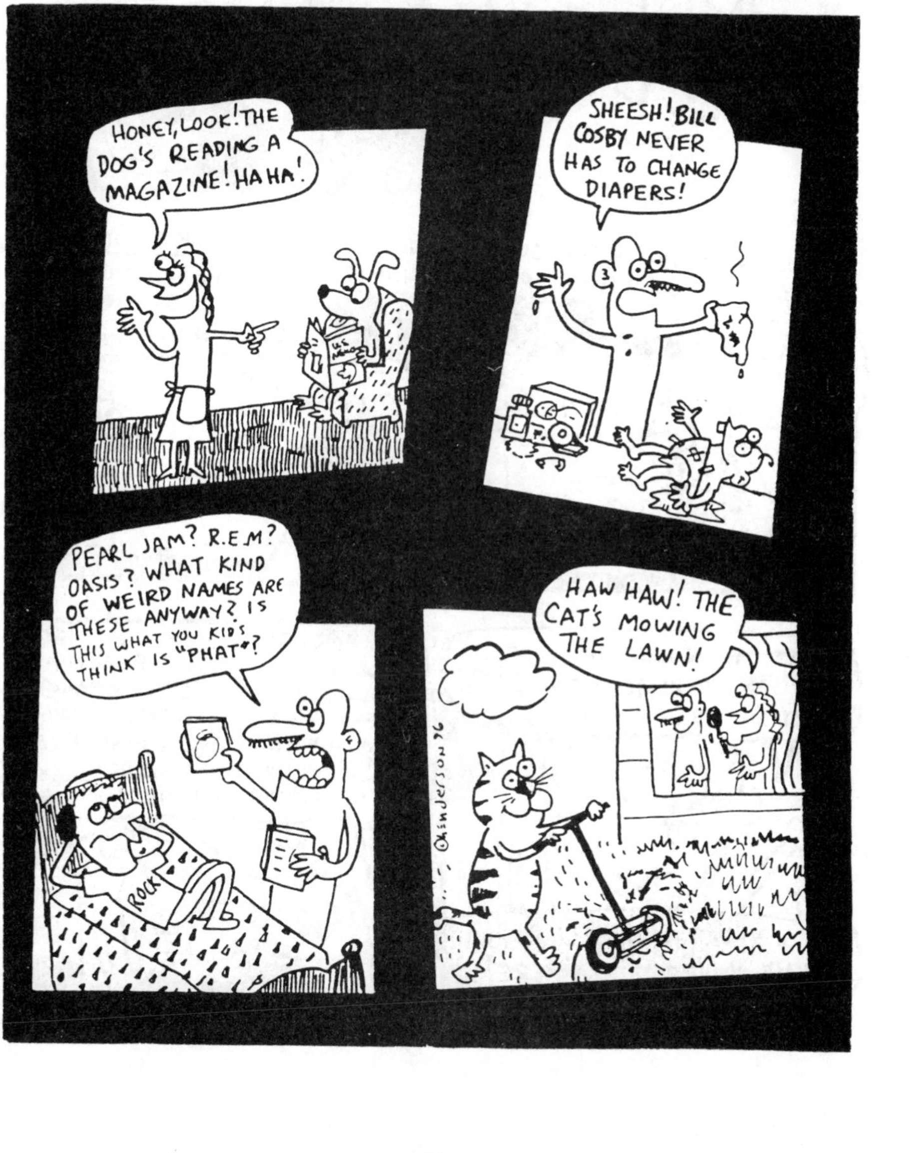
HONEY, LOOK! THE DOG'S READING A MAGAZINE! HA HA!
SHEESH! BILL COSBY NEVER HAS TO CHANGE DIAPERS!
PEARL JAM? R.E.M? OASIS? WHAT KIND OF WEIRD NAMES ARE THESE ANYWAY? IS THIS WHAT YOU KIDS THINK IS "PHAT"?
ROCK
HAW HAW! THE CAT'S MOWING THE LAWN!
©HENDERSON '96

"MY BEST SUMMER JOB EVER"

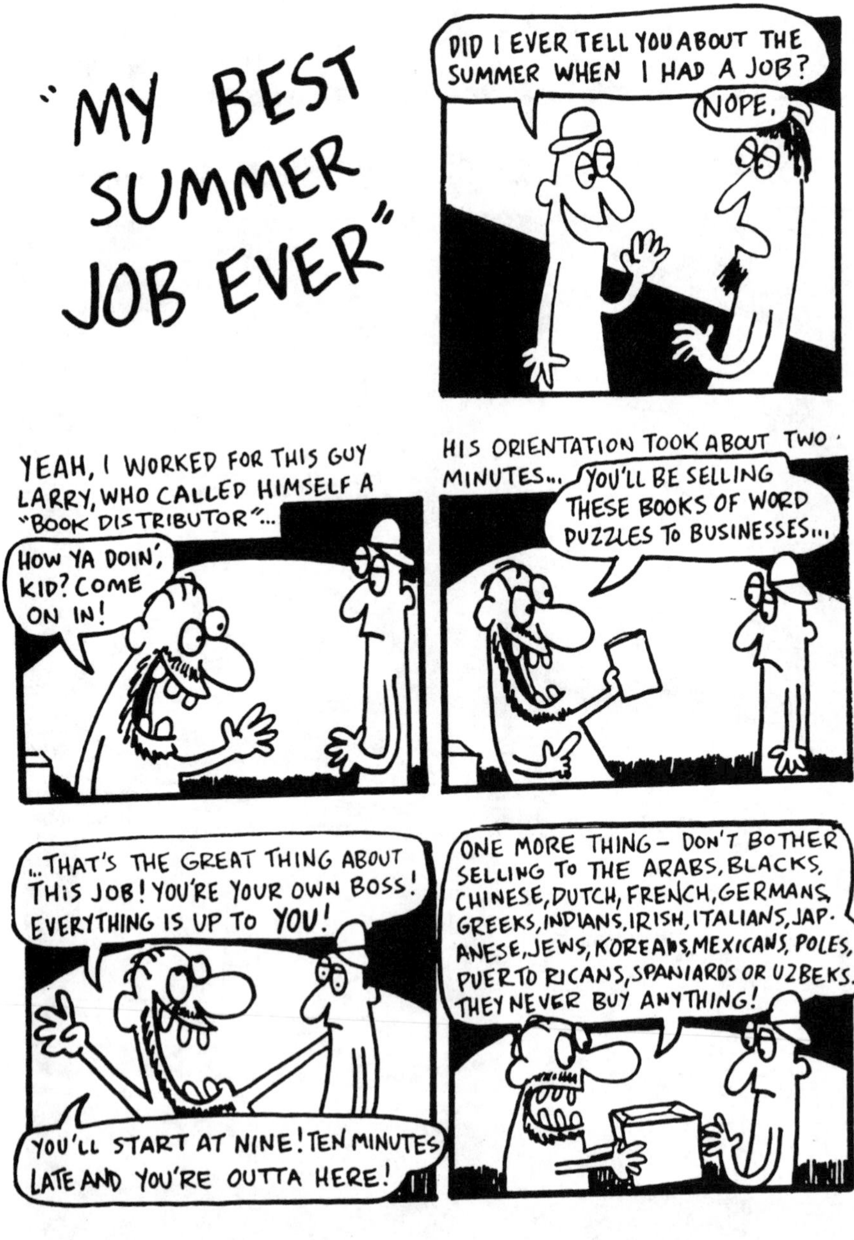
DID I EVER TELL YOU ABOUT THE SUMMER WHEN I HAD A JOB?
NOPE.
YEAH, I WORKED FOR THIS GUY LARRY, WHO CALLED HIMSELF A "BOOK DISTRIBUTOR"...
HOW YA DOIN', KID? COME ON IN!
HIS ORIENTATION TOOK ABOUT TWO MINUTES...
YOU'LL BE SELLING THESE BOOKS OF WORD PUZZLES TO BUSINESSES...
...THAT'S THE GREAT THING ABOUT THIS JOB! YOU'RE YOUR OWN BOSS! EVERYTHING IS UP TO YOU!
YOU'LL START AT NINE! TEN MINUTES LATE AND YOU'RE OUTTA HERE!
ONE MORE THING – DON'T BOTHER SELLING TO THE ARABS, BLACKS, CHINESE, DUTCH, FRENCH, GERMANS, GREEKS, INDIANS, IRISH, ITALIANS, JAP-ANESE, JEWS, KOREANS, MEXICANS, POLES, PUERTO RICANS, SPANIARDS OR UZBEKS! THEY NEVER BUY ANYTHING!

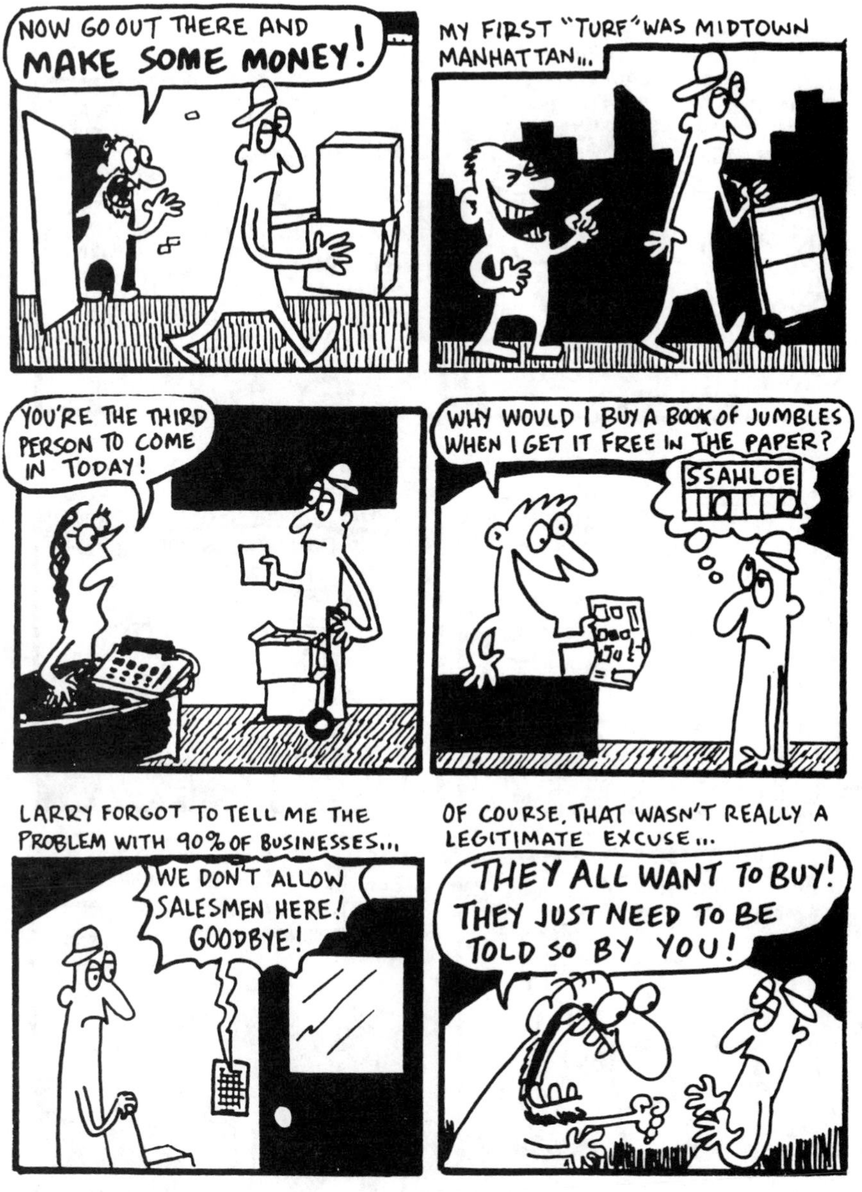
NOW GO OUT THERE AND MAKE SOME MONEY!
MY FIRST "TURF" WAS MIDTOWN MANHATTAN...
YOU'RE THE THIRD PERSON TO COME IN TODAY!
WHY WOULD I BUY A BOOK OF JUMBLES WHEN I GET IT FREE IN THE PAPER?
SSAHLOE
LARRY FORGOT TO TELL ME THE PROBLEM WITH 90% OF BUSINESSES...
WE DON'T ALLOW SALESMEN HERE! GOODBYE!
OF COURSE, THAT WASN'T REALLY A LEGITIMATE EXCUSE...
THEY ALL WANT TO BUY! THEY JUST NEED TO BE TOLD SO BY YOU!

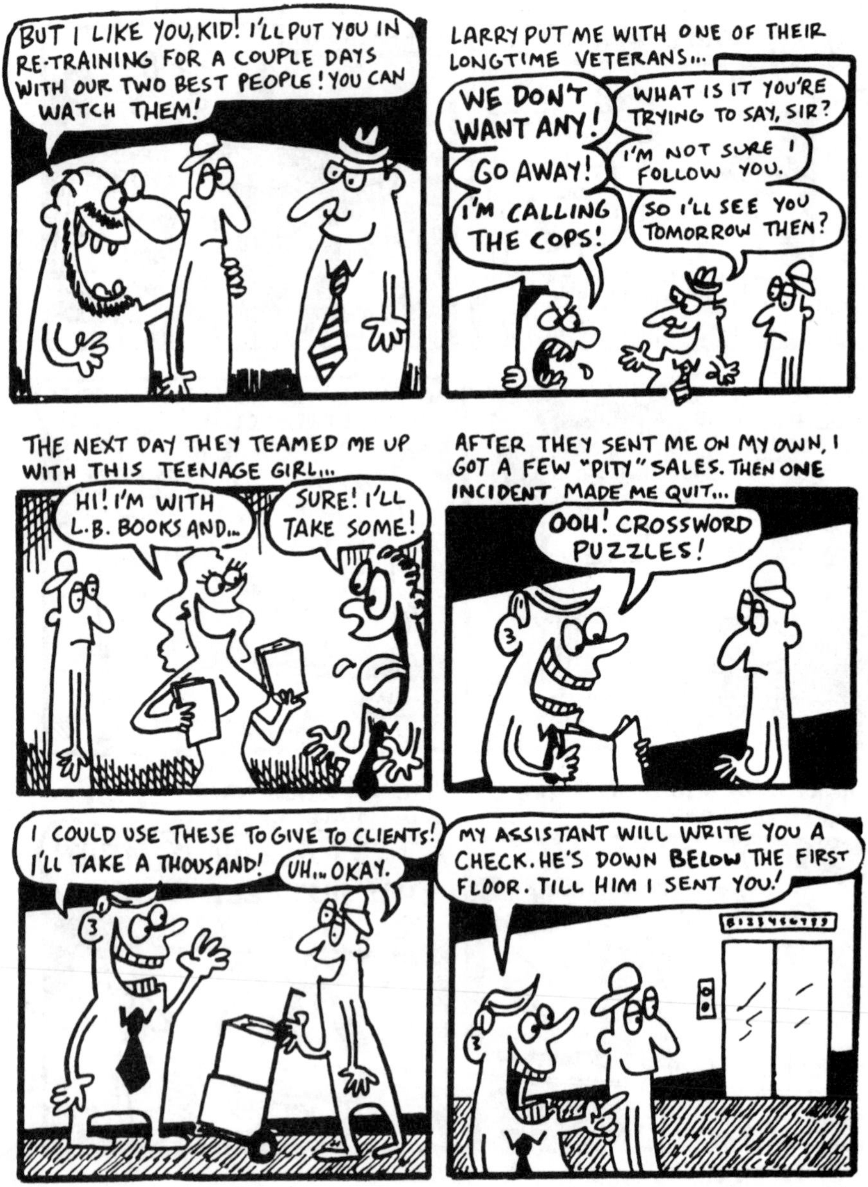
BUT I LIKE YOU, KID! I'LL PUT YOU IN RE-TRAINING FOR A COUPLE DAYS WITH OUR TWO BEST PEOPLE! YOU CAN WATCH THEM!
LARRY PUT ME WITH ONE OF THEIR LONGTIME VETERANS...
WE DON'T WANT ANY!
WHAT IS IT YOU'RE TRYING TO SAY, SIR?
GO AWAY!
I'M NOT SURE I FOLLOW YOU.
I'M CALLING THE COPS!
SO I'LL SEE YOU TOMORROW THEN?
THE NEXT DAY THEY TEAMED ME UP WITH THIS TEENAGE GIRL...
HI! I'M WITH L.B. BOOKS AND...
SURE! I'LL TAKE SOME!
AFTER THEY SENT ME ON MY OWN, I GOT A FEW "PITY" SALES. THEN ONE INCIDENT MADE ME QUIT...
OOH! CROSSWORD PUZZLES!
I COULD USE THESE TO GIVE TO CLIENTS! I'LL TAKE A THOUSAND!
UH... OKAY.
MY ASSISTANT WILL WRITE YOU A CHECK. HE'S DOWN BELOW THE FIRST FLOOR. TILL HIM I SENT YOU!

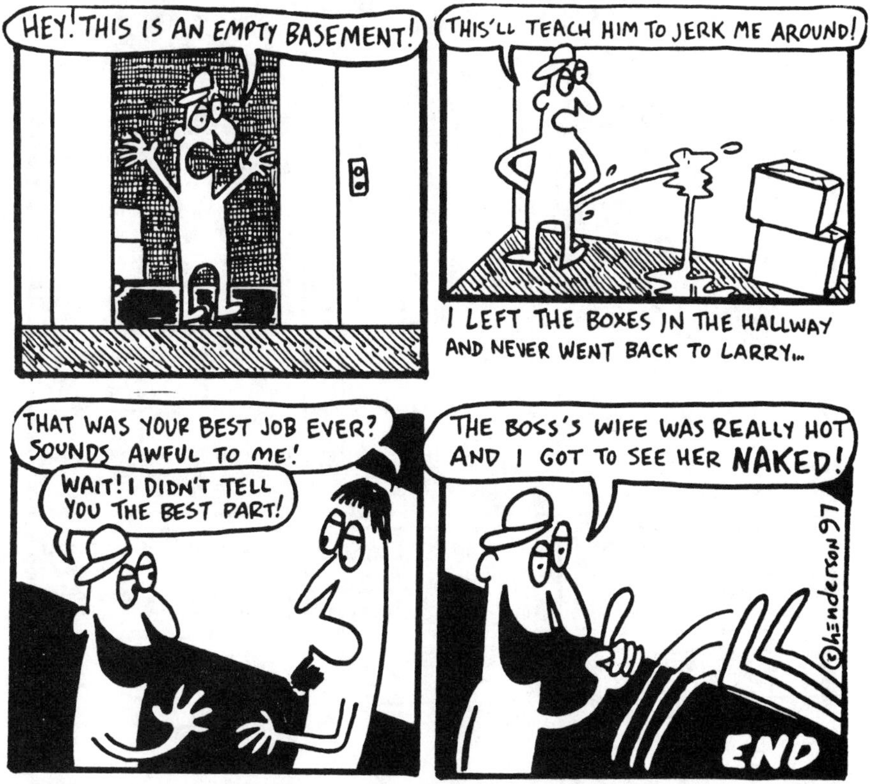
HEY! THIS IS AN EMPTY BASEMENT!
THIS'LL TEACH HIM TO JERK ME AROUND!
I LEFT THE BOXES IN THE HALLWAY AND NEVER WENT BACK TO LARRY...
THAT WAS YOUR BEST JOB EVER? SOUNDS AWFUL TO ME!
WAIT! I DIDN'T TELL YOU THE BEST PART!
THE BOSS'S WIFE WAS REALLY HOT AND I GOT TO SEE HER NAKED!
©henderson97
END

©SAM HENDERSON

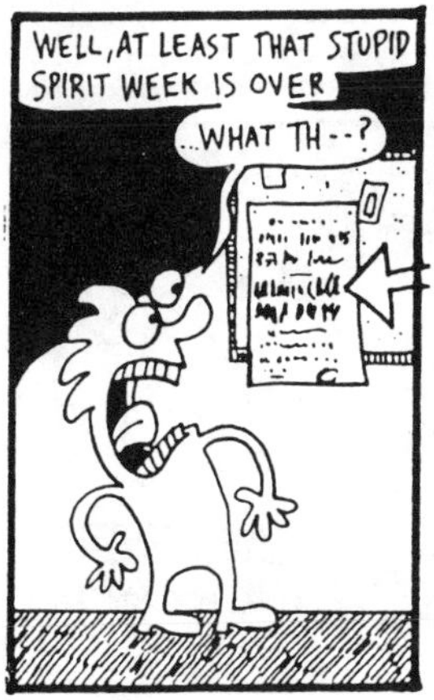
WELL, AT LEAST THAT STUPID SPIRIT WEEK IS OVER
...WHAT TH--?

MAD MAGAZINE RECENTLY PREMIERED ITS "NEW LOOK", WHICH INCLUDES A RECURRING CHARACTER NAMED MONROE. LONGTIME *MAGIC WHISTLE* FANS MAY BE FAMILIAR WITH ANOTHER MONROE, WHICH HAS APPEARED IN MINI AND ALTERNATIVE COMICS SINCE 1990. THE ORIGINAL AUTHOR SEEKS NO COMPENSATION, BUT APOLOGIZES FOR ALL HIS POTSHOTS AT DAVE BERG OVER THE YEARS.

©E C PUBLICATIONS

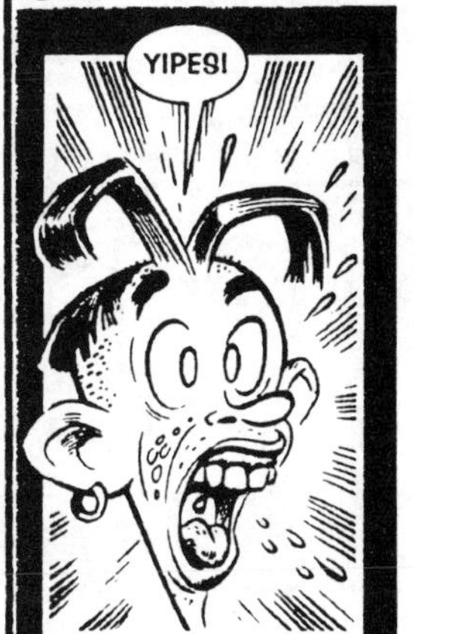
YIPES!

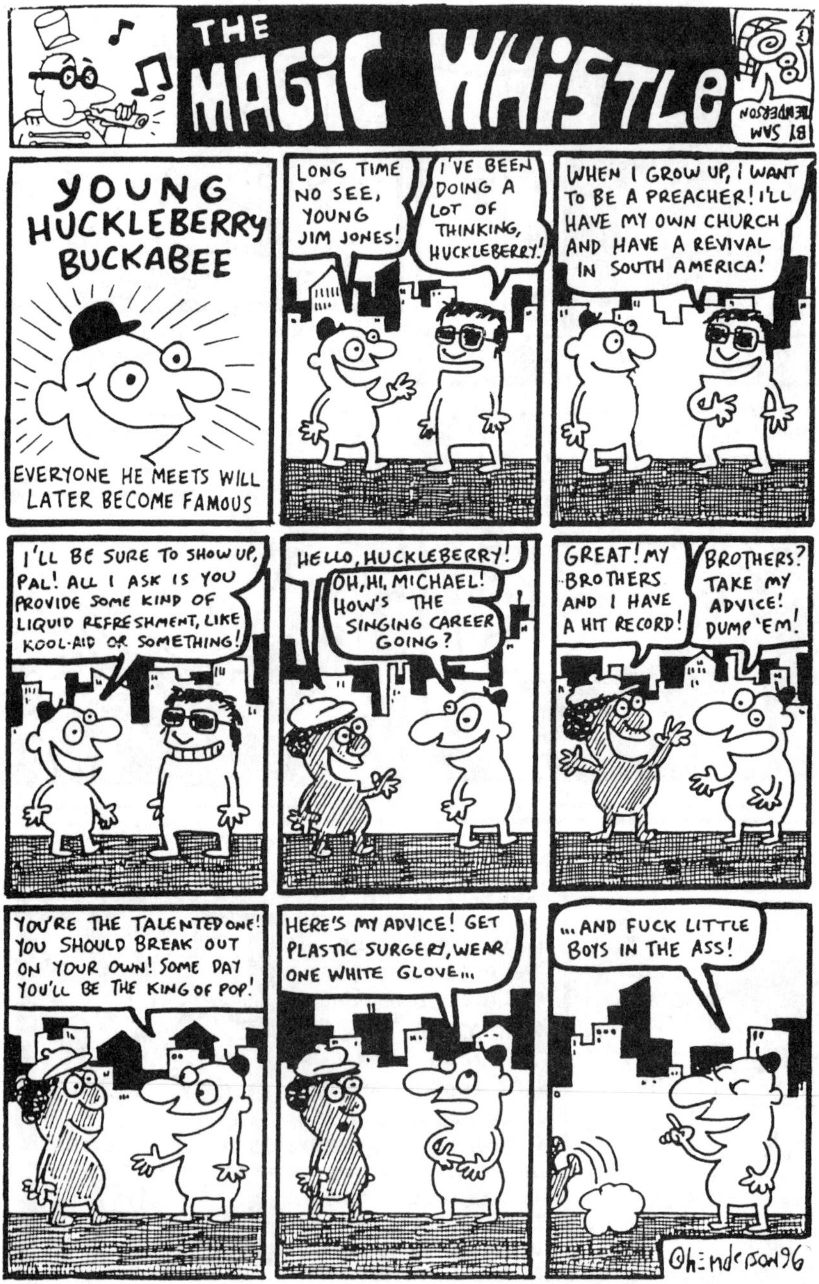
THE MAGIC WHISTLE
BY SAM HENDERSON
YOUNG HUCKLEBERRY BUCKABEE
EVERYONE HE MEETS WILL LATER BECOME FAMOUS
LONG TIME NO SEE, YOUNG JIM JONES!
I'VE BEEN DOING A LOT OF THINKING, HUCKLEBERRY!
WHEN I GROW UP, I WANT TO BE A PREACHER! I'LL HAVE MY OWN CHURCH AND HAVE A REVIVAL IN SOUTH AMERICA!
I'LL BE SURE TO SHOW UP, PAL! ALL I ASK IS YOU PROVIDE SOME KIND OF LIQUID REFRESHMENT, LIKE KOOL-AID OR SOMETHING!
HELLO, HUCKLEBERRY!
OH, HI, MICHAEL! HOW'S THE SINGING CAREER GOING?
GREAT! MY BROTHERS AND I HAVE A HIT RECORD!
BROTHERS? TAKE MY ADVICE! DUMP 'EM!
YOU'RE THE TALENTED ONE! YOU SHOULD BREAK OUT ON YOUR OWN! SOME DAY YOU'LL BE THE KING OF POP!
HERE'S MY ADVICE! GET PLASTIC SURGERY, WEAR ONE WHITE GLOVE...
...AND FUCK LITTLE BOYS IN THE ASS!
©henderson96

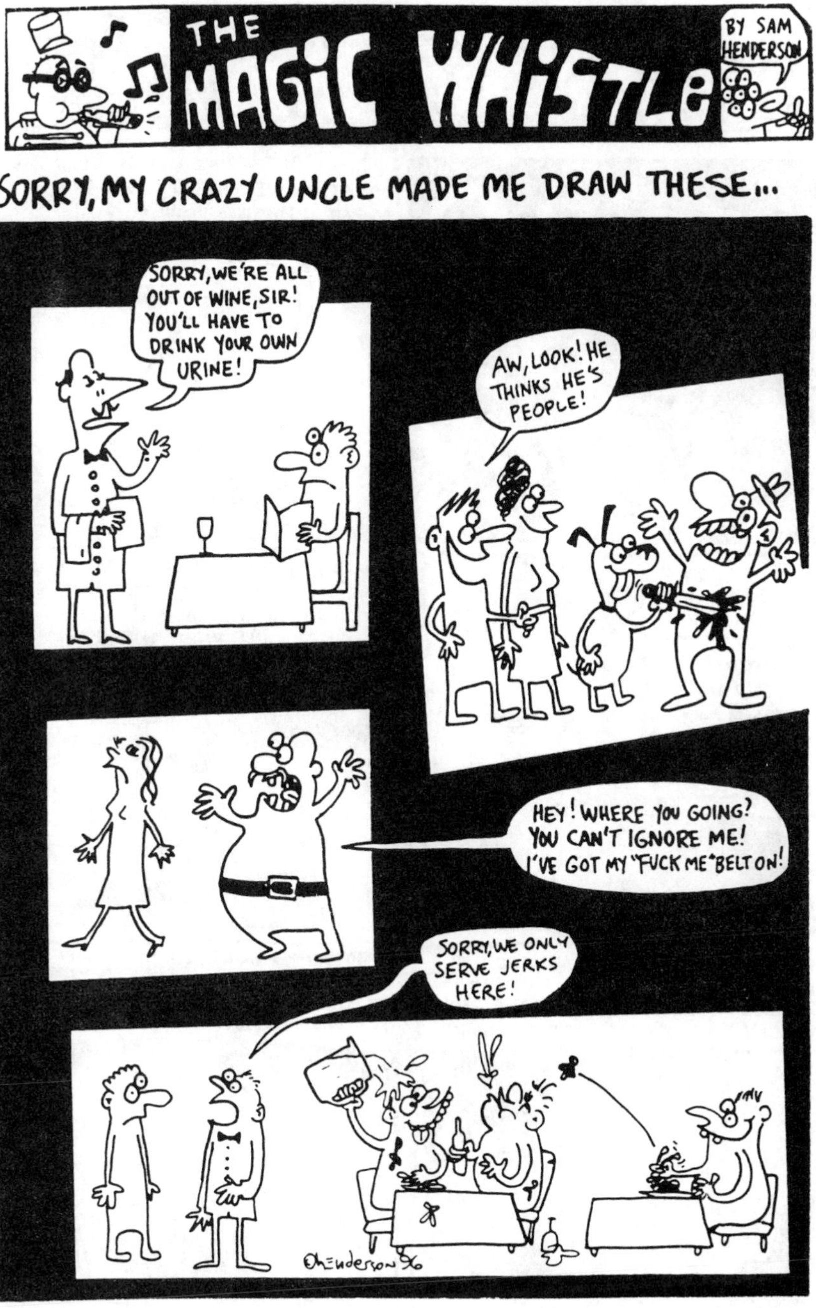
THE MAGIC WHISTLE
BY SAM HENDERSON
SORRY, MY CRAZY UNCLE MADE ME DRAW THESE...
SORRY, WE'RE ALL OUT OF WINE, SIR! YOU'LL HAVE TO DRINK YOUR OWN URINE!
AW, LOOK! HE THINKS HE'S PEOPLE!
HEY! WHERE YOU GOING? YOU CAN'T IGNORE ME! I'VE GOT MY "FUCK ME" BELT ON!
SORRY, WE ONLY SERVE JERKS HERE!
©HENDERSON 96

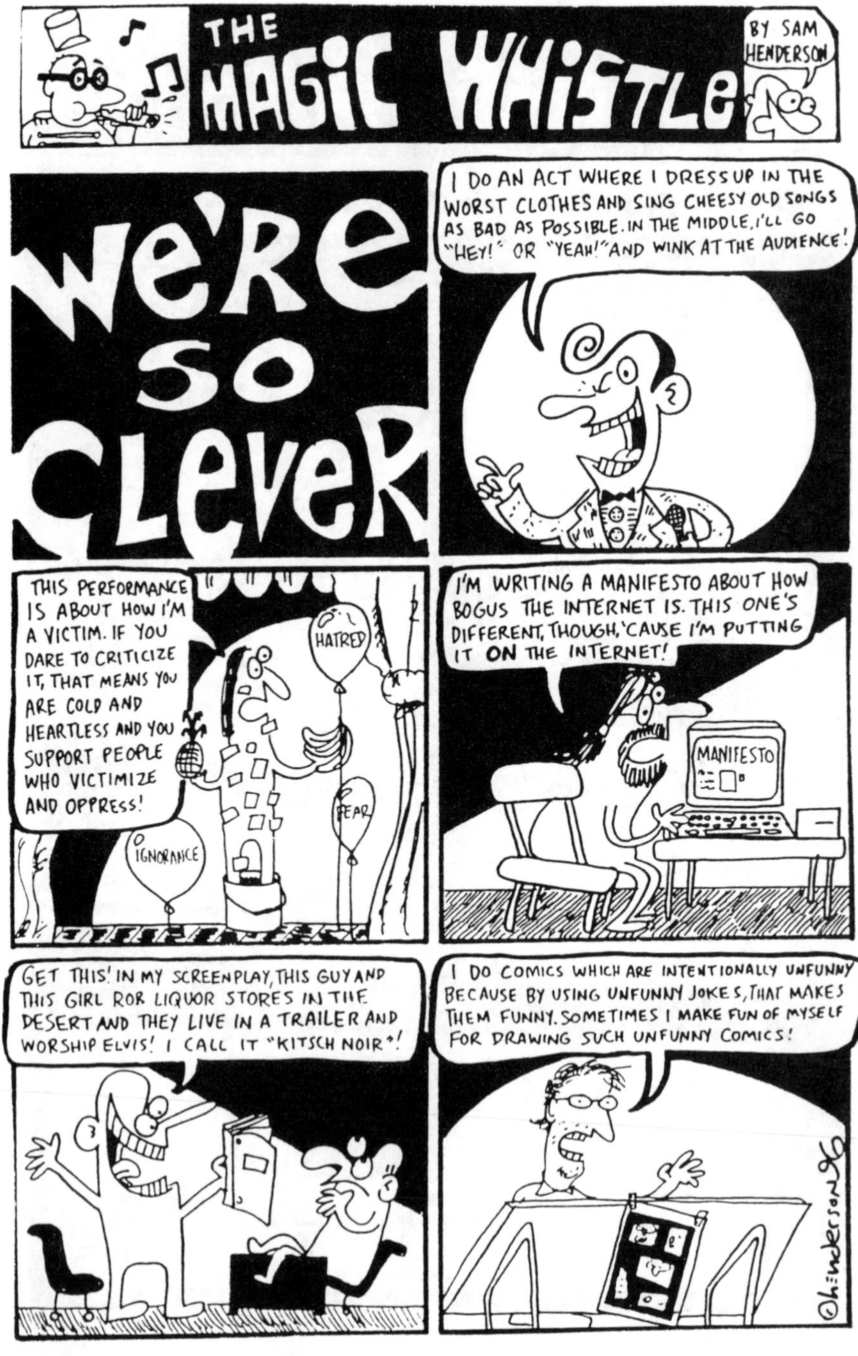
THE MAGIC WHISTLE
BY SAM HENDERSON
WE'RE SO CLEVER
I DO AN ACT WHERE I DRESS UP IN THE WORST CLOTHES AND SING CHEESY OLD SONGS AS BAD AS POSSIBLE. IN THE MIDDLE, I'LL GO "HEY!" OR "YEAH!" AND WINK AT THE AUDIENCE!
THIS PERFORMANCE IS ABOUT HOW I'M A VICTIM. IF YOU DARE TO CRITICIZE IT, THAT MEANS YOU ARE COLD AND HEARTLESS AND YOU SUPPORT PEOPLE WHO VICTIMIZE AND OPPRESS!
HATRED
FEAR
IGNORANCE
I'M WRITING A MANIFESTO ABOUT HOW BOGUS THE INTERNET IS. THIS ONE'S DIFFERENT, THOUGH, 'CAUSE I'M PUTTING IT ON THE INTERNET!
MANIFESTO
GET THIS! IN MY SCREENPLAY, THIS GUY AND THIS GIRL ROB LIQUOR STORES IN THE DESERT AND THEY LIVE IN A TRAILER AND WORSHIP ELVIS! I CALL IT "KITSCH NOIR"!
I DO COMICS WHICH ARE INTENTIONALLY UNFUNNY BECAUSE BY USING UNFUNNY JOKES, THAT MAKES THEM FUNNY. SOMETIMES I MAKE FUN OF MYSELF FOR DRAWING SUCH UNFUNNY COMICS!
©henderson 96

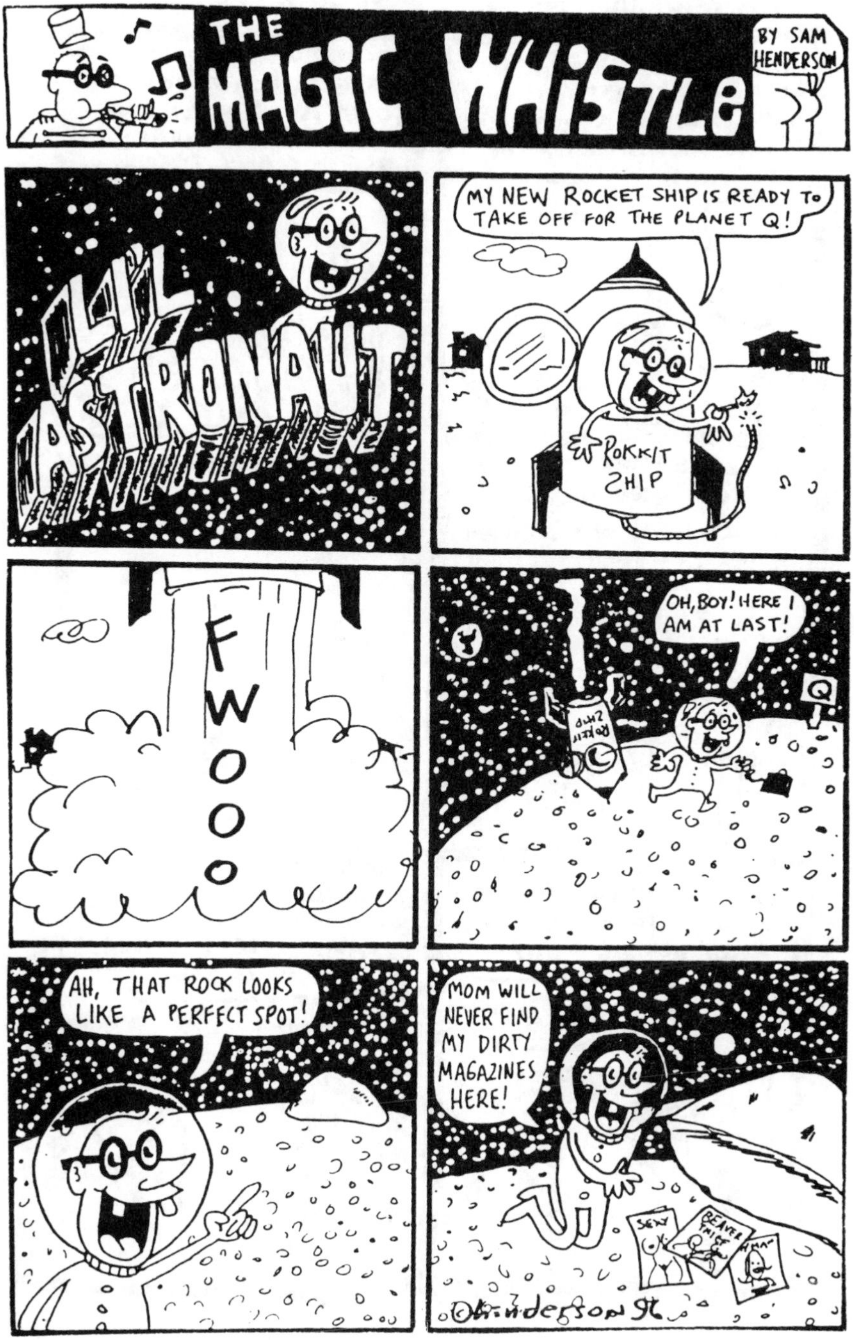
THE MAGIC WHISTLE
BY SAM HENDERSON
LI'L ASTRONAUT
MY NEW ROCKET SHIP IS READY TO TAKE OFF FOR THE PLANET Q!
ROKKIT ZHIP
FWOOO
OH, BOY! HERE I AM AT LAST!
Q
AH, THAT ROCK LOOKS LIKE A PERFECT SPOT!
MOM WILL NEVER FIND MY DIRTY MAGAZINES HERE!
SEXY
BEAVER THIEF
©Henderson 96

HOMOPHOBIA IN THE WORKPLACE

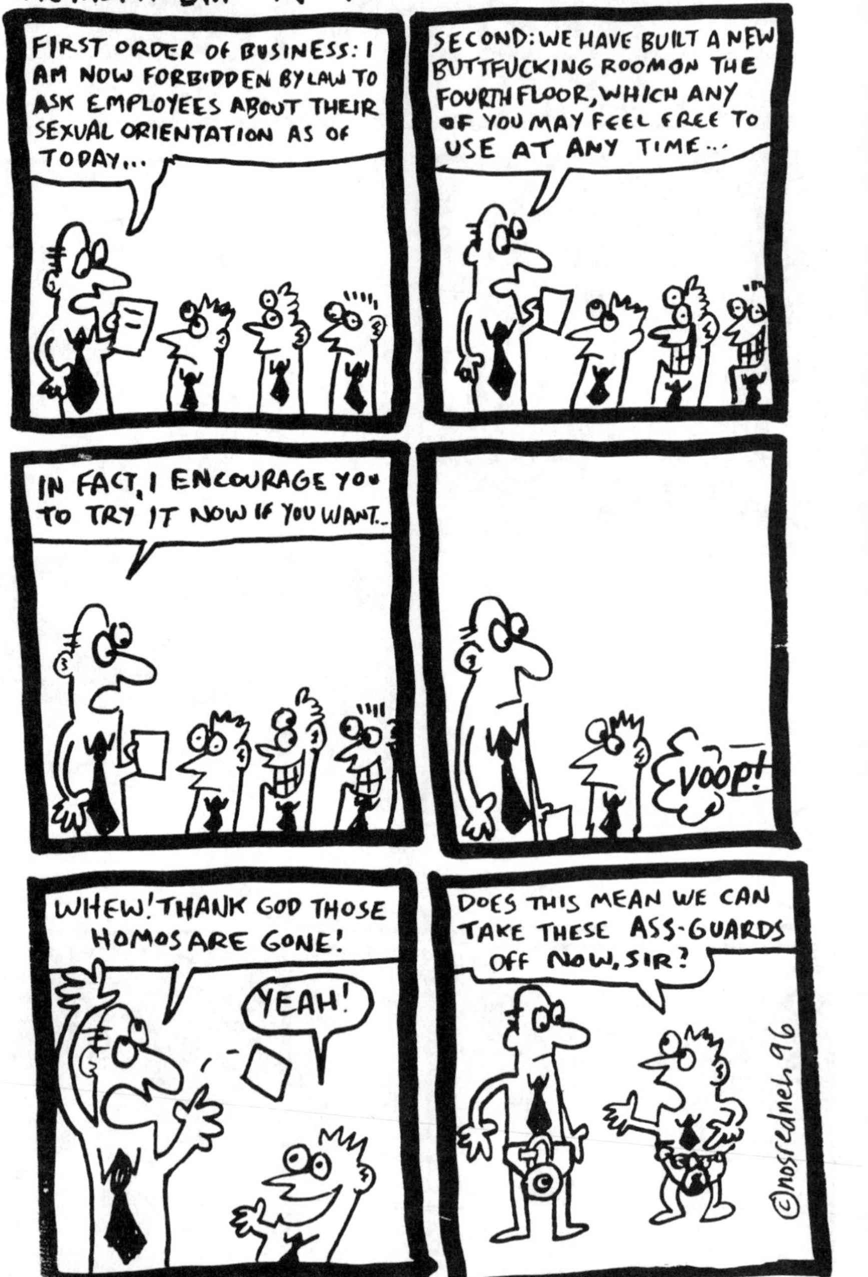

FIRST ORDER OF BUSINESS: I AM NOW FORBIDDEN BY LAW TO ASK EMPLOYEES ABOUT THEIR SEXUAL ORIENTATION AS OF TODAY...
SECOND: WE HAVE BUILT A NEW BUTTFUCKING ROOM ON THE FOURTH FLOOR, WHICH ANY OF YOU MAY FEEL FREE TO USE AT ANY TIME...
IN FACT, I ENCOURAGE YOU TO TRY IT NOW IF YOU WANT...
VOOP!
WHEW! THANK GOD THOSE HOMOS ARE GONE!
YEAH!
DOES THIS MEAN WE CAN TAKE THESE ASS-GUARDS OFF NOW, SIR?
©nosredneh 96

(YOU WOULDN'T HESITATE TO LAUGH IF THIS WAS ABOUT FAT PEOPLE)

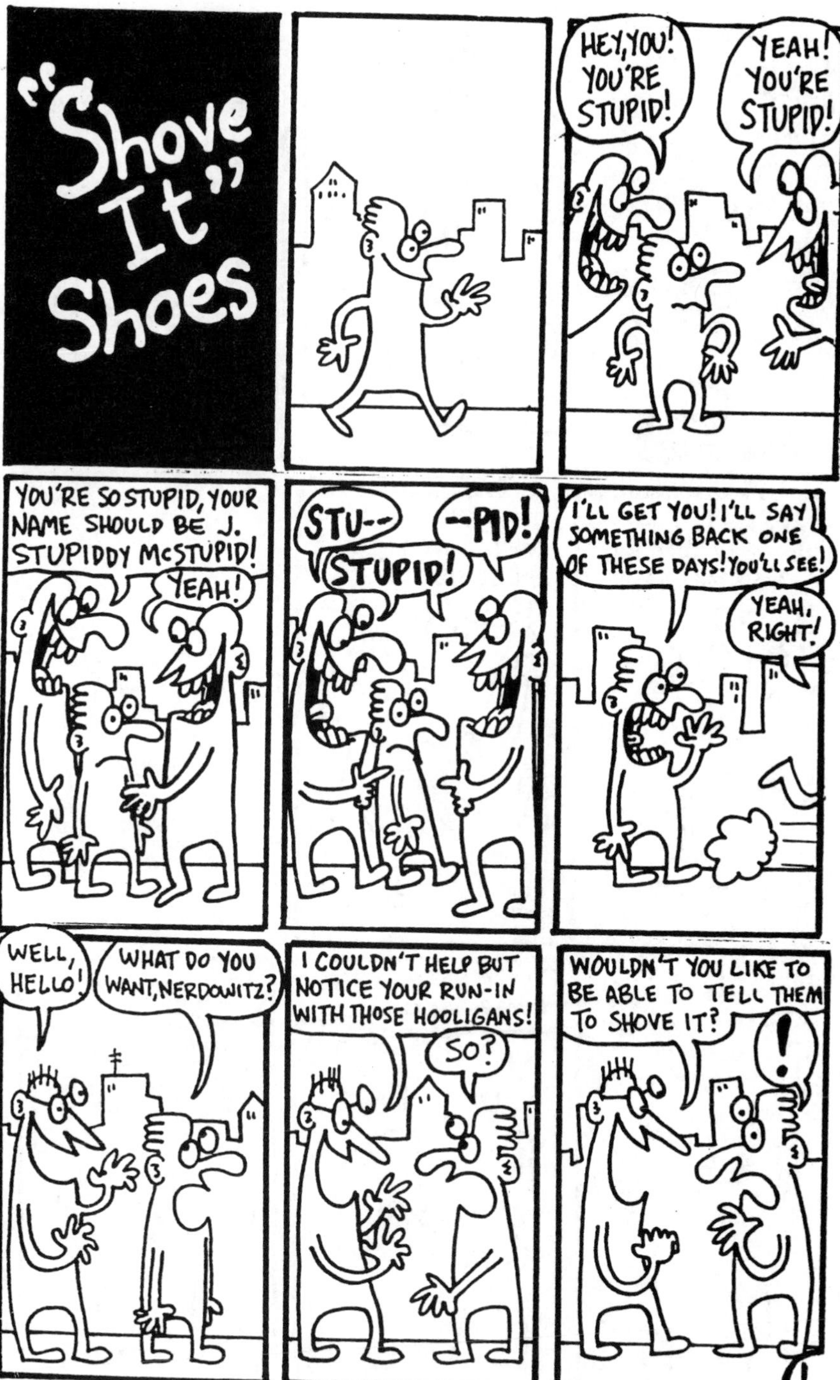

"Shove It" Shoes
HEY, YOU! YOU'RE STUPID!
YEAH! YOU'RE STUPID!
YOU'RE SO STUPID, YOUR NAME SHOULD BE J. STUPIDDY McSTUPID!
YEAH!
STU--
--PID!
STUPID!
I'LL GET YOU! I'LL SAY SOMETHING BACK ONE OF THESE DAYS! YOU'LL SEE!
YEAH, RIGHT!
WELL, HELLO!
WHAT DO YOU WANT, NERDOWITZ?
I COULDN'T HELP BUT NOTICE YOUR RUN-IN WITH THOSE HOOLIGANS!
SO?
WOULDN'T YOU LIKE TO BE ABLE TO TELL THEM TO SHOVE IT?
!

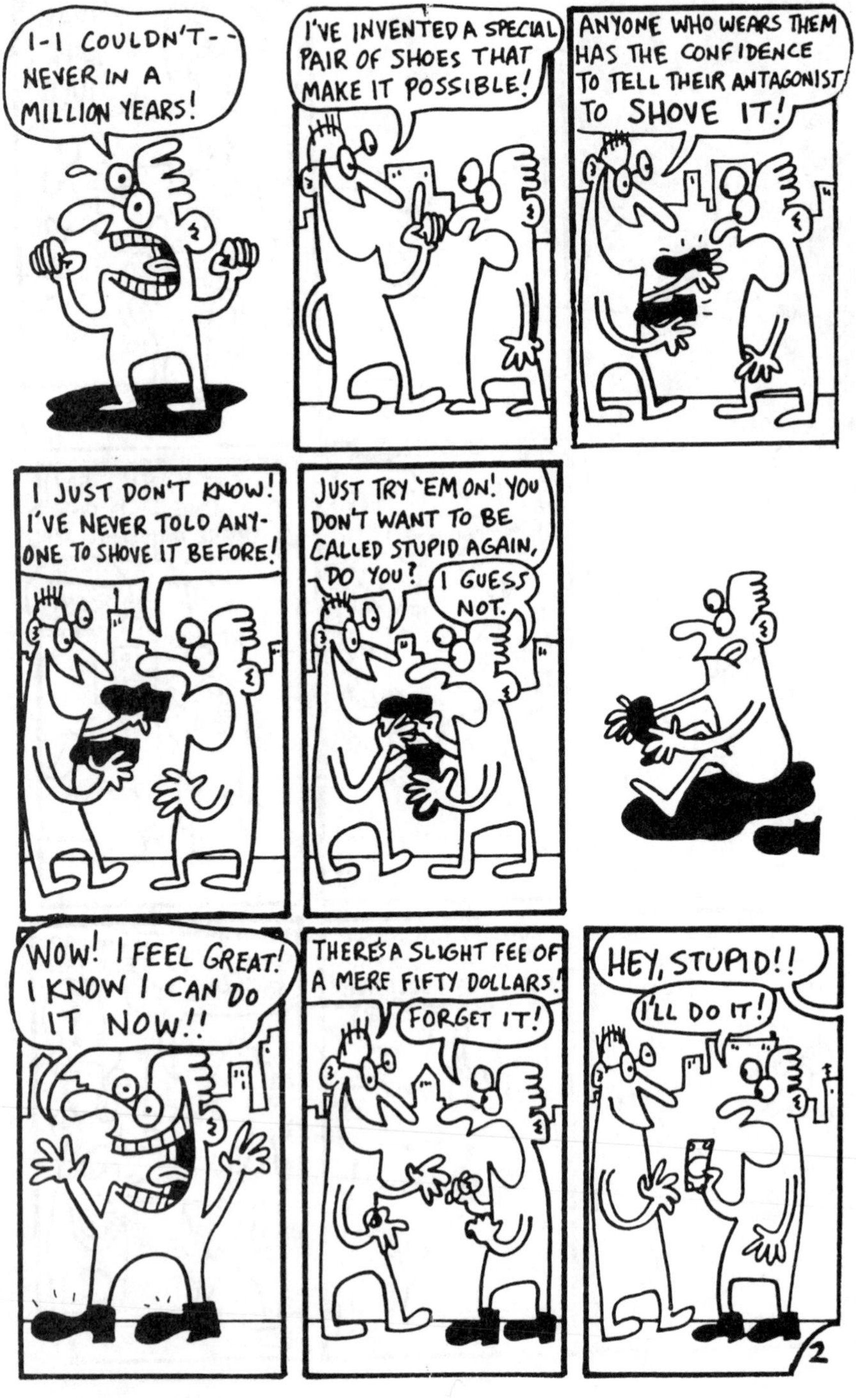
I-I COULDN'T--
NEVER IN A
MILLION YEARS!
I'VE INVENTED A SPECIAL PAIR OF SHOES THAT MAKE IT POSSIBLE!
ANYONE WHO WEARS THEM HAS THE CONFIDENCE TO TELL THEIR ANTAGONIST TO SHOVE IT!
I JUST DON'T KNOW! I'VE NEVER TOLD ANYONE TO SHOVE IT BEFORE!
JUST TRY 'EM ON! YOU DON'T WANT TO BE CALLED STUPID AGAIN, DO YOU?
I GUESS NOT.
WOW! I FEEL GREAT! I KNOW I CAN DO IT NOW!!
THERE'S A SLIGHT FEE OF A MERE FIFTY DOLLARS!
FORGET IT!
HEY, STUPID!!
I'LL DO IT!
2

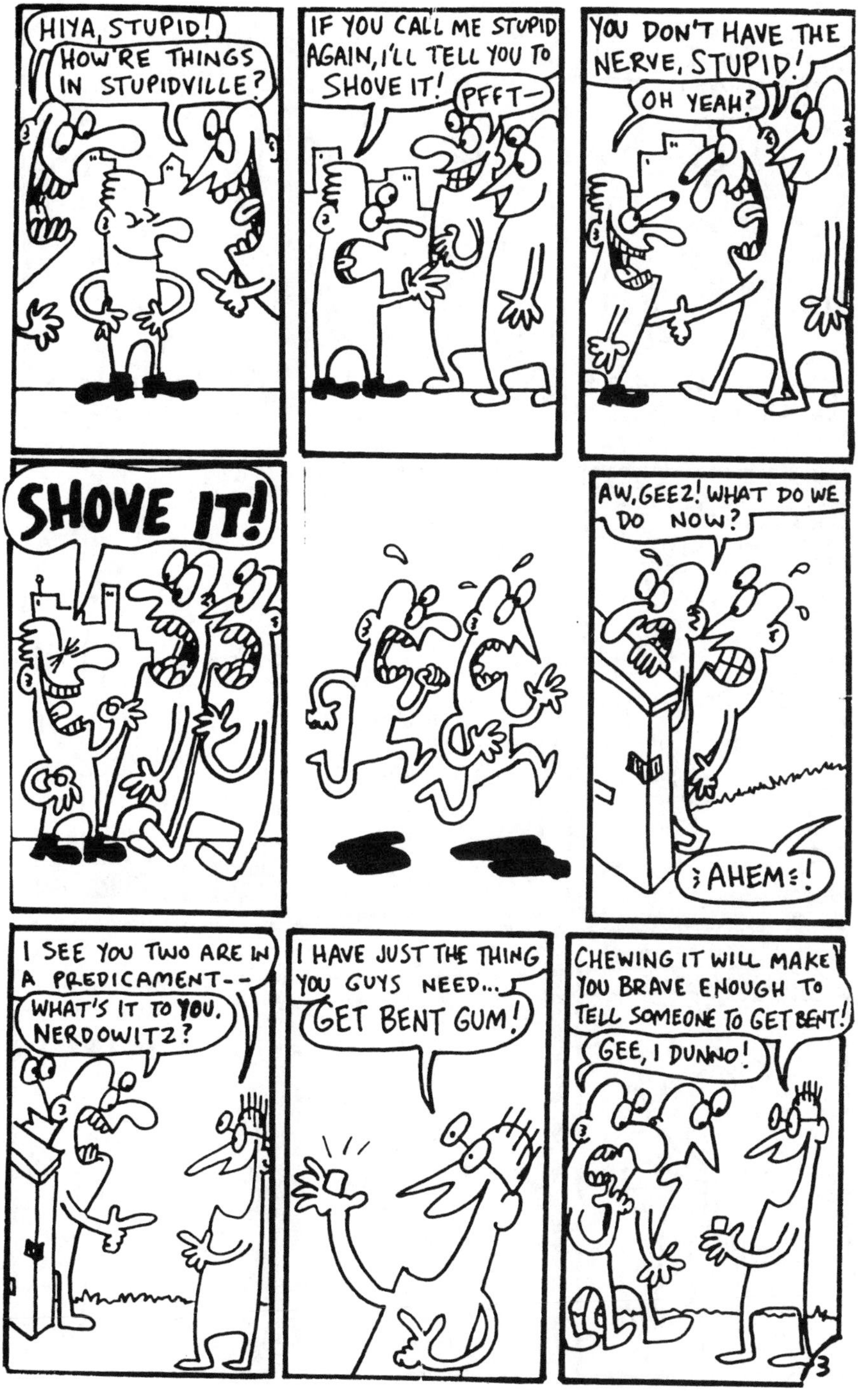
HIYA, STUPID!
HOW'RE THINGS IN STUPIDVILLE?
IF YOU CALL ME STUPID AGAIN, I'LL TELL YOU TO SHOVE IT!
PFFT—
YOU DON'T HAVE THE NERVE, STUPID!
OH YEAH?
SHOVE IT!
AW, GEEZ! WHAT DO WE DO NOW?
AHEM!
I SEE YOU TWO ARE IN A PREDICAMENT--
WHAT'S IT TO YOU, NERDOWITZ?
I HAVE JUST THE THING YOU GUYS NEED...
GET BENT GUM!
CHEWING IT WILL MAKE YOU BRAVE ENOUGH TO TELL SOMEONE TO GET BENT!
GEE, I DUNNO!
3

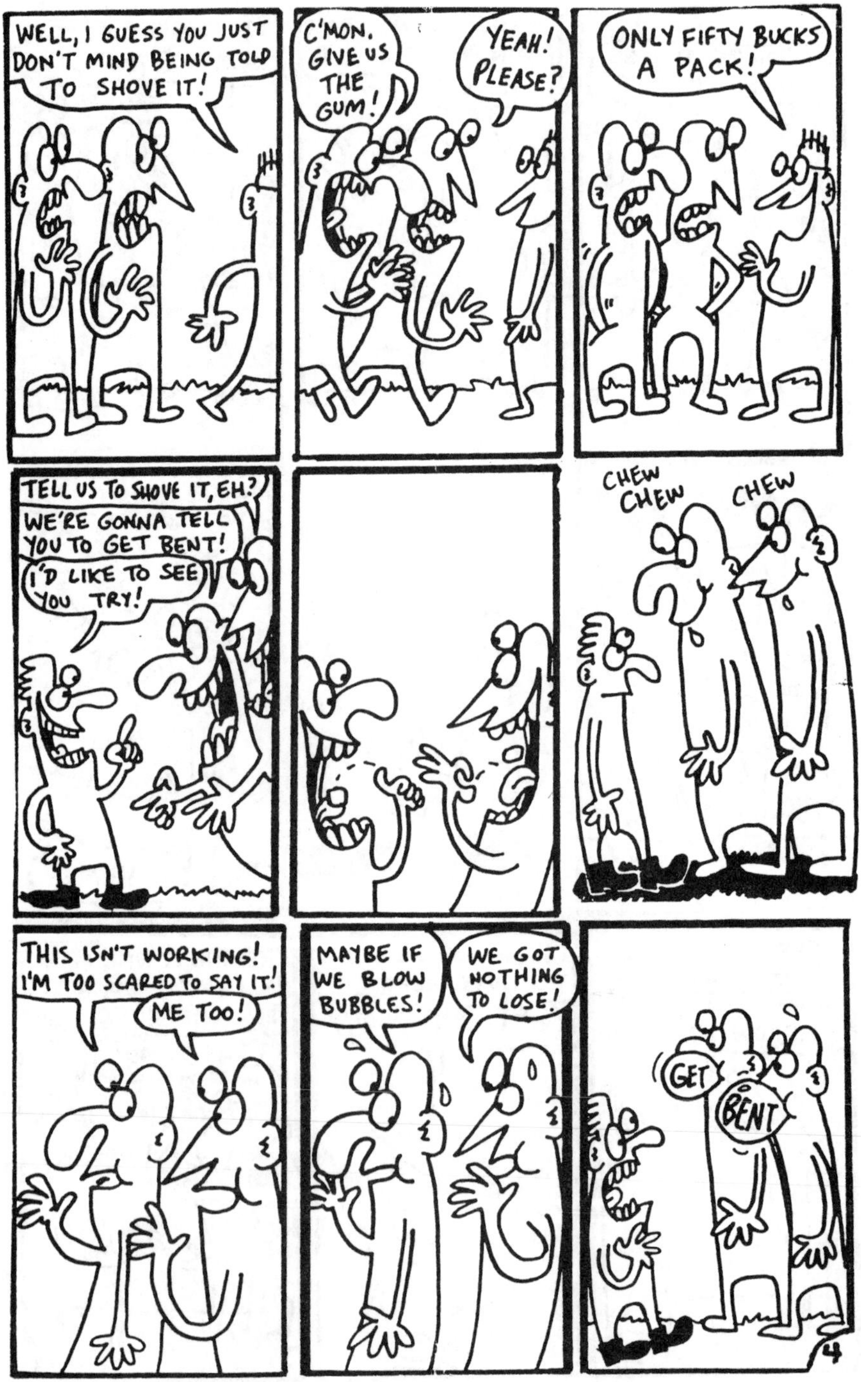

WELL, I GUESS YOU JUST DON'T MIND BEING TOLD TO SHOVE IT!
C'MON. GIVE US THE GUM!
YEAH! PLEASE?
ONLY FIFTY BUCKS A PACK!
TELL US TO SHOVE IT, EH?
WE'RE GONNA TELL YOU TO GET BENT!
I'D LIKE TO SEE YOU TRY!
CHEW CHEW
CHEW
THIS ISN'T WORKING! I'M TOO SCARED TO SAY IT!
ME TOO!
MAYBE IF WE BLOW BUBBLES!
WE GOT NOTHING TO LOSE!
GET
BENT

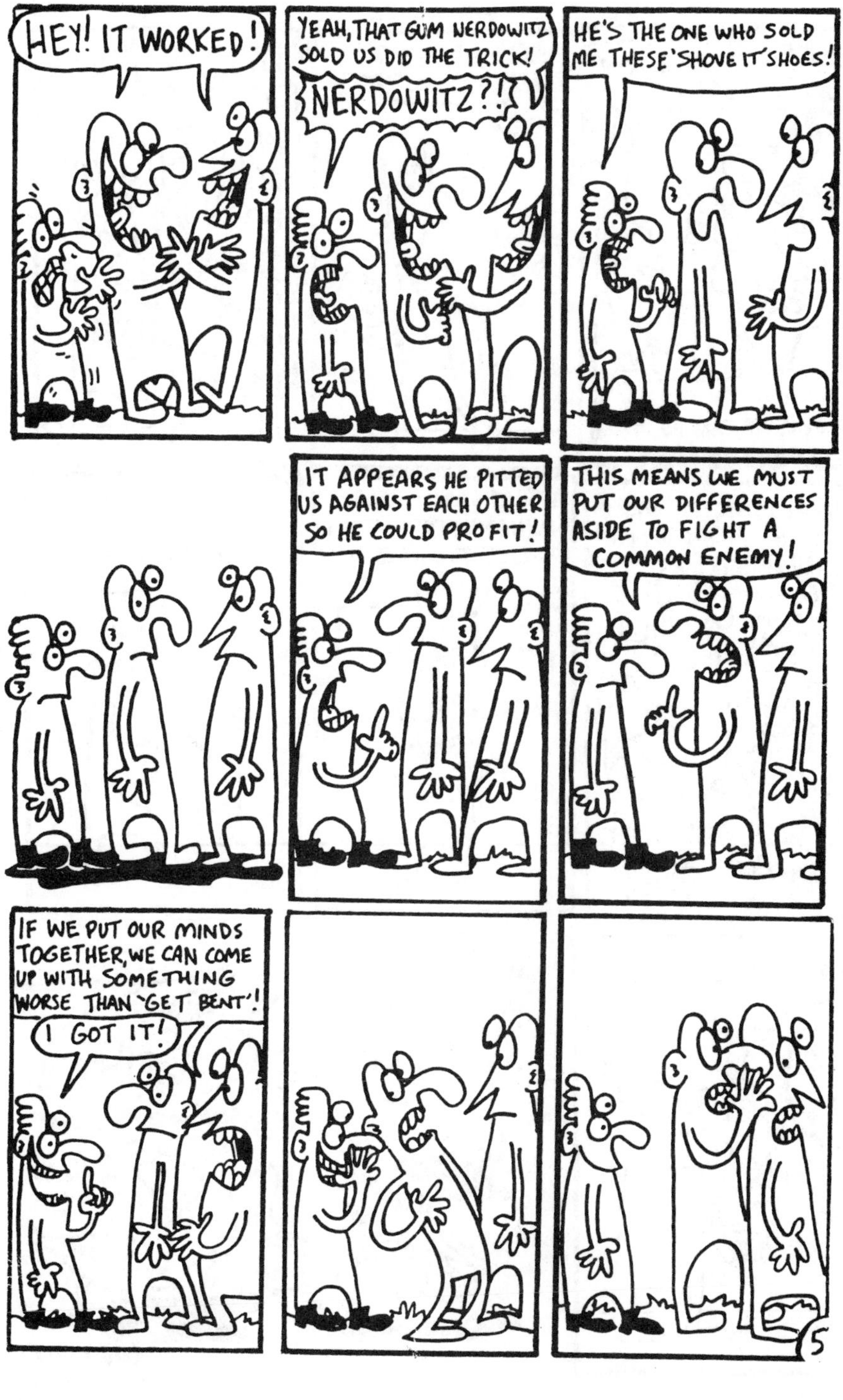
HEY! IT WORKED!
YEAH, THAT GUM NERDOWITZ SOLD US DID THE TRICK!
NERDOWITZ?!
HE'S THE ONE WHO SOLD ME THESE 'SHOVE IT' SHOES!
IT APPEARS HE PITTED US AGAINST EACH OTHER SO HE COULD PROFIT!
THIS MEANS WE MUST PUT OUR DIFFERENCES ASIDE TO FIGHT A COMMON ENEMY!
IF WE PUT OUR MINDS TOGETHER, WE CAN COME UP WITH SOMETHING WORSE THAN 'GET BENT'!
I GOT IT!

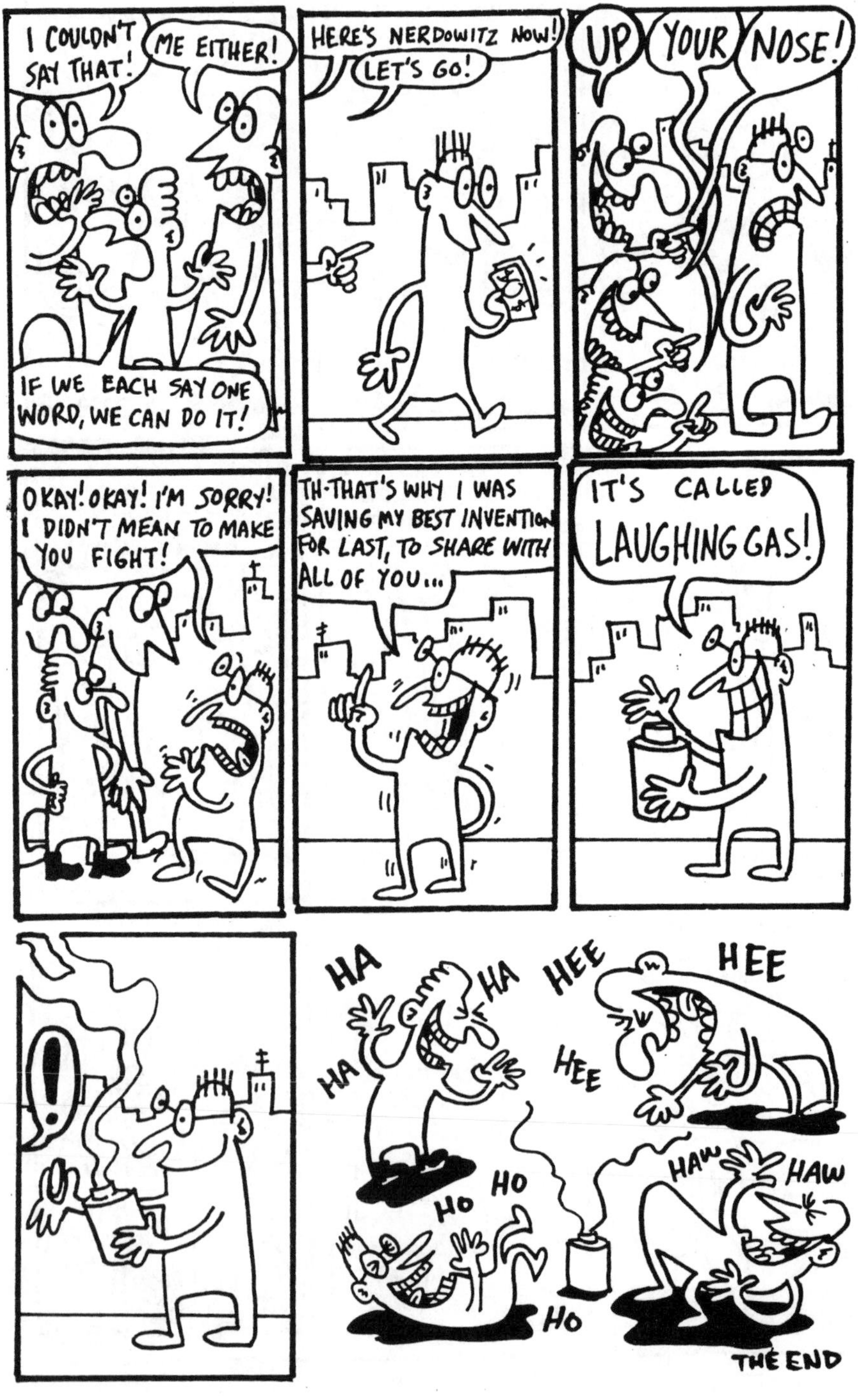
I COULDN'T SAY THAT!
ME EITHER!
IF WE EACH SAY ONE WORD, WE CAN DO IT!
HERE'S NERDOWITZ NOW!
LET'S GO!
UP
YOUR
NOSE!
OKAY! OKAY! I'M SORRY! I DIDN'T MEAN TO MAKE YOU FIGHT!
TH-THAT'S WHY I WAS SAVING MY BEST INVENTION FOR LAST, TO SHARE WITH ALL OF YOU...
IT'S CALLED LAUGHING GAS!
!
HA
HA
HA
HEE
HEE
HEE
HO
HO
HO
HAW
HAW
THE END

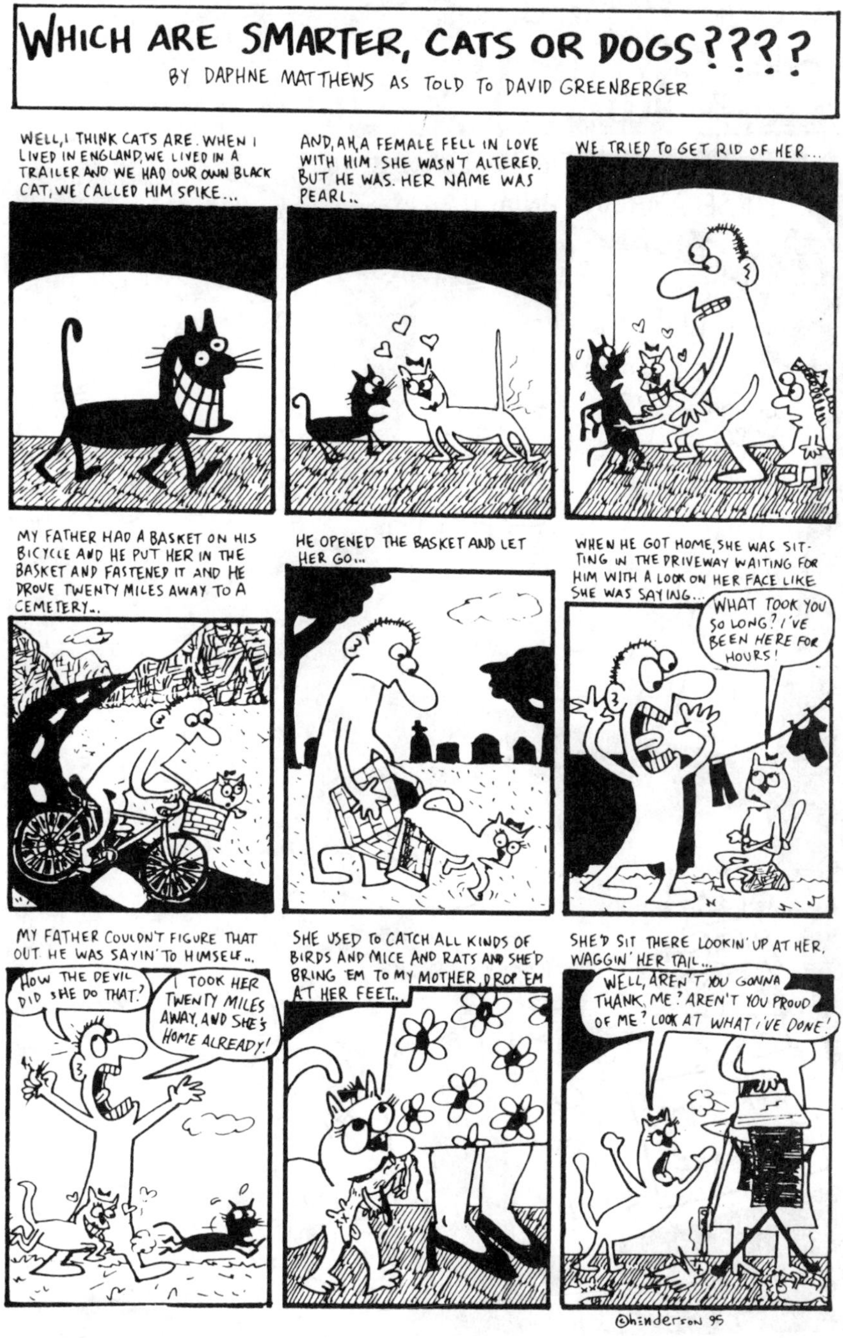
WHICH ARE SMARTER, CATS OR DOGS????
BY DAPHNE MATTHEWS AS TOLD TO DAVID GREENBERGER
WELL, I THINK CATS ARE. WHEN I LIVED IN ENGLAND, WE LIVED IN A TRAILER AND WE HAD OUR OWN BLACK CAT, WE CALLED HIM SPIKE...
AND, AH, A FEMALE FELL IN LOVE WITH HIM. SHE WASN'T ALTERED. BUT HE WAS. HER NAME WAS PEARL..
WE TRIED TO GET RID OF HER...
MY FATHER HAD A BASKET ON HIS BICYCLE AND HE PUT HER IN THE BASKET AND FASTENED IT AND HE DROVE TWENTY MILES AWAY TO A CEMETERY..
HE OPENED THE BASKET AND LET HER GO...
WHEN HE GOT HOME, SHE WAS SITTING IN THE DRIVEWAY WAITING FOR HIM WITH A LOOK ON HER FACE LIKE SHE WAS SAYING...
WHAT TOOK YOU SO LONG? I'VE BEEN HERE FOR HOURS!
MY FATHER COULDN'T FIGURE THAT OUT. HE WAS SAYIN' TO HIMSELF...
HOW THE DEVIL DID SHE DO THAT?
I TOOK HER TWENTY MILES AWAY, AND SHE'S HOME ALREADY!
SHE USED TO CATCH ALL KINDS OF BIRDS AND MICE AND RATS AND SHE'D BRING 'EM TO MY MOTHER, DROP 'EM AT HER FEET..
SHE'D SIT THERE LOOKIN' UP AT HER, WAGGIN' HER TAIL...
WELL, AREN'T YOU GONNA THANK ME? AREN'T YOU PROUD OF ME? LOOK AT WHAT I'VE DONE!
©henderson 95

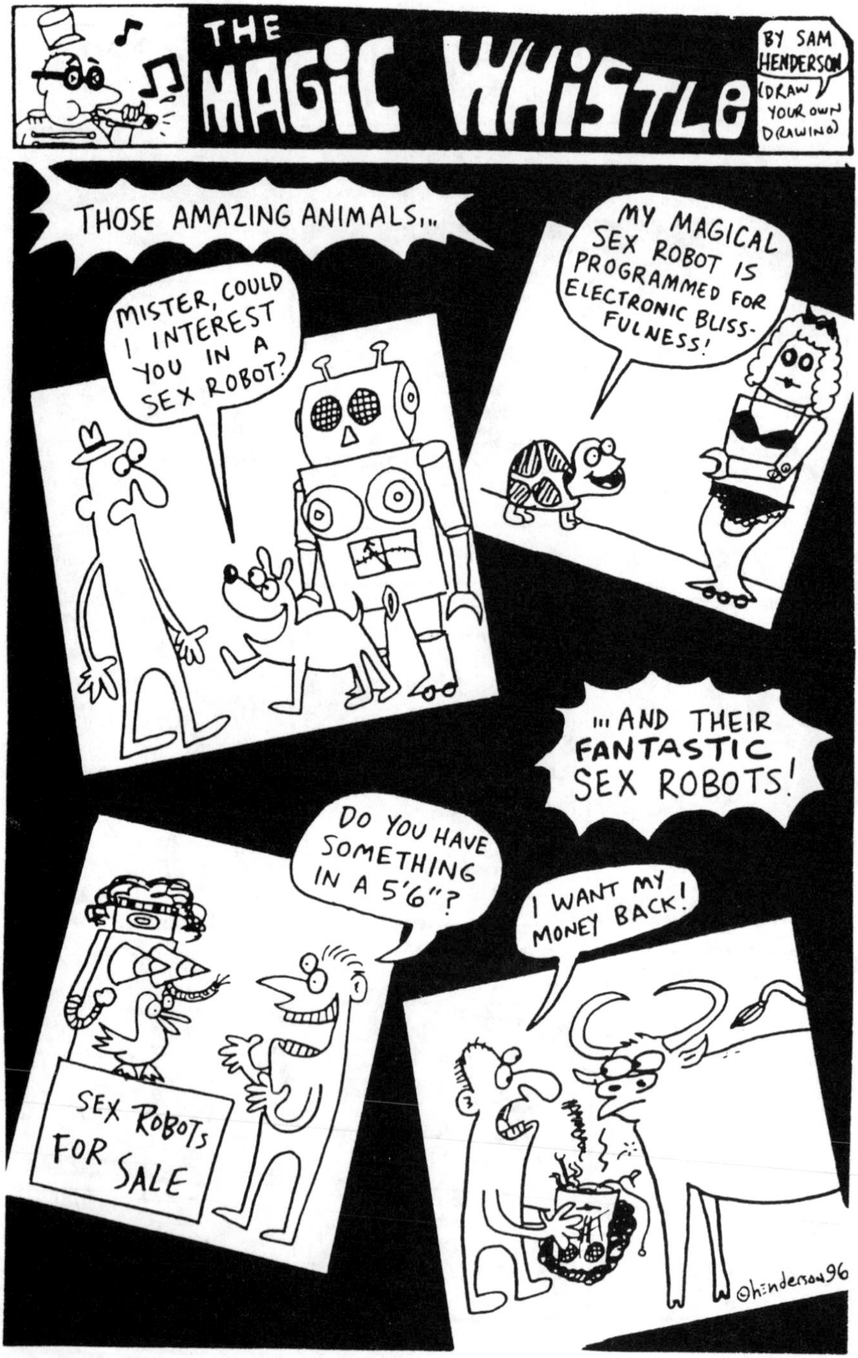
THE MAGIC WHISTLE
BY SAM HENDERSON (DRAW YOUR OWN DRAWING)
THOSE AMAZING ANIMALS...
MISTER, COULD I INTEREST YOU IN A SEX ROBOT?
MY MAGICAL SEX ROBOT IS PROGRAMMED FOR ELECTRONIC BLISS-FULNESS!
...AND THEIR FANTASTIC SEX ROBOTS!
SEX ROBOTS FOR SALE
DO YOU HAVE SOMETHING IN A 5'6"?
I WANT MY MONEY BACK!
©henderson96

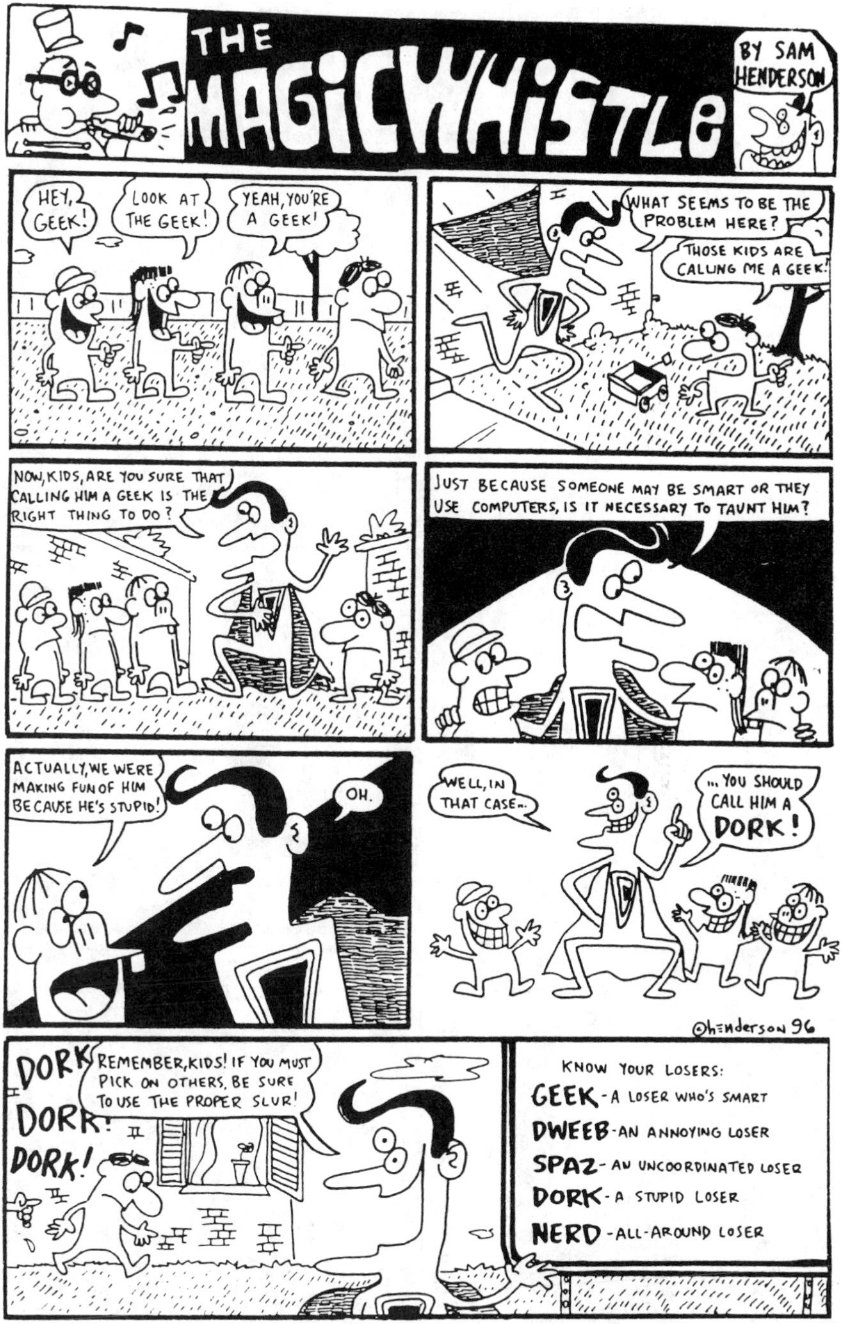
THE MAGIC WHISTLE
BY SAM HENDERSON
HEY, GEEK!
LOOK AT THE GEEK!
YEAH, YOU'RE A GEEK!
WHAT SEEMS TO BE THE PROBLEM HERE?
THOSE KIDS ARE CALLING ME A GEEK!
NOW, KIDS, ARE YOU SURE THAT CALLING HIM A GEEK IS THE RIGHT THING TO DO?
JUST BECAUSE SOMEONE MAY BE SMART OR THEY USE COMPUTERS, IS IT NECESSARY TO TAUNT HIM?
ACTUALLY, WE WERE MAKING FUN OF HIM BECAUSE HE'S STUPID!
OH.
WELL, IN THAT CASE..
...YOU SHOULD CALL HIM A DORK!
©henderson 96
DORK
DORK!
DORK!
REMEMBER, KIDS! IF YOU MUST PICK ON OTHERS, BE SURE TO USE THE PROPER SLUR!
KNOW YOUR LOSERS:
GEEK - A LOSER WHO'S SMART
DWEEB - AN ANNOYING LOSER
SPAZ - AN UNCOORDINATED LOSER
DORK - A STUPID LOSER
NERD - ALL-AROUND LOSER

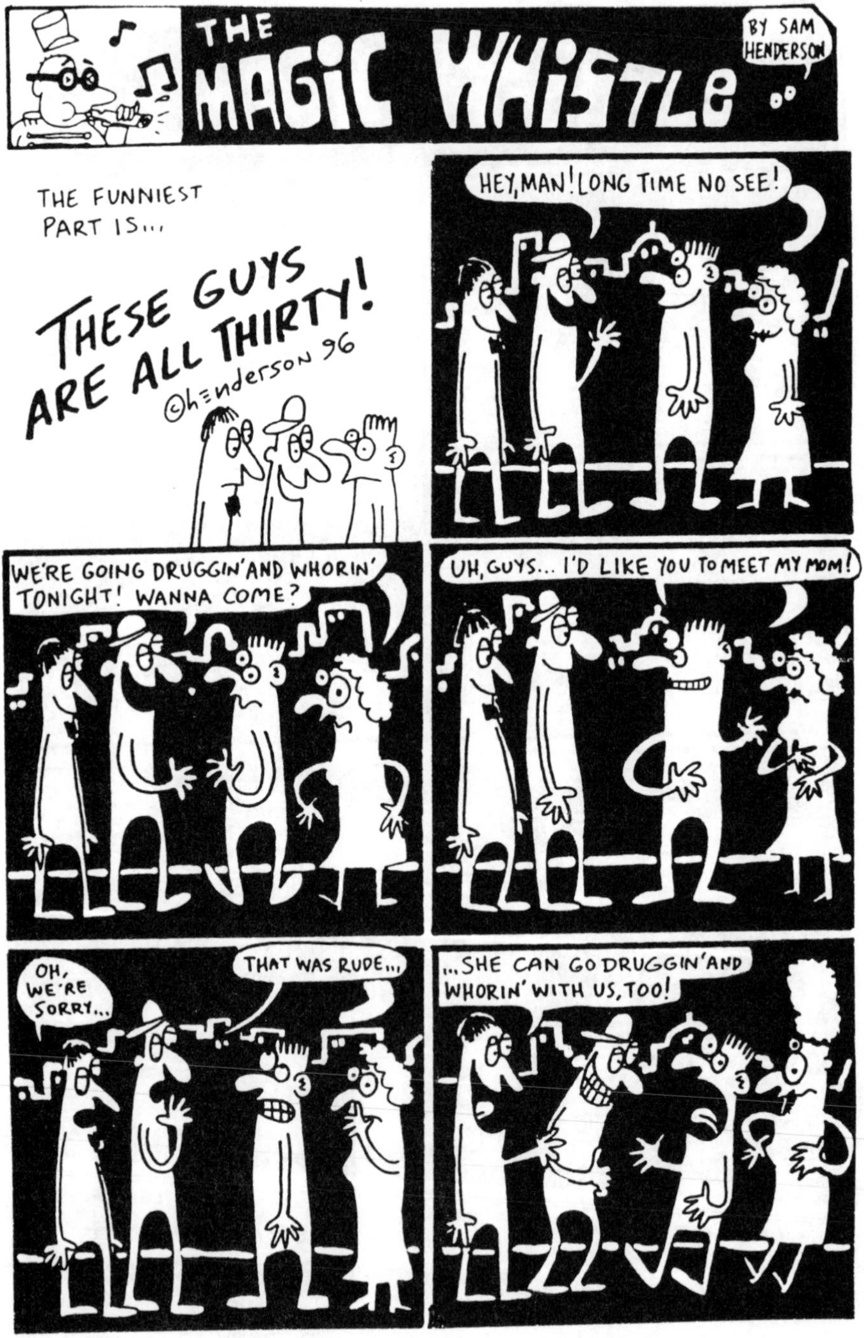
THE MAGIC WHISTLE
BY SAM HENDERSON
HEY, MAN! LONG TIME NO SEE!
WE'RE GOING DRUGGIN' AND WHORIN' TONIGHT! WANNA COME?
UH, GUYS... I'D LIKE YOU TO MEET MY MOM!
OH, WE'RE SORRY...
THAT WAS RUDE...
...SHE CAN GO DRUGGIN' AND WHORIN' WITH US, TOO!
THE FUNNIEST PART IS...
THESE GUYS ARE ALL THIRTY!
©henderson 96

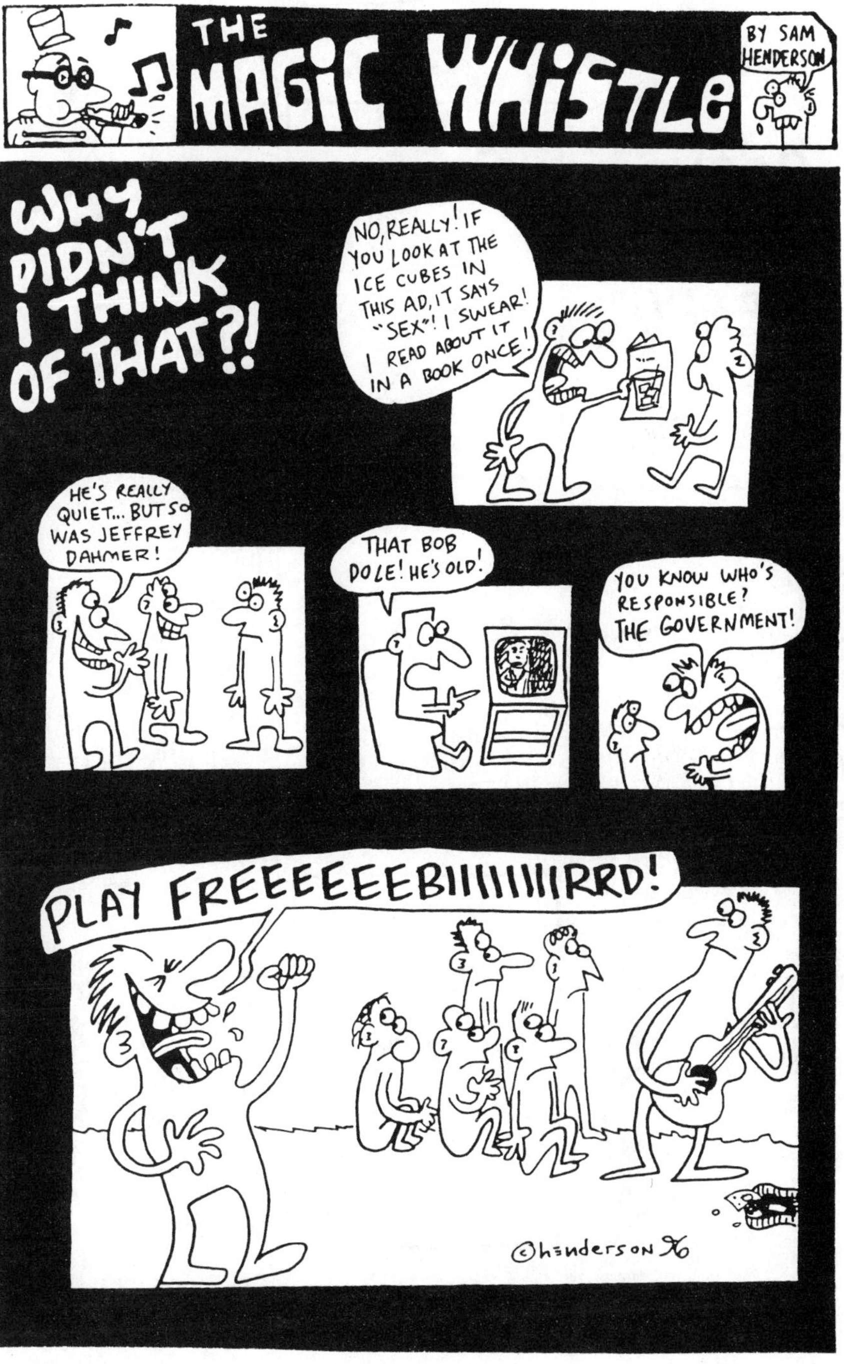
THE MAGIC WHISTLE
BY SAM HENDERSON
WHY DIDN'T I THINK OF THAT?!
NO, REALLY! IF YOU LOOK AT THE ICE CUBES IN THIS AD, IT SAYS "SEX"! I SWEAR! I READ ABOUT IT IN A BOOK ONCE!
HE'S REALLY QUIET... BUT SO WAS JEFFREY DAHMER!
THAT BOB DOLE! HE'S OLD!
YOU KNOW WHO'S RESPONSIBLE? THE GOVERNMENT!
PLAY FREEEEEEEBIIIIIIIIIRRD!
©henderson 96

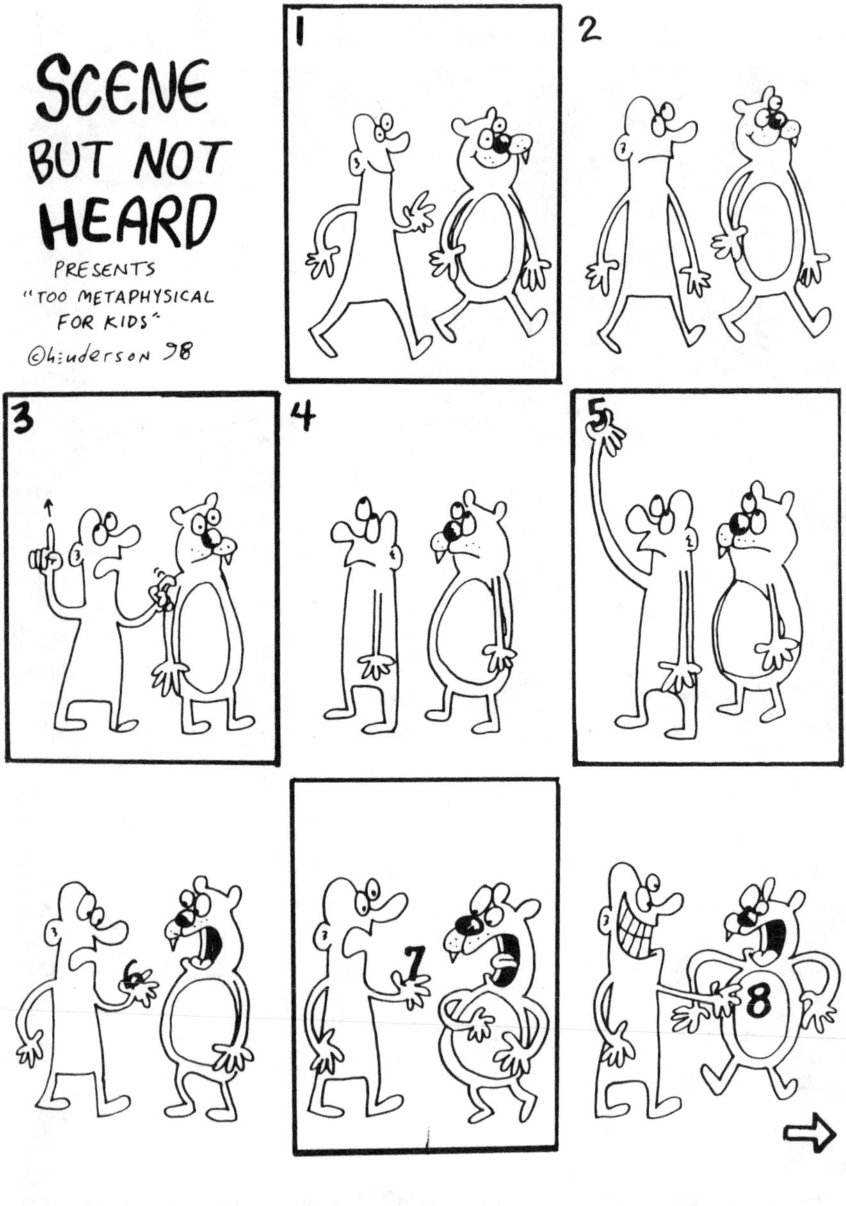
SCENE BUT NOT HEARD
PRESENTS
"TOO METAPHYSICAL FOR KIDS"
©henderson 98
1
2
3
4
5
6
7
8

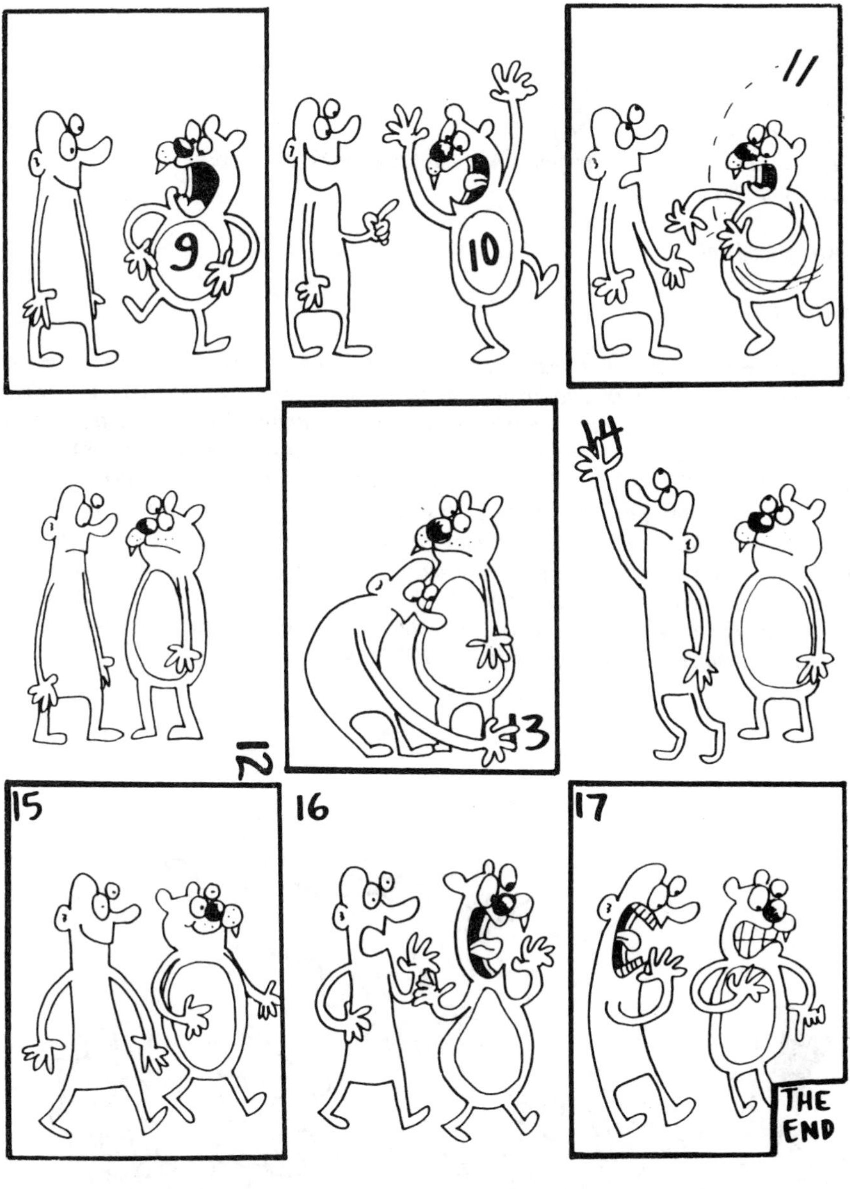

9
10
11
12
13
14
15
16
17
THE END

RECIPE FOR FUN #1

ingredients:

1 Heiress
1 Fiancé and group of 5-10 Preppies
1 Regular Guy and equally proportioned entourage of Ne'er-do-wells
50-200 Socialites
1 Butler
1 Swimming Pool

directions:

Start multi-million dollar business and give birth to daughter. Allow daughter to mature for about twenty-one years, and arrange marriage to recent Ivy League graduate who is also potential business partner. Forbid daughter from dating regular guy from wrong side of tracks. Throw engagement party. Regular guy and friends will then crash party disguised as socialites. Allow fiancé to pick fight with regular guy and accidentally fall in swimming pool, provoking fights between respective entourages who also fall in pool and knock actual socialites and you into pool in the process. Allow 2-5 minutes for other socialites to jump into pool fully clothed and laughing followed by uptight butler who shrugs and jumps in. Allow regular guy to show evidence of fiancé's plan to take over business before cursing him and telling daughter she can do what she wants to do. Serves millions and teaches valuable lesson in ROCKIN' ON.

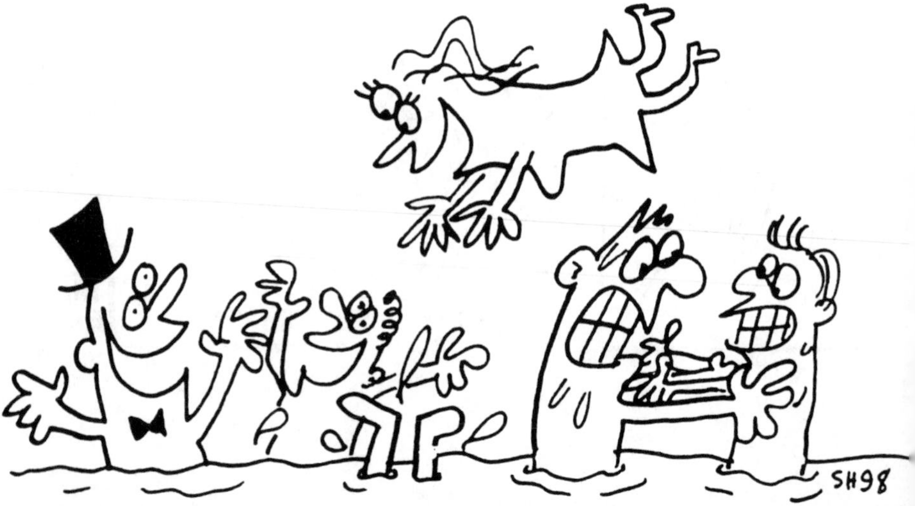
SH98

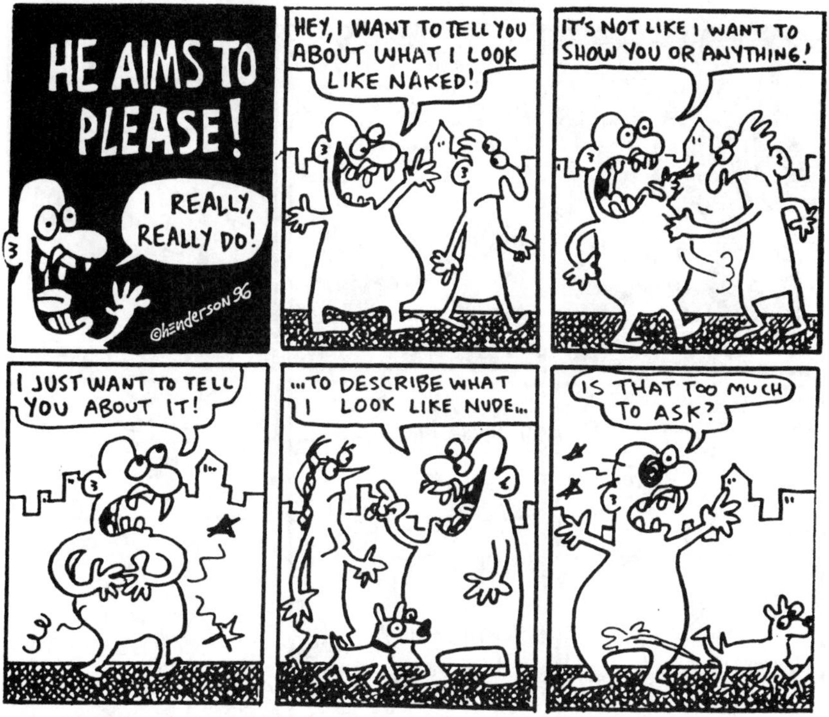
HE AIMS TO PLEASE!
I REALLY, REALLY DO!
©henderson 96
HEY, I WANT TO TELL YOU ABOUT WHAT I LOOK LIKE NAKED!
IT'S NOT LIKE I WANT TO SHOW YOU OR ANYTHING!
I JUST WANT TO TELL YOU ABOUT IT!
...TO DESCRIBE WHAT I LOOK LIKE NUDE...
IS THAT TOO MUCH TO ASK?

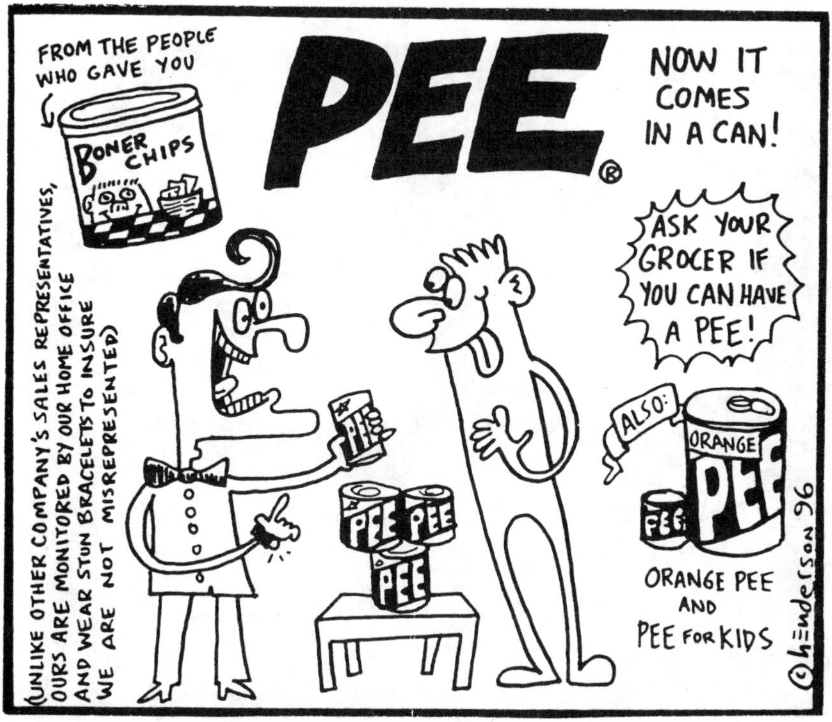
FROM THE PEOPLE WHO GAVE YOU
BONER CHIPS
PEE®
NOW IT COMES IN A CAN!
ASK YOUR GROCER IF YOU CAN HAVE A PEE!
(UNLIKE OTHER COMPANY'S SALES REPRESENTATIVES, OURS ARE MONITORED BY OUR HOME OFFICE AND WEAR STUN BRACELETS TO INSURE WE ARE NOT MISREPRESENTED)
ALSO:
ORANGE PEE
ORANGE PEE AND PEE FOR KIDS
©henderson 96

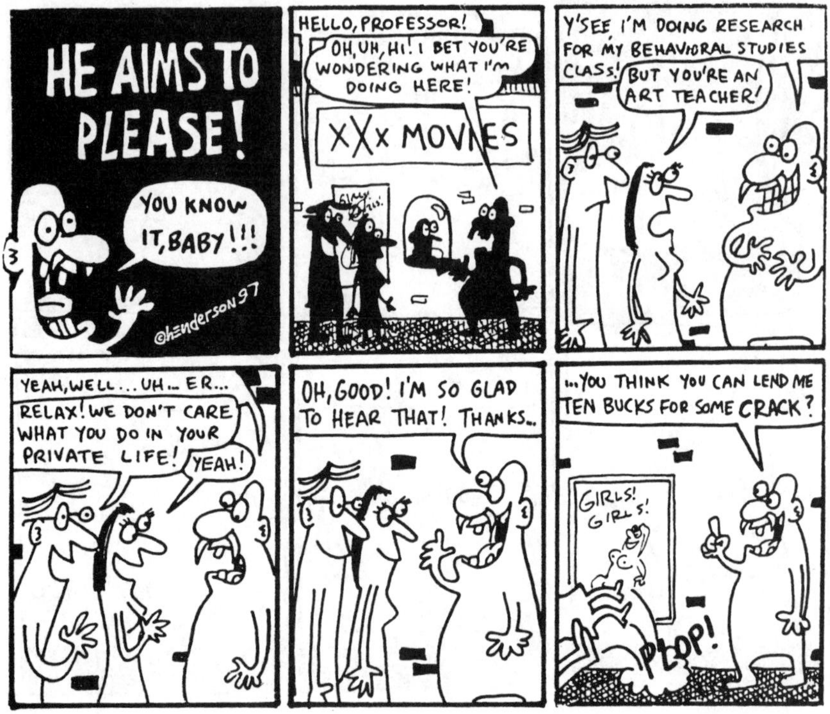
HE AIMS TO PLEASE!
YOU KNOW IT, BABY!!!
©henderson97
HELLO, PROFESSOR!
OH, UH, HI! I BET YOU'RE WONDERING WHAT I'M DOING HERE!
XXx MOVIES
Y'SEE I'M DOING RESEARCH FOR MY BEHAVIORAL STUDIES CLASS!
BUT YOU'RE AN ART TEACHER!
YEAH, WELL... UH... ER...
RELAX! WE DON'T CARE WHAT YOU DO IN YOUR PRIVATE LIFE!
YEAH!
OH, GOOD! I'M SO GLAD TO HEAR THAT! THANKS...
...YOU THINK YOU CAN LEND ME TEN BUCKS FOR SOME CRACK?
GIRLS! GIRLS!
PLOP!

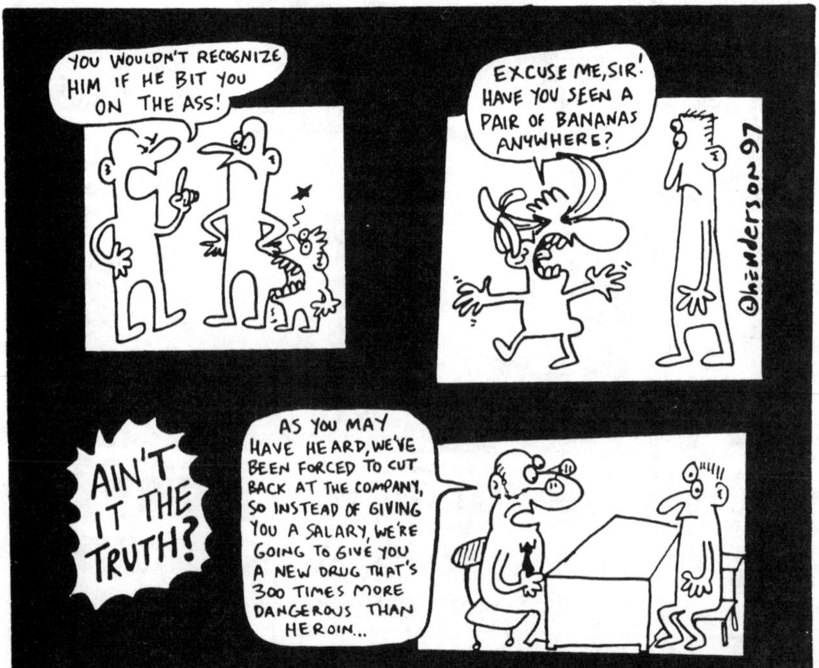
YOU WOULDN'T RECOGNIZE HIM IF HE BIT YOU ON THE ASS!
EXCUSE ME, SIR! HAVE YOU SEEN A PAIR OF BANANAS ANYWHERE?
©henderson97
AIN'T IT THE TRUTH?
AS YOU MAY HAVE HEARD, WE'VE BEEN FORCED TO CUT BACK AT THE COMPANY, SO INSTEAD OF GIVING YOU A SALARY, WE'RE GOING TO GIVE YOU A NEW DRUG THAT'S 300 TIMES MORE DANGEROUS THAN HEROIN...

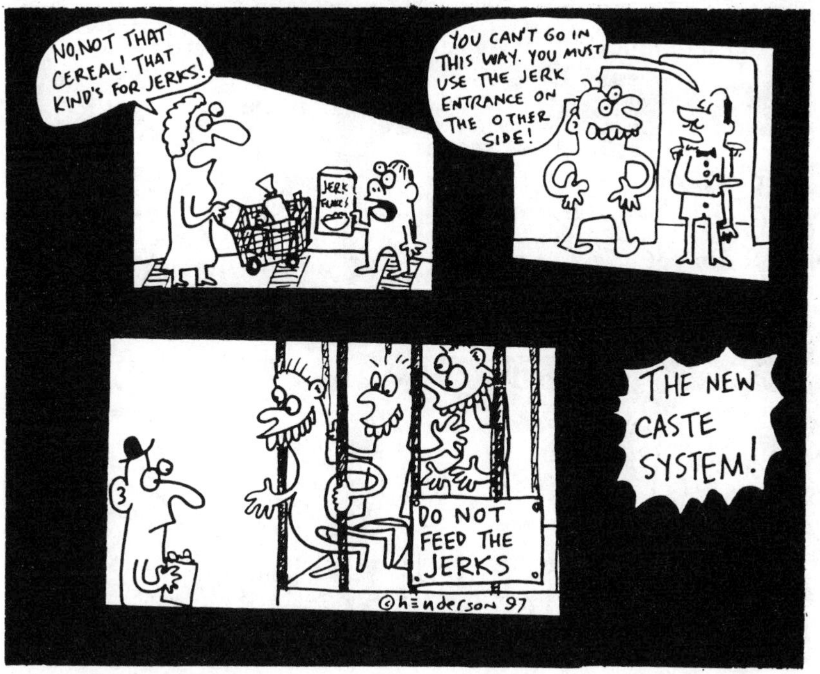
THE NEW CASTE SYSTEM!
NO, NOT THAT CEREAL! THAT KIND'S FOR JERKS!
JERK FLAKES!
YOU CAN'T GO IN THIS WAY. YOU MUST USE THE JERK ENTRANCE ON THE OTHER SIDE!
DO NOT FEED THE JERKS
©henderson 97

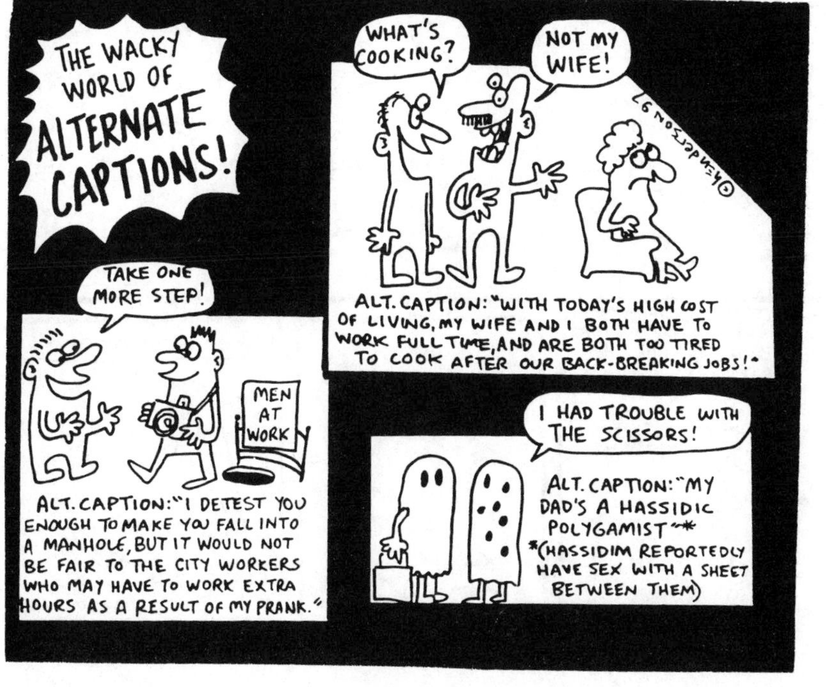
THE WACKY WORLD OF ALTERNATE CAPTIONS!
WHAT'S COOKING?
NOT MY WIFE!
©henderson 97
ALT. CAPTION: "WITH TODAY'S HIGH COST OF LIVING, MY WIFE AND I BOTH HAVE TO WORK FULL TIME, AND ARE BOTH TOO TIRED TO COOK AFTER OUR BACK-BREAKING JOBS!"
TAKE ONE MORE STEP!
MEN AT WORK
ALT. CAPTION: "I DETEST YOU ENOUGH TO MAKE YOU FALL INTO A MANHOLE, BUT IT WOULD NOT BE FAIR TO THE CITY WORKERS WHO MAY HAVE TO WORK EXTRA HOURS AS A RESULT OF MY PRANK."
I HAD TROUBLE WITH THE SCISSORS!
ALT. CAPTION: "MY DAD'S A HASSIDIC POLYGAMIST"*
*(HASSIDIM REPORTEDLY HAVE SEX WITH A SHEET BETWEEN THEM)

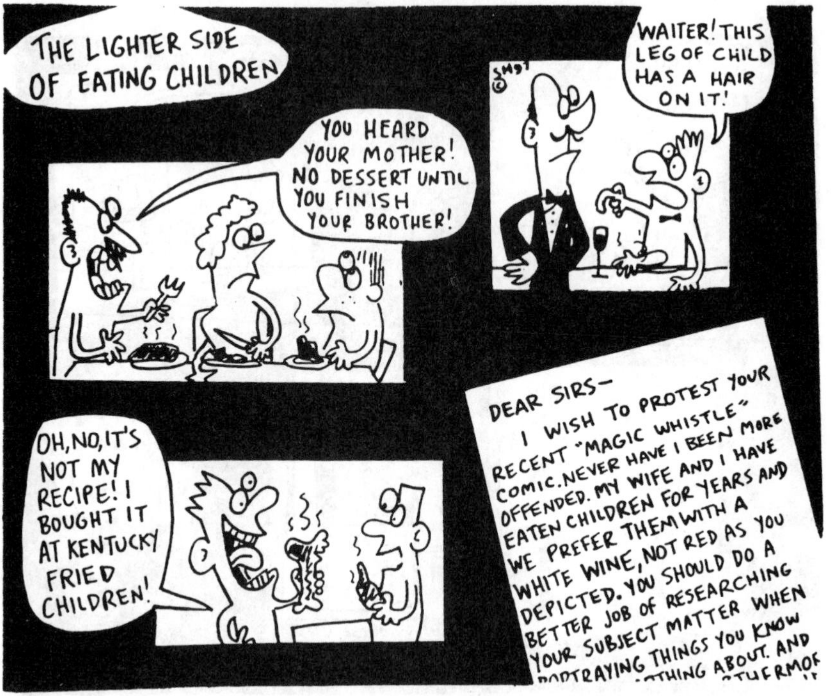
THE LIGHTER SIDE OF EATING CHILDREN
YOU HEARD YOUR MOTHER! NO DESSERT UNTIL YOU FINISH YOUR BROTHER!
WAITER! THIS LEG OF CHILD HAS A HAIR ON IT!
SM97
OH, NO, IT'S NOT MY RECIPE! I BOUGHT IT AT KENTUCKY FRIED CHILDREN!
DEAR SIRS—
I WISH TO PROTEST YOUR RECENT "MAGIC WHISTLE" COMIC. NEVER HAVE I BEEN MORE OFFENDED. MY WIFE AND I HAVE EATEN CHILDREN FOR YEARS AND WE PREFER THEM WITH A WHITE WINE, NOT RED AS YOU DEPICTED. YOU SHOULD DO A BETTER JOB OF RESEARCHING YOUR SUBJECT MATTER WHEN PORTRAYING THINGS YOU KNOW

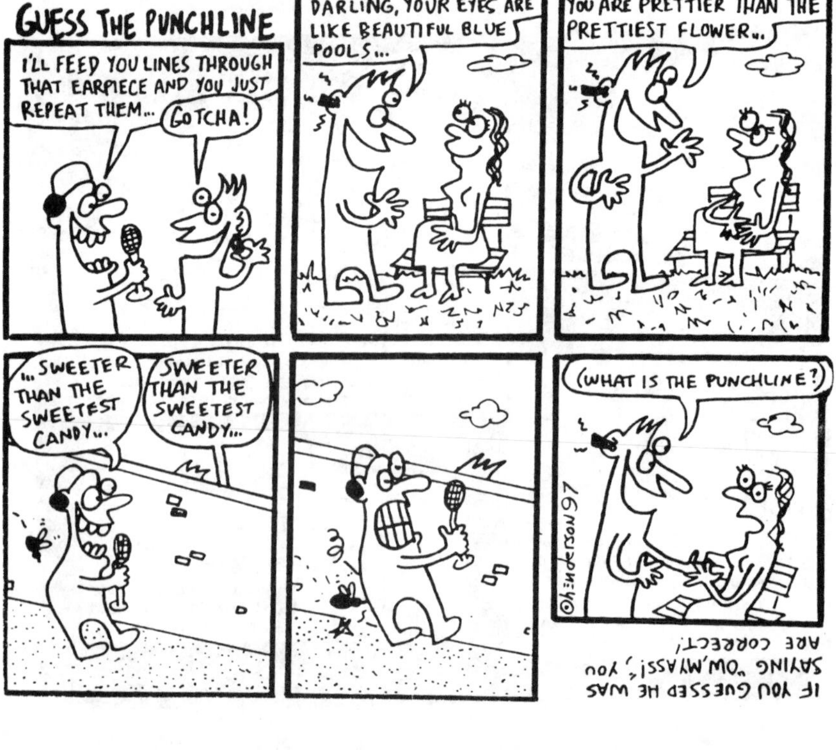
GUESS THE PUNCHLINE
I'LL FEED YOU LINES THROUGH THAT EARPIECE AND YOU JUST REPEAT THEM...
GOTCHA!
DARLING, YOUR EYES ARE LIKE BEAUTIFUL BLUE POOLS...
YOU ARE PRETTIER THAN THE PRETTIEST FLOWER...
...SWEETER THAN THE SWEETEST CANDY...
SWEETER THAN THE SWEETEST CANDY...
(WHAT IS THE PUNCHLINE?)
©henderson97
IF YOU GUESSED HE WAS SAYING "OW, MY ASS!", YOU ARE CORRECT!

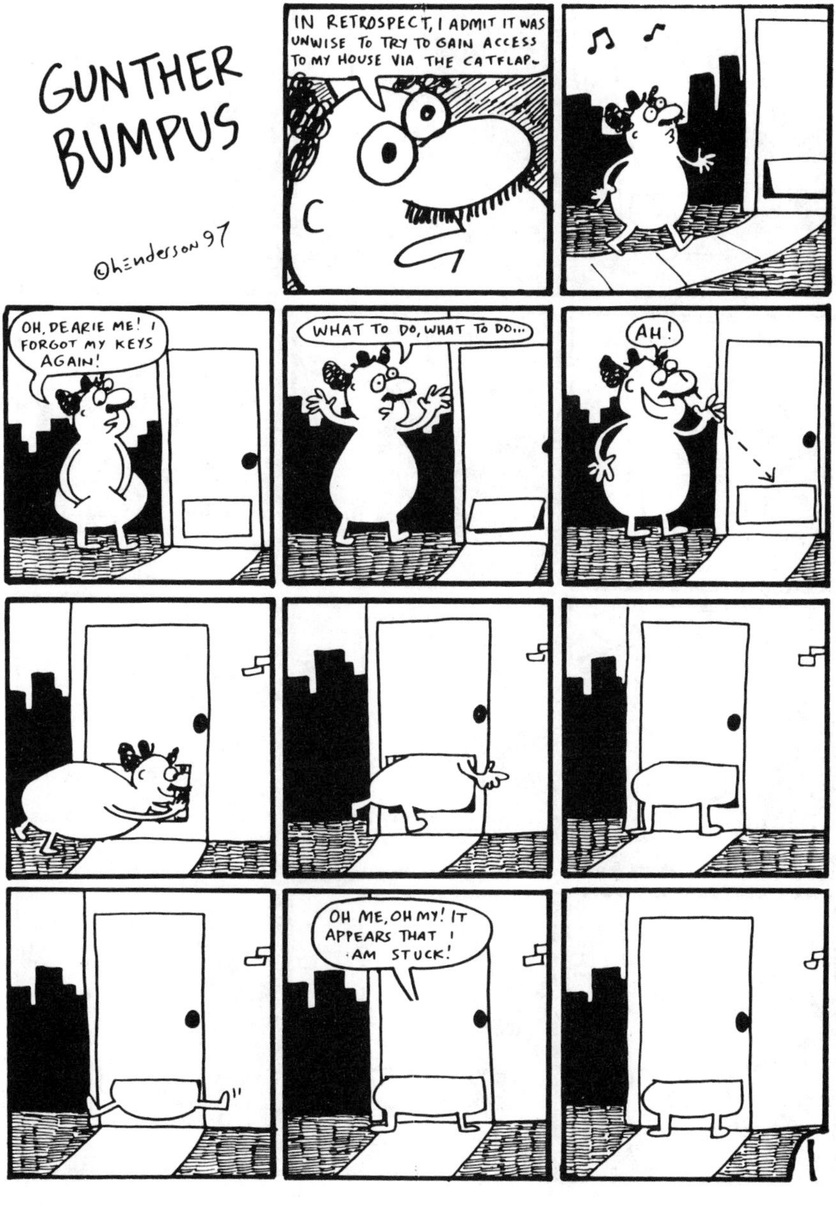
GUNTHER BUMPUS
©henderson 97
IN RETROSPECT, I ADMIT IT WAS UNWISE TO TRY TO GAIN ACCESS TO MY HOUSE VIA THE CATFLAP.
OH, DEARIE ME! I FORGOT MY KEYS AGAIN!
WHAT TO DO, WHAT TO DO...
AH!
OH ME, OH MY! IT APPEARS THAT I AM STUCK!

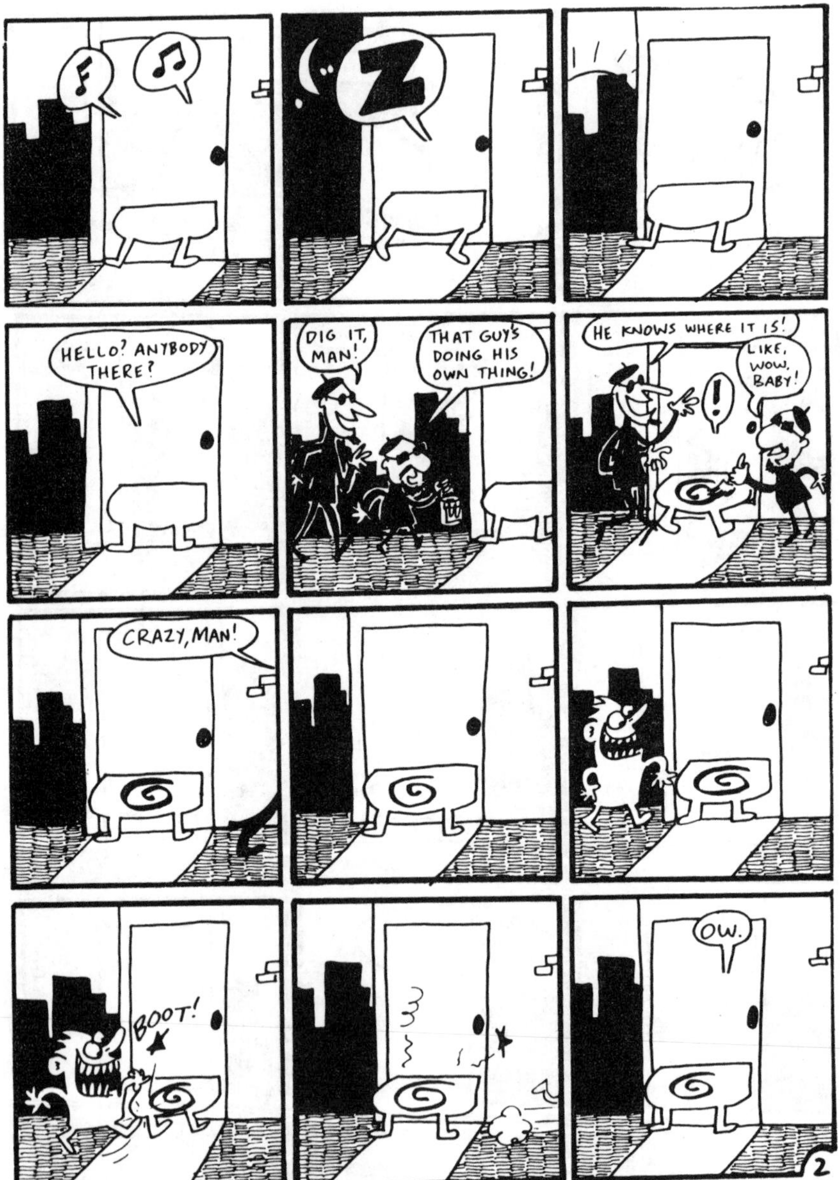

Z
HELLO? ANYBODY THERE?
DIG IT, MAN!
THAT GUY'S DOING HIS OWN THING!
HE KNOWS WHERE IT IS!
!
LIKE, WOW, BABY!
CRAZY, MAN!
BOOT!
OW.

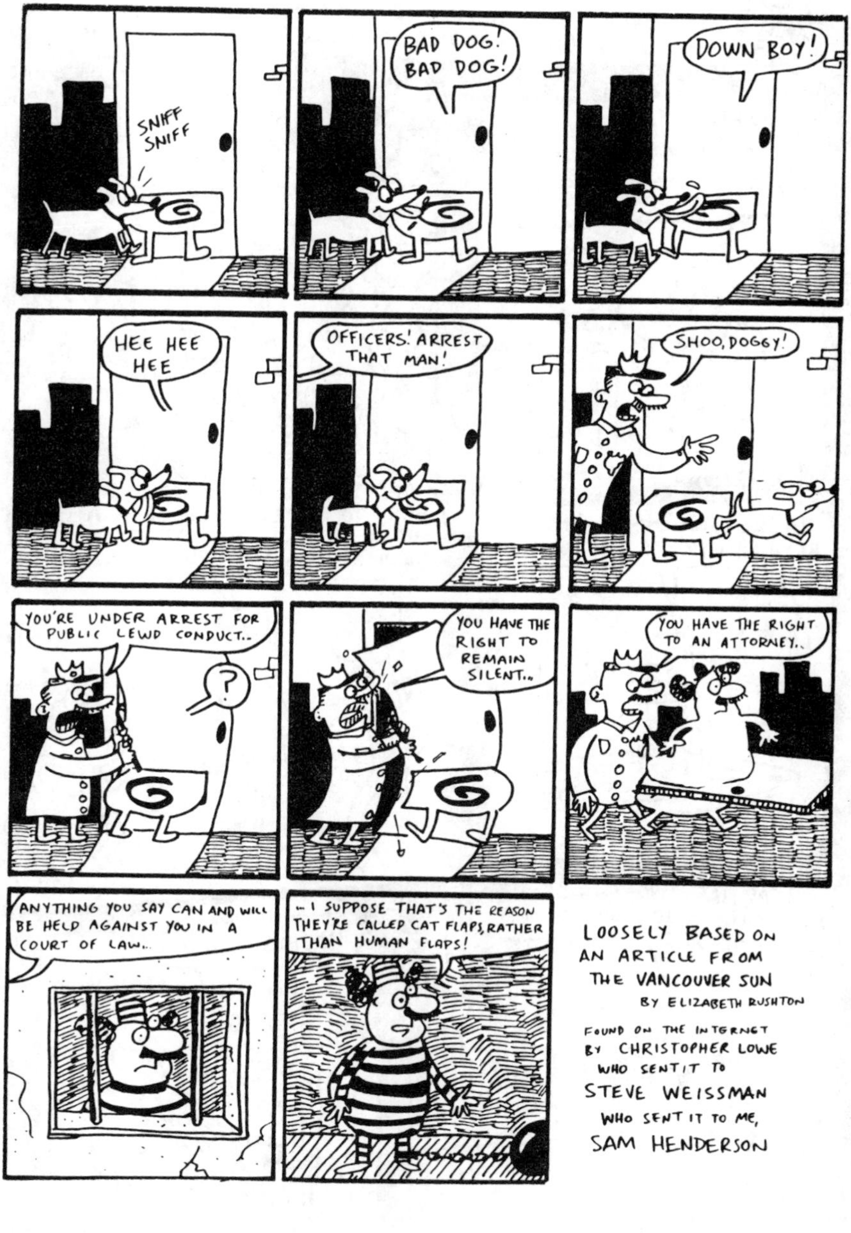
SNIFF SNIFF
BAD DOG! BAD DOG!
DOWN BOY!
HEE HEE HEE
OFFICERS! ARREST THAT MAN!
SHOO, DOGGY!
YOU'RE UNDER ARREST FOR PUBLIC LEWD CONDUCT..
?
YOU HAVE THE RIGHT TO REMAIN SILENT..
YOU HAVE THE RIGHT TO AN ATTORNEY..
ANYTHING YOU SAY CAN AND WILL BE HELD AGAINST YOU IN A COURT OF LAW..
..I SUPPOSE THAT'S THE REASON THEY'RE CALLED CAT FLAPS, RATHER THAN HUMAN FLAPS!
LOOSELY BASED ON AN ARTICLE FROM THE VANCOUVER SUN
BY ELIZABETH RUSHTON
FOUND ON THE INTERNET BY CHRISTOPHER LOWE WHO SENT IT TO STEVE WEISSMAN WHO SENT IT TO ME, SAM HENDERSON

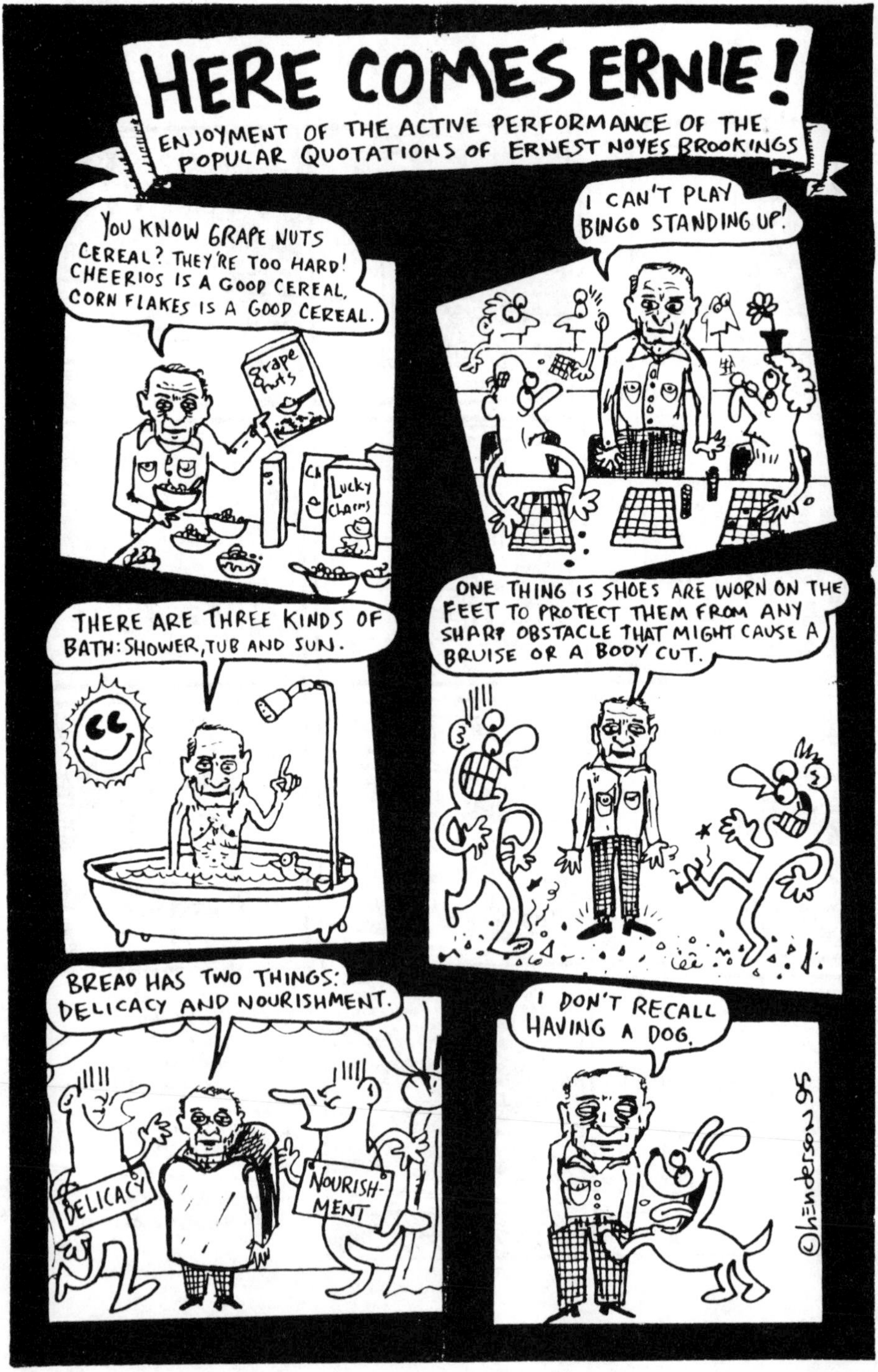
HERE COMES ERNIE!
ENJOYMENT OF THE ACTIVE PERFORMANCE OF THE POPULAR QUOTATIONS OF ERNEST NOYES BROOKINGS
YOU KNOW GRAPE NUTS CEREAL? THEY'RE TOO HARD! CHEERIOS IS A GOOD CEREAL, CORN FLAKES IS A GOOD CEREAL.
Grape Nuts
Lucky Charms
I CAN'T PLAY BINGO STANDING UP!
THERE ARE THREE KINDS OF BATH: SHOWER, TUB AND SUN.
ONE THING IS SHOES ARE WORN ON THE FEET TO PROTECT THEM FROM ANY SHARP OBSTACLE THAT MIGHT CAUSE A BRUISE OR A BODY CUT.
BREAD HAS TWO THINGS: DELICACY AND NOURISHMENT.
DELICACY
NOURISH-MENT
I DON'T RECALL HAVING A DOG.
©henderson 95

MAGIC WHISTLE'S TOP 20 CARTOON ARCHETYPE COUNTDOWN

RANK		YEAR DEBUTED ON CHART	RANK		DEBUT ON CHART
1	SLACKERS	1991	11	HOBOES	1933
2	ALCOHOLICS	1643	12	REDNECK COPS	1976
3	BEATNIKS	1957	13	MOBSTERS	1928
4	HILLBILLIES	1939	14	SHOWBIZ AGENTS	1961
5	FRENCHMEN†	1964	15	GREASERS	1955
6	DANDIES	1896	16	HIPPIES	1967
7	PUNK-ROCKERS	1979	17	NERDS*	1985
8	PIMPS	1971	18	ROBOTS	1932
9	RICH TEXANS	1980	19	HENPECKED HUSBANDS	1947
10	SNOOTY WAITERS	1954	20	IRISH PIRATE ROBOTS**	1997

†DENOTES BOHEMIAN FRENCHMAN *NOT TO BE CONFUSED WITH GEEKS OR DWEEBS OR 50'S NERD ARCHETYPE.
**I JUST MADE THIS ONE UP RIGHT NOW

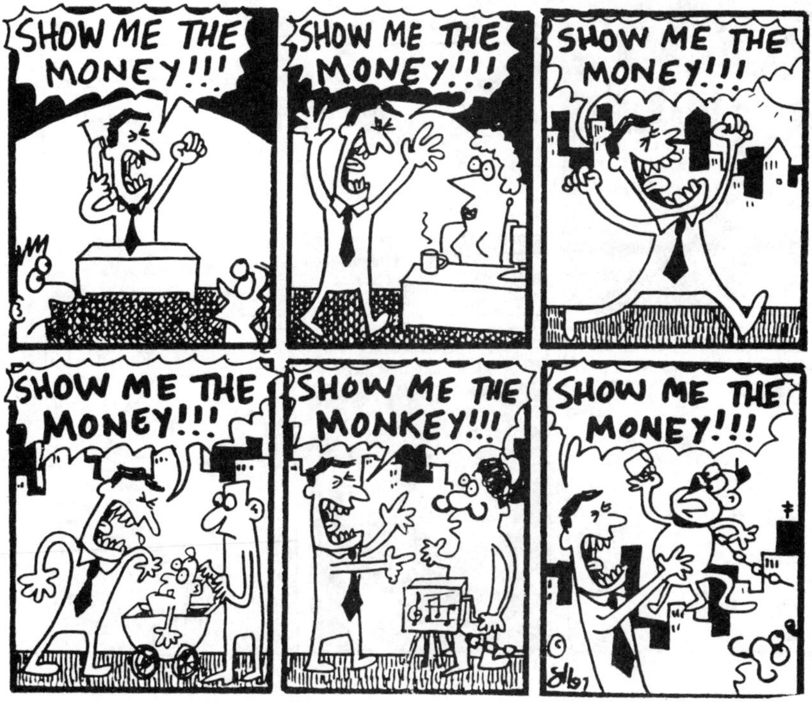
SHOW ME THE MONEY!!!
SHOW ME THE MONEY!!!
SHOW ME THE MONEY!!!
SHOW ME THE MONEY!!!
SHOW ME THE MONKEY!!!
SHOW ME THE MONEY!!!

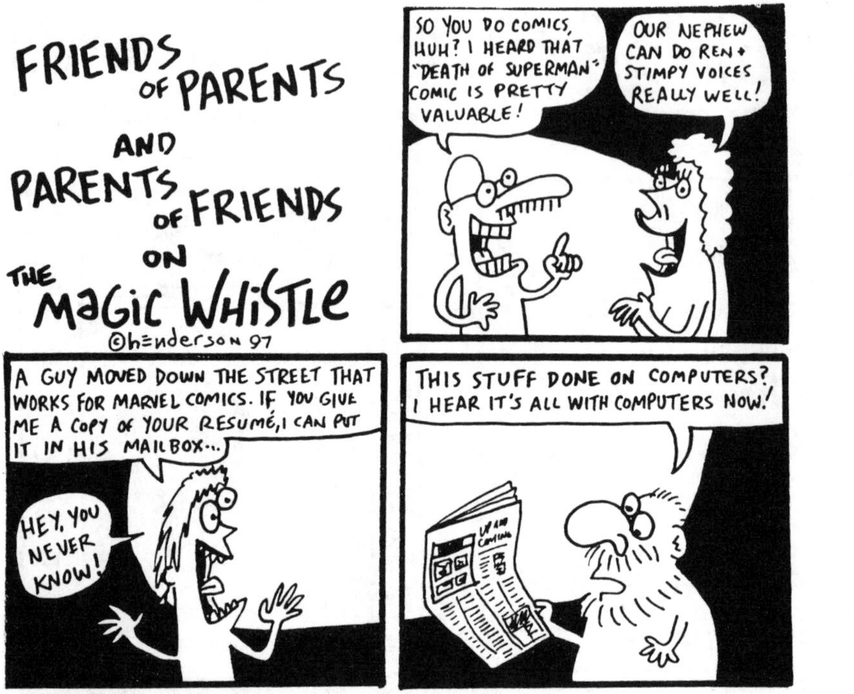
FRIENDS OF PARENTS AND PARENTS OF FRIENDS ON THE MAGIC WHISTLE
©henderson 97
SO YOU DO COMICS, HUH? I HEARD THAT "DEATH OF SUPERMAN" COMIC IS PRETTY VALUABLE!
OUR NEPHEW CAN DO REN + STIMPY VOICES REALLY WELL!
A GUY MOVED DOWN THE STREET THAT WORKS FOR MARVEL COMICS. IF YOU GIVE ME A COPY OF YOUR RESUMÉ, I CAN PUT IT IN HIS MAILBOX...
HEY, YOU NEVER KNOW!
THIS STUFF DONE ON COMPUTERS? I HEAR IT'S ALL WITH COMPUTERS NOW!

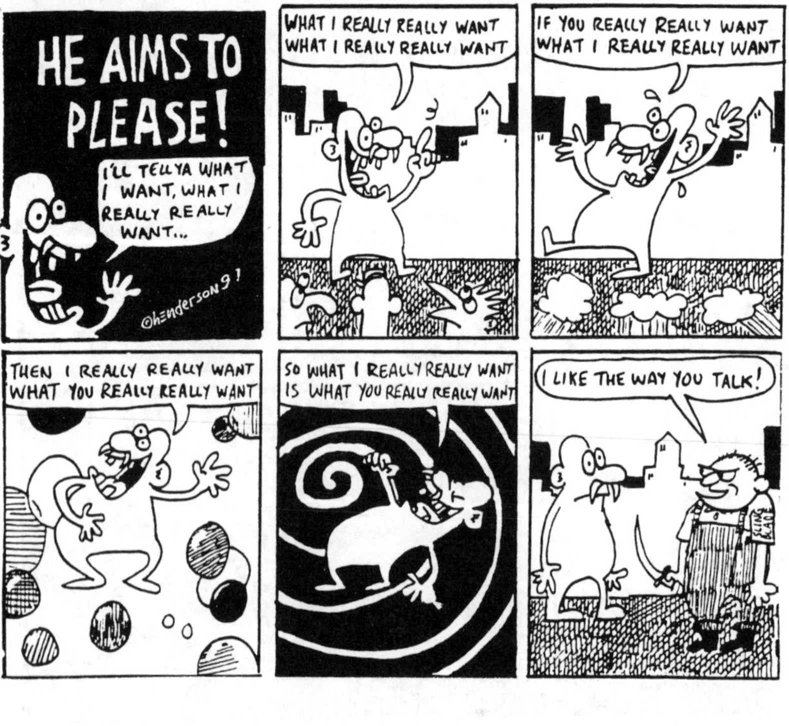
HE AIMS TO PLEASE!
I'LL TELLYA WHAT I WANT, WHAT I REALLY REALLY WANT...
©henderson 97
WHAT I REALLY REALLY WANT WHAT I REALLY REALLY WANT
IF YOU REALLY REALLY WANT WHAT I REALLY REALLY WANT
THEN I REALLY REALLY WANT WHAT YOU REALLY REALLY WANT
SO WHAT I REALLY REALLY WANT IS WHAT YOU REALLY REALLY WANT
I LIKE THE WAY YOU TALK!

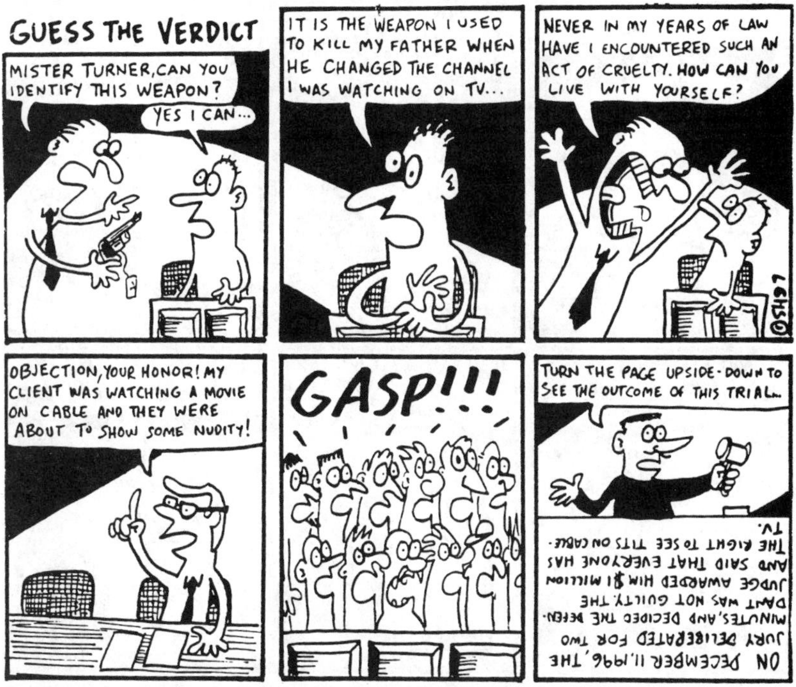
GUESS THE VERDICT
MISTER TURNER, CAN YOU IDENTIFY THIS WEAPON?
YES I CAN...
IT IS THE WEAPON I USED TO KILL MY FATHER WHEN HE CHANGED THE CHANNEL I WAS WATCHING ON TV...
NEVER IN MY YEARS OF LAW HAVE I ENCOUNTERED SUCH AN ACT OF CRUELTY. HOW CAN YOU LIVE WITH YOURSELF?
OBJECTION, YOUR HONOR! MY CLIENT WAS WATCHING A MOVIE ON CABLE AND THEY WERE ABOUT TO SHOW SOME NUDITY!
GASP!!!
TURN THE PAGE UPSIDE-DOWN TO SEE THE OUTCOME OF THIS TRIAL...
ON DECEMBER 11, 1996, THE JURY DELIBERATED FOR TWO MINUTES, AND DECIDED THE DEFENDANT WAS NOT GUILTY. THE JUDGE AWARDED HIM $1 MILLION AND SAID THAT EVERYONE HAS THE RIGHT TO SEE TITS ON CABLE-TV.

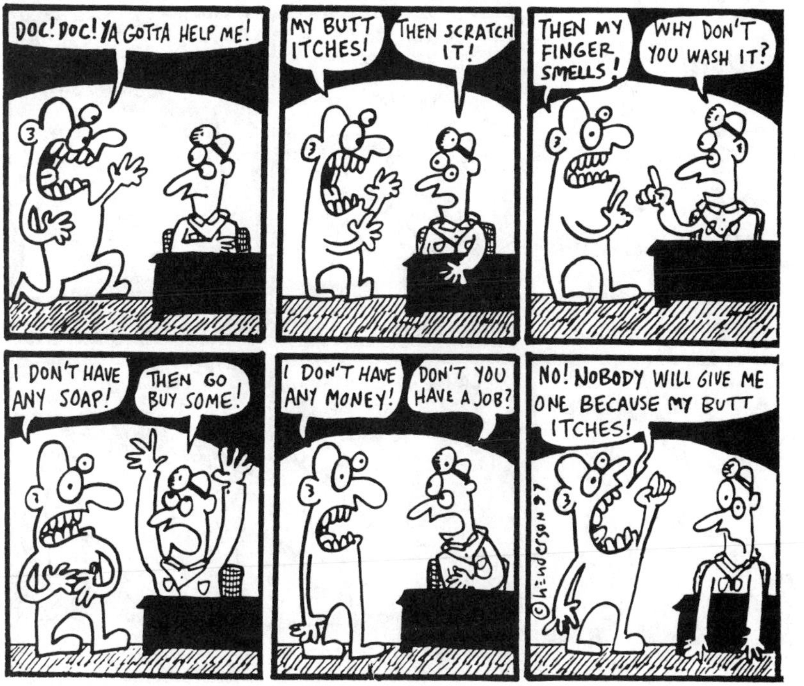
DOC! DOC! YA GOTTA HELP ME!
MY BUTT ITCHES!
THEN SCRATCH IT!
THEN MY FINGER SMELLS!
WHY DON'T YOU WASH IT?
I DON'T HAVE ANY SOAP!
THEN GO BUY SOME!
I DON'T HAVE ANY MONEY!
DON'T YOU HAVE A JOB?
NO! NOBODY WILL GIVE ME ONE BECAUSE MY BUTT ITCHES!
© henderson 97

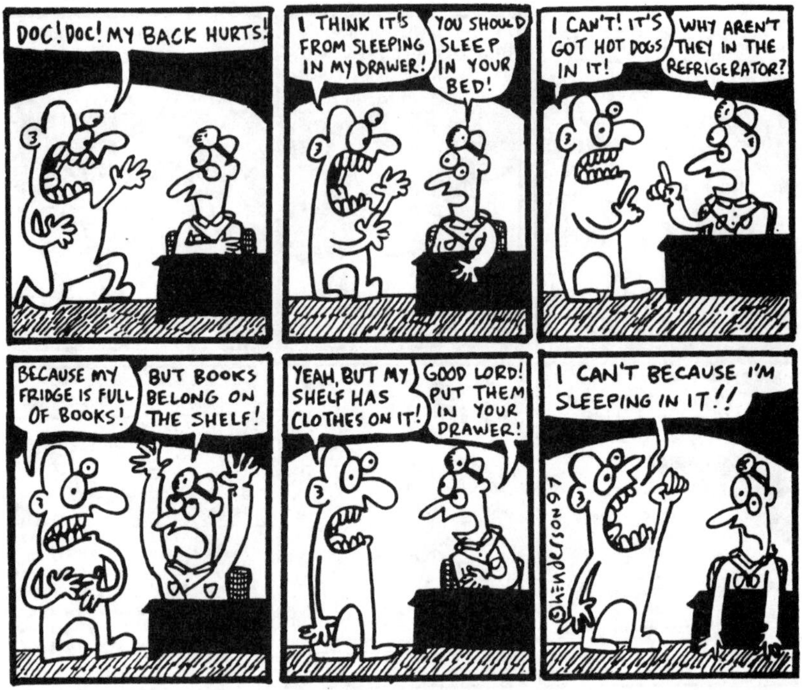

DOC! DOC! MY BACK HURTS!
I THINK IT'S FROM SLEEPING IN MY DRAWER!
YOU SHOULD SLEEP IN YOUR BED!
I CAN'T! IT'S GOT HOT DOGS IN IT!
WHY AREN'T THEY IN THE REFRIGERATOR?
BECAUSE MY FRIDGE IS FULL OF BOOKS!
BUT BOOKS BELONG ON THE SHELF!
YEAH, BUT MY SHELF HAS CLOTHES ON IT!
GOOD LORD! PUT THEM IN YOUR DRAWER!
I CAN'T BECAUSE I'M SLEEPING IN IT!!
©henderson 97

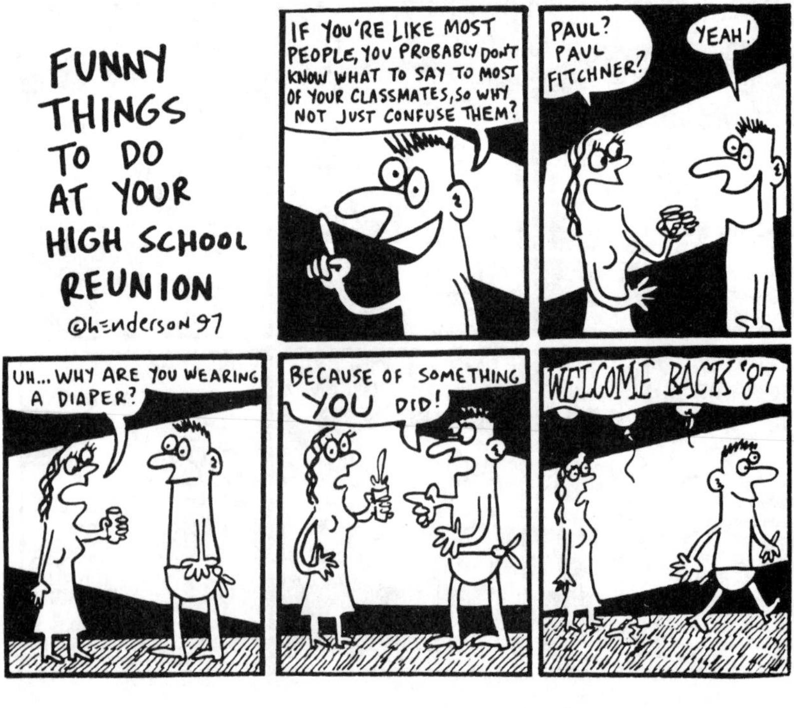

FUNNY THINGS TO DO AT YOUR HIGH SCHOOL REUNION
©henderson 97
IF YOU'RE LIKE MOST PEOPLE, YOU PROBABLY DON'T KNOW WHAT TO SAY TO MOST OF YOUR CLASSMATES, SO WHY NOT JUST CONFUSE THEM?
PAUL? PAUL FITCHNER?
YEAH!
UH... WHY ARE YOU WEARING A DIAPER?
BECAUSE OF SOMETHING YOU DID!
WELCOME BACK '87

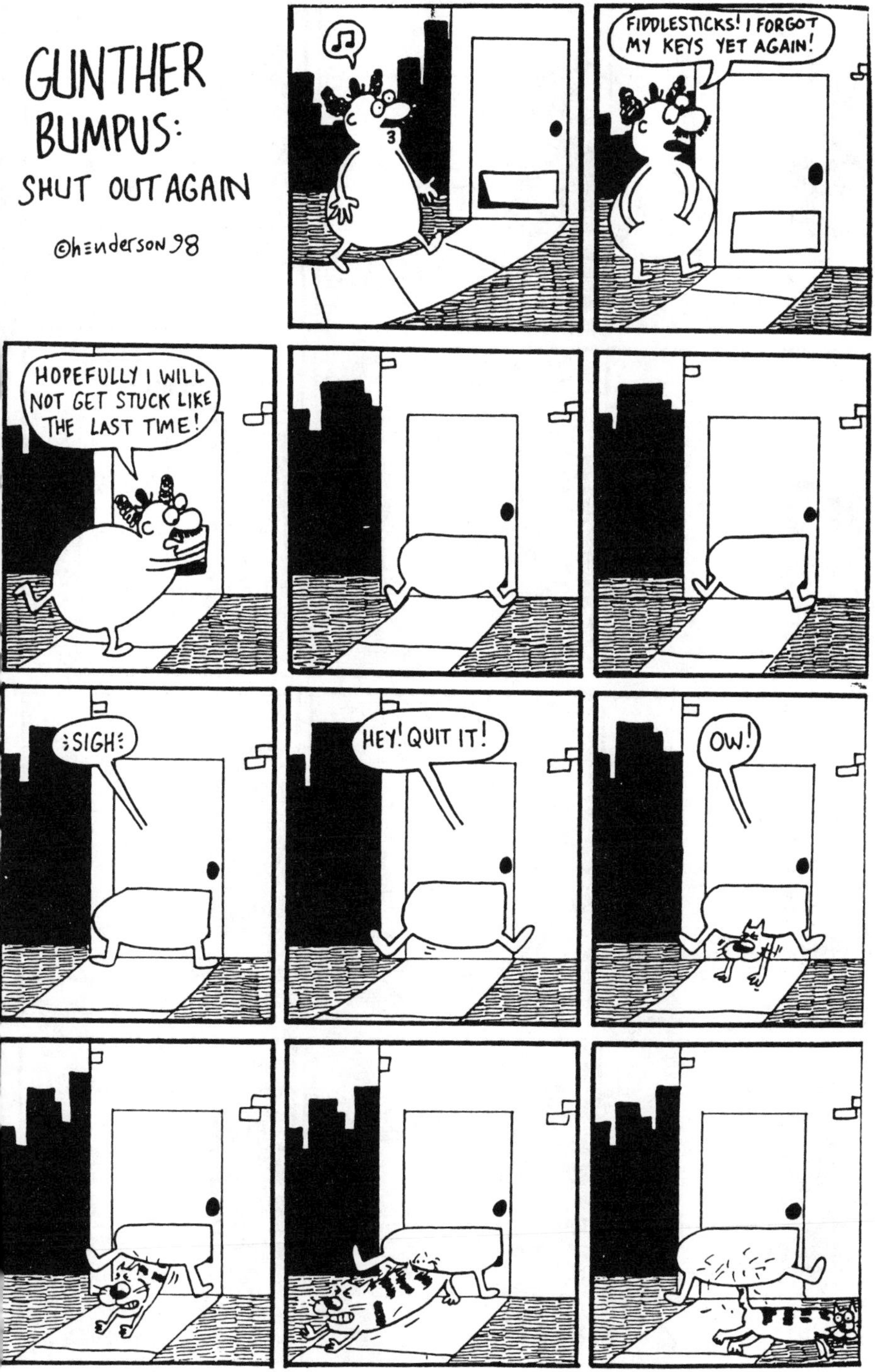
GUNTHER BUMPUS:
SHUT OUT AGAIN
©henderson 98
FIDDLESTICKS! I FORGOT MY KEYS YET AGAIN!
HOPEFULLY I WILL NOT GET STUCK LIKE THE LAST TIME!
SIGH
HEY! QUIT IT!
OW!

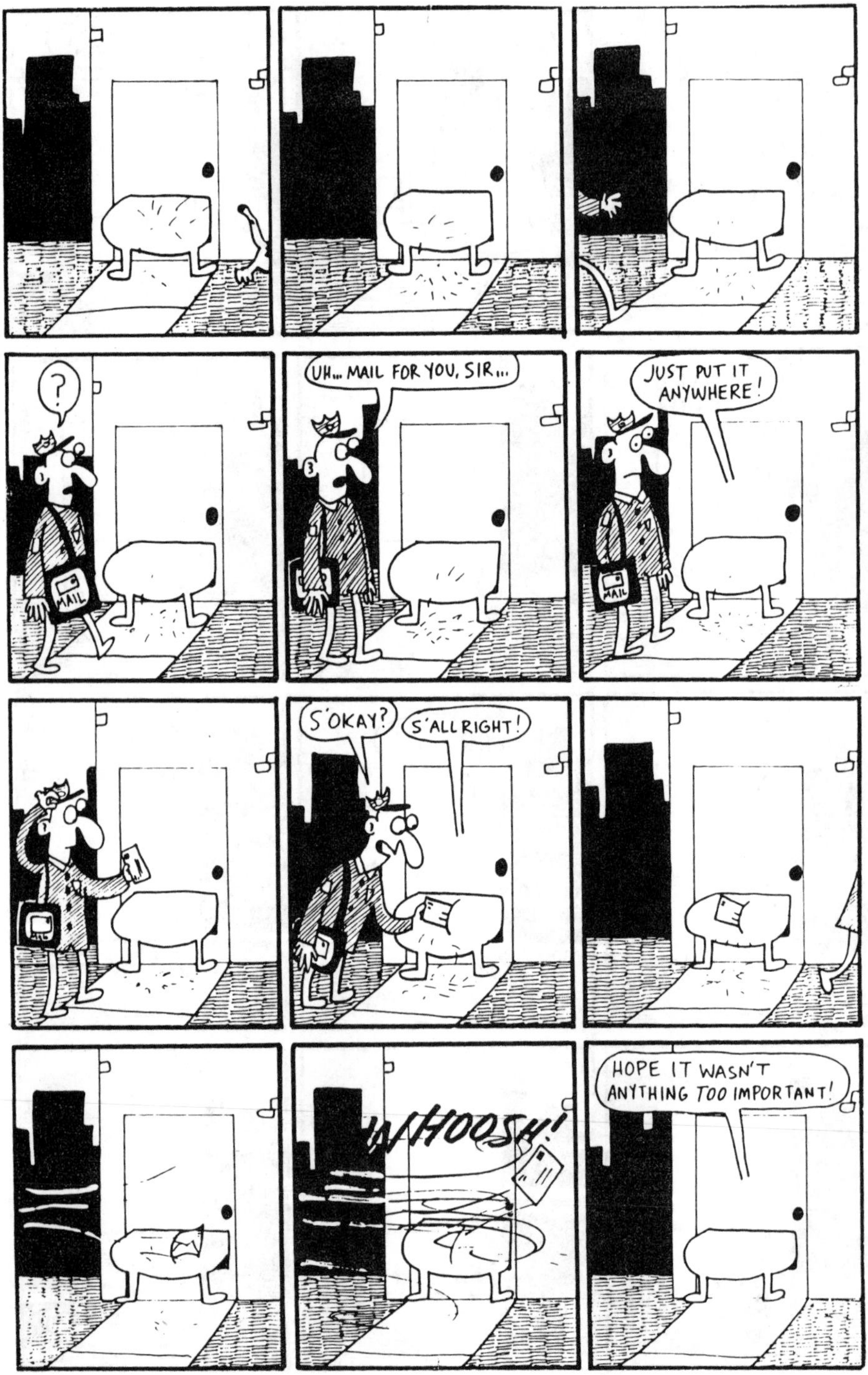
?
UH... MAIL FOR YOU, SIR...
JUST PUT IT ANYWHERE!
S'OKAY?
S'ALL RIGHT!
WHOOSH!
HOPE IT WASN'T ANYTHING TOO IMPORTANT!

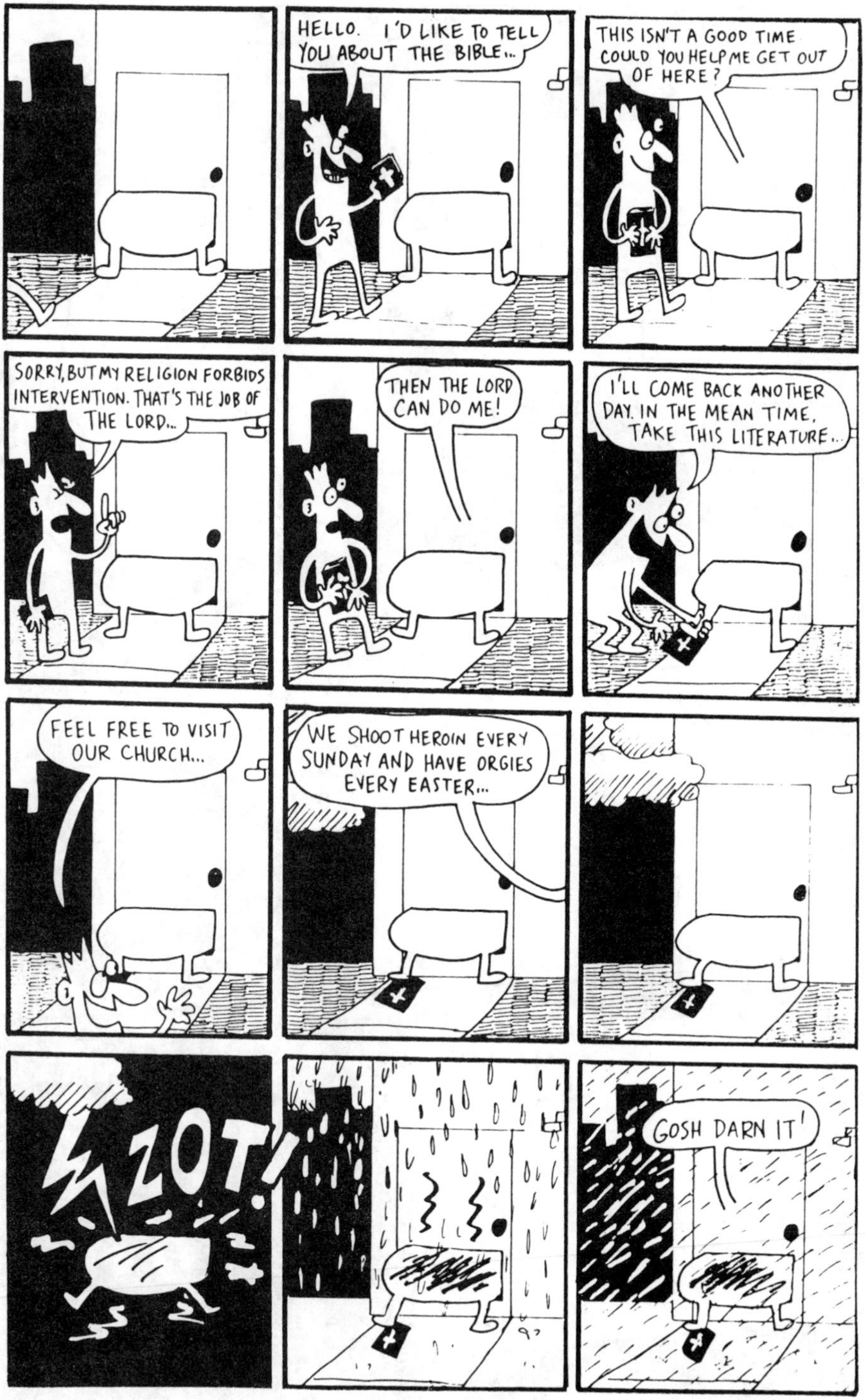
HELLO. I'D LIKE TO TELL YOU ABOUT THE BIBLE...
THIS ISN'T A GOOD TIME COULD YOU HELP ME GET OUT OF HERE?
SORRY, BUT MY RELIGION FORBIDS INTERVENTION. THAT'S THE JOB OF THE LORD...
THEN THE LORD CAN DO ME!
I'LL COME BACK ANOTHER DAY. IN THE MEAN TIME, TAKE THIS LITERATURE...
FEEL FREE TO VISIT OUR CHURCH...
WE SHOOT HEROIN EVERY SUNDAY AND HAVE ORGIES EVERY EASTER...
ZOT!
GOSH DARN IT!

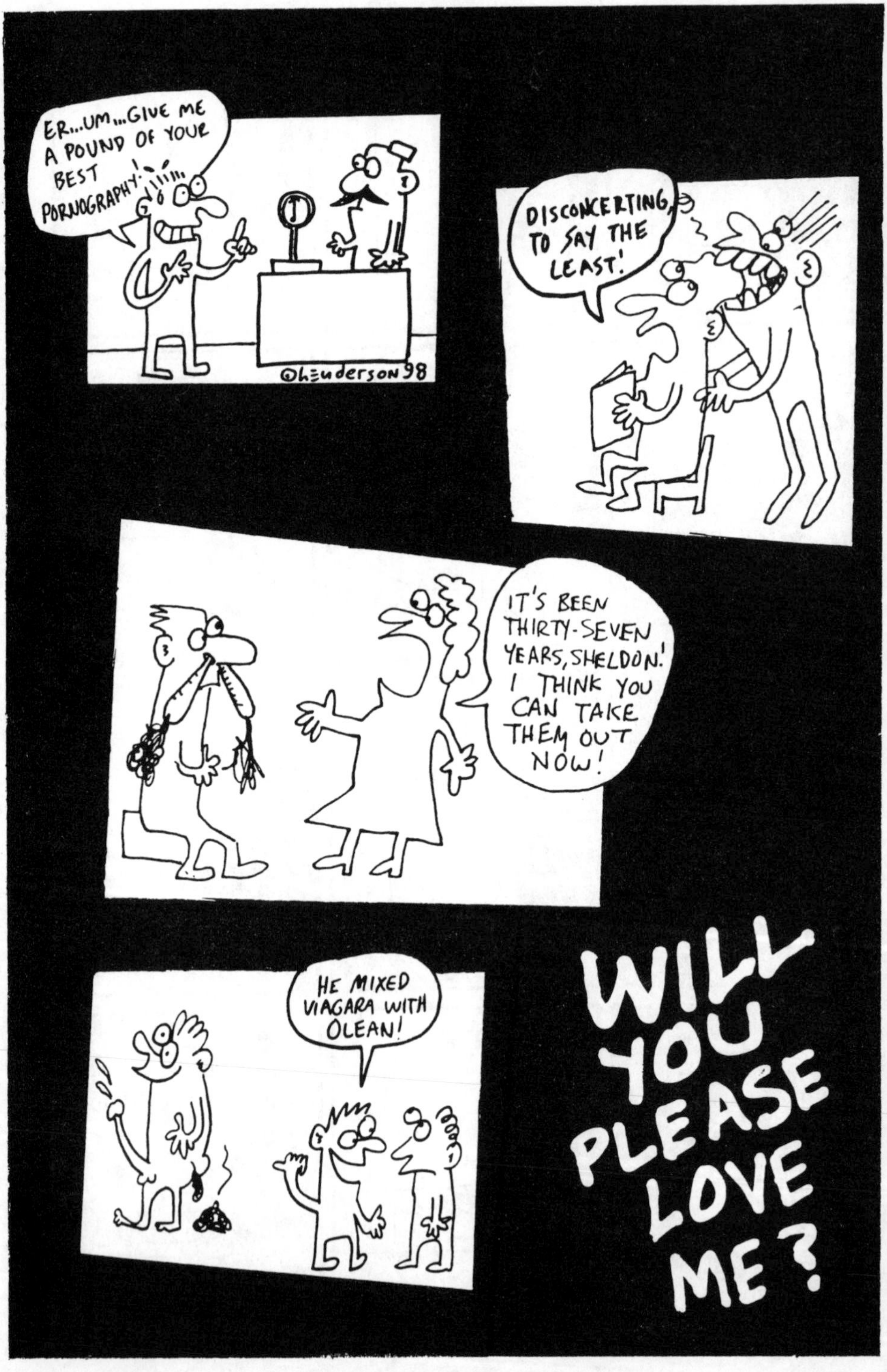
ER...UM...GIVE ME A POUND OF YOUR BEST PORNOGRAPHY!
©henderson98
DISCONCERTING, TO SAY THE LEAST!
IT'S BEEN THIRTY-SEVEN YEARS, SHELDON! I THINK YOU CAN TAKE THEM OUT NOW!
HE MIXED VIAGARA WITH OLEAN!
WILL YOU PLEASE LOVE ME?

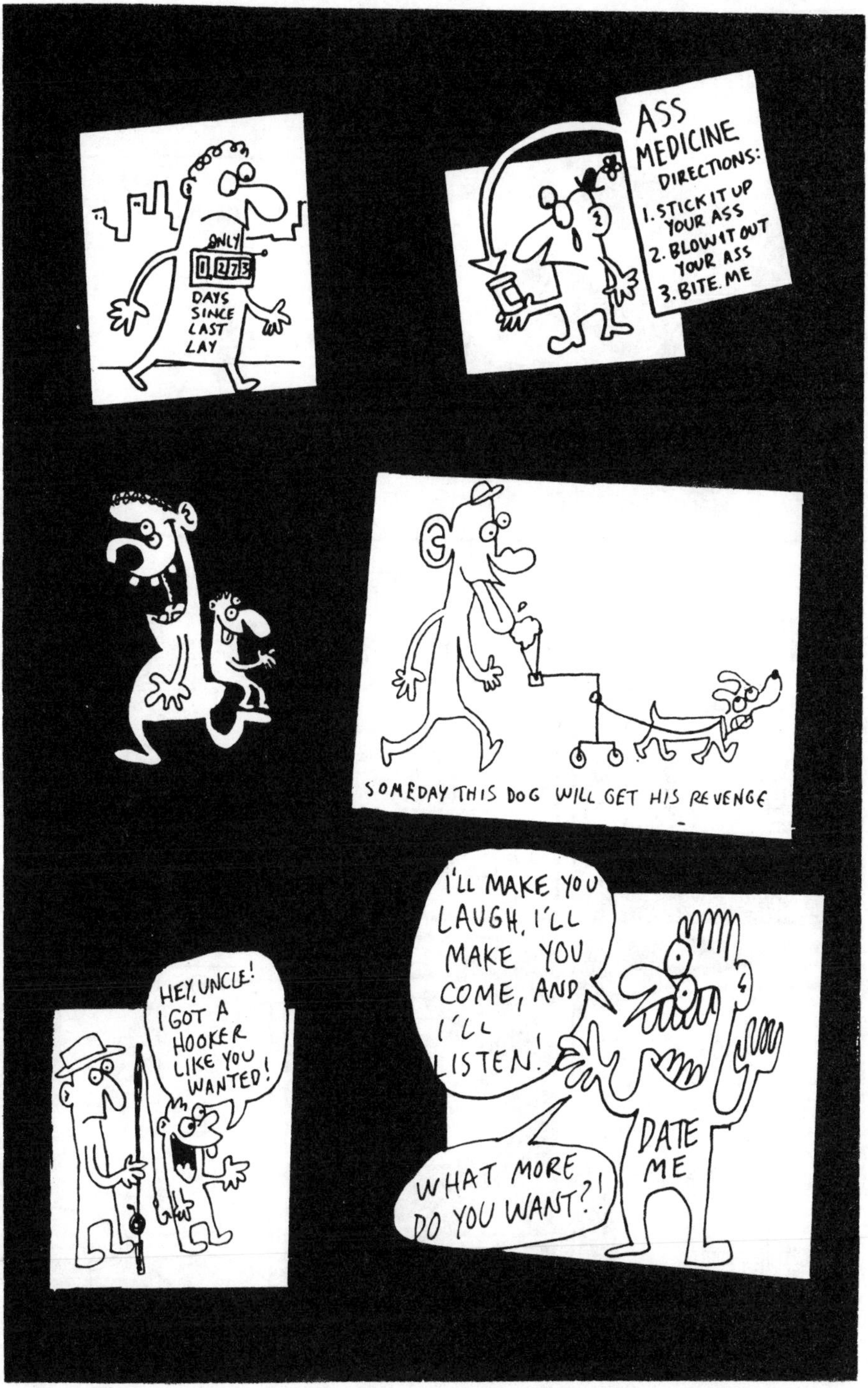
ONLY
0,273
DAYS SINCE LAST LAY
ASS MEDICINE
DIRECTIONS:
1. STICK IT UP YOUR ASS
2. BLOW IT OUT YOUR ASS
3. BITE ME
SOMEDAY THIS DOG WILL GET HIS REVENGE
HEY, UNCLE! I GOT A HOOKER LIKE YOU WANTED!
I'LL MAKE YOU LAUGH, I'LL MAKE YOU COME, AND I'LL LISTEN!
WHAT MORE DO YOU WANT?!
DATE ME

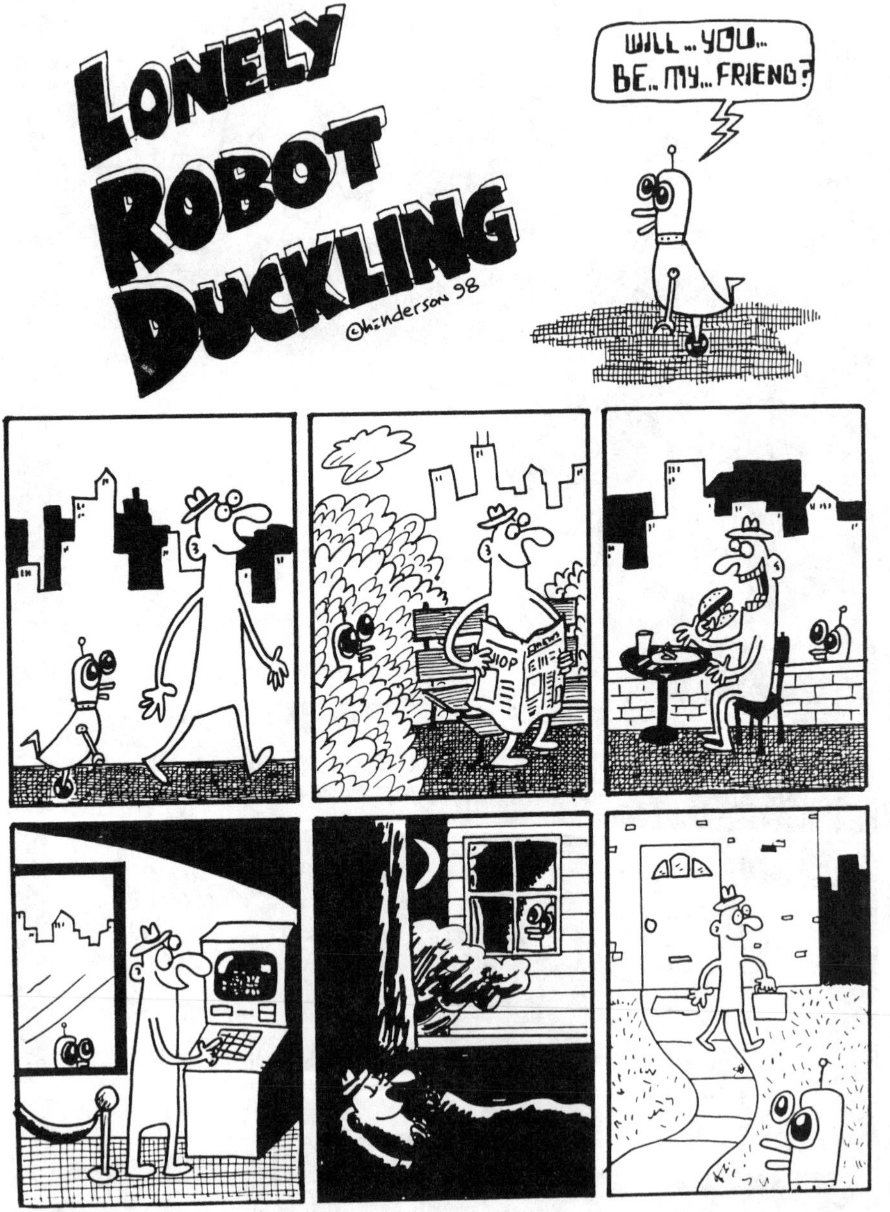
LONELY ROBOT DUCKLING
©hinderson 98
WILL... YOU... BE... MY... FRIEND?
NEWS

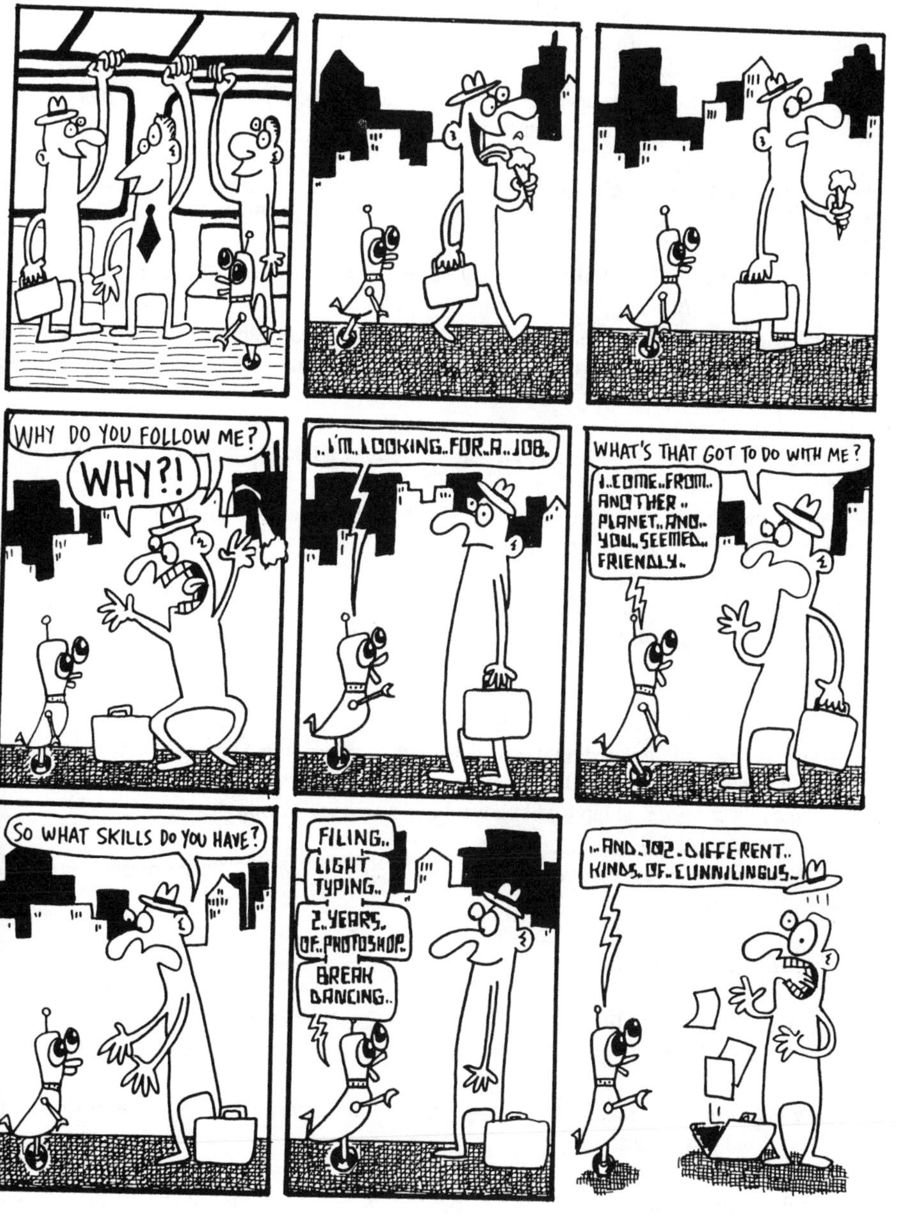
WHY DO YOU FOLLOW ME?
WHY?!
..I'M..LOOKING..FOR..A..JOB..
WHAT'S THAT GOT TO DO WITH ME?
I..COME..FROM..ANOTHER..PLANET..AND..YOU..SEEMED..FRIENDLY..
SO WHAT SKILLS DO YOU HAVE?
FILING..
LIGHT TYPING..
2..YEARS..OF..PHOTOSHOP..
BREAK DANCING..
..AND..702..DIFFERENT..KINDS..OF..CUNNILINGUS..

• HR BILL #9999F: REFORM IN HUMOROLOGY

WHEREAS we live in an age where irony, iconoclasm, and irreverence are now the standard and "post-modernism" is an excuse for recycling tired old material,

WHEREAS the information age has introduced more venues for comedy and has made it possible for anyone to find an audience for their work,

WHEREAS we approach a new millenium and yesterday's observations are tomorrow's cliches, and what was once "always funny" is now "no longer funny",

IT IS RESOLVED that the following premises be eliminated from comedy:

- Torturing somebody by making him or her listen to a certain piece of music, watch a certain television program, or otherwise expose them to a particular pop culture artifact which is generally considered mediocre.

- Facial distortions, either through a fish-eye lens or a fast wind blowing in one's face.

- Any sketch in which a famous person shows up at the end to show the actor who has just impersonated them "how it's really done".

- The "A makes B look like Z" formula (i.e.; something new makes this slightly less extreme item look like something completely benign, or vice-versa)

- Psychotic postal workers or referring to a violent act as "going postal".

- Implications of unwanted anal intrusion such as a prisoner blowing a kiss to a fellow inmate, a police chief ordering a cavity search. aliens with ostentatious probing devices, or a doctor snapping his/her rubber glove and smiling.

- The following phrases: "bad hair day", "panties in a bunch", "from hell", "on acid", and "with an attitude".

- Victims being "toast".

- Anything with the title "[It's/Oh][Those/That][Wacky/Nutty/Crazy][...]", "(You Gotta) Love That[...]", "I Was a Teenage [...]", or any combinations thereof.

- Any fake interview in which the same shot of the interviewer nodding knowingly is later edited in several times

- Movie trailers that begin with text saying "Once in a lifetime comes a movie that defines a generation..." followed by a record scratching and a voice saying "...This is not one of them!"

HI! I'M HERE FOR THE ASS MEASURERS CLUB MEETING!
WRONG ROOM!
GO AWAY!
YOU SUCK!
OH... SORRY...
IS HE GONE?
YEAH!
©henderson 97

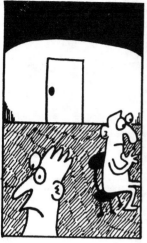

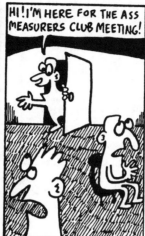

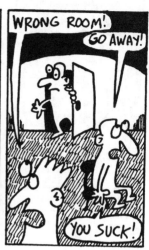

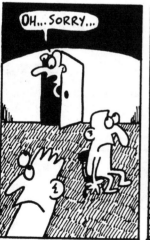

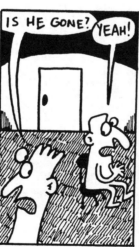

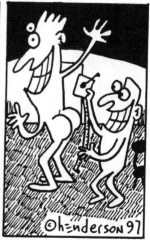

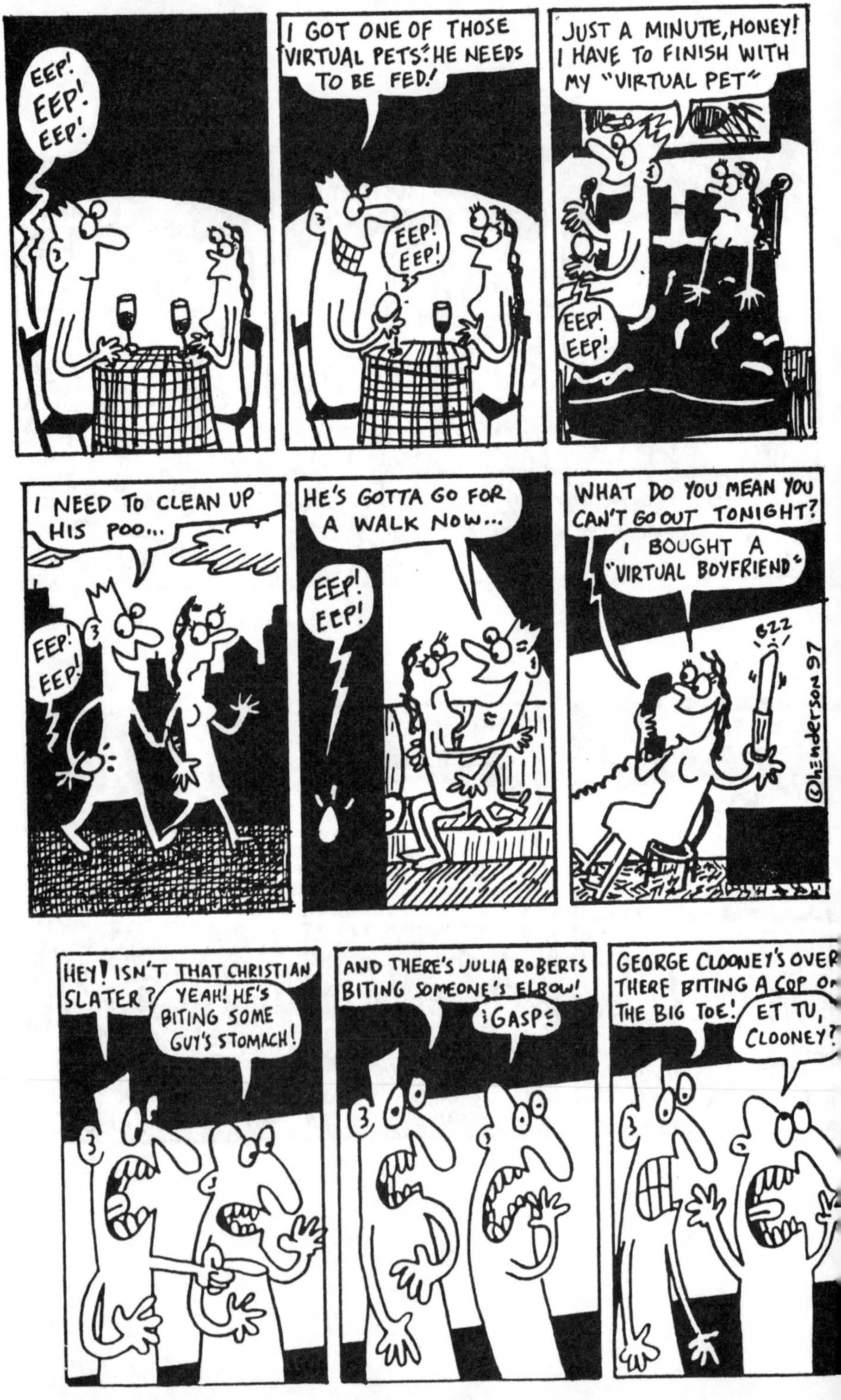
EEP! EEP! EEP!
I GOT ONE OF THOSE "VIRTUAL PETS"! HE NEEDS TO BE FED!
EEP! EEP!
JUST A MINUTE, HONEY! I HAVE TO FINISH WITH MY "VIRTUAL PET"
EEP! EEP!
I NEED TO CLEAN UP HIS POO...
EEP! EEP!
HE'S GOTTA GO FOR A WALK NOW...
EEP! EEP!
WHAT DO YOU MEAN YOU CAN'T GO OUT TONIGHT?
I BOUGHT A "VIRTUAL BOYFRIEND"
BZZ
©henderson 97
HEY! ISN'T THAT CHRISTIAN SLATER?
YEAH! HE'S BITING SOME GUY'S STOMACH!
AND THERE'S JULIA ROBERTS BITING SOMEONE'S ELBOW!
GASP
GEORGE CLOONEY'S OVER THERE BITING A COP ON THE BIG TOE!
ET TU, CLOONEY?

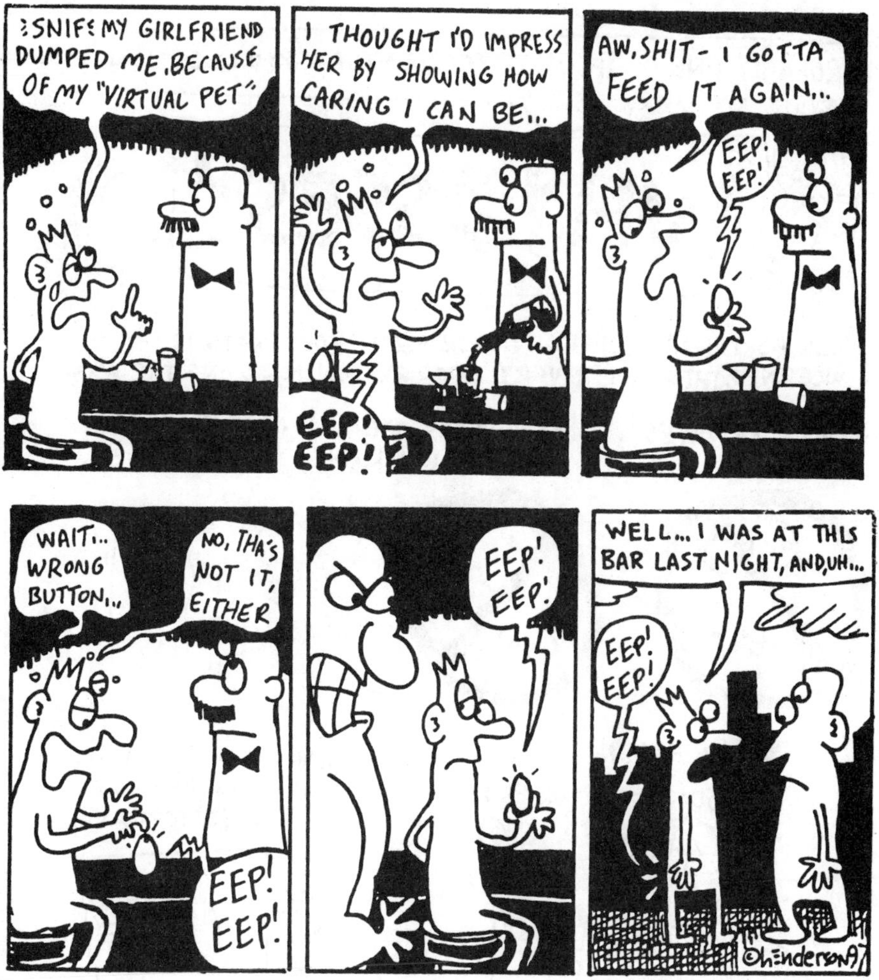
:SNIF: MY GIRLFRIEND DUMPED ME, BECAUSE OF MY "VIRTUAL PET"
I THOUGHT I'D IMPRESS HER BY SHOWING HOW CARING I CAN BE...
EEP! EEP!
AW, SHIT - I GOTTA FEED IT AGAIN...
EEP! EEP!
WAIT... WRONG BUTTON...
NO, THA'S NOT IT, EITHER
EEP! EEP!
EEP! EEP!
WELL... I WAS AT THIS BAR LAST NIGHT, AND, UH...
EEP! EEP!
©henderson97

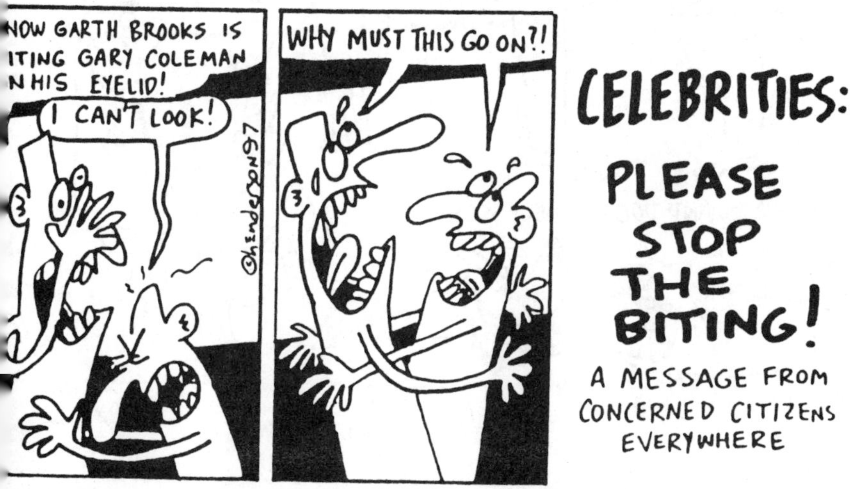
NOW GARTH BROOKS IS ITING GARY COLEMAN N HIS EYELID!
I CAN'T LOOK!
©henderson97
WHY MUST THIS GO ON?!
CELEBRITIES:
PLEASE STOP THE BITING!
A MESSAGE FROM CONCERNED CITIZENS EVERYWHERE

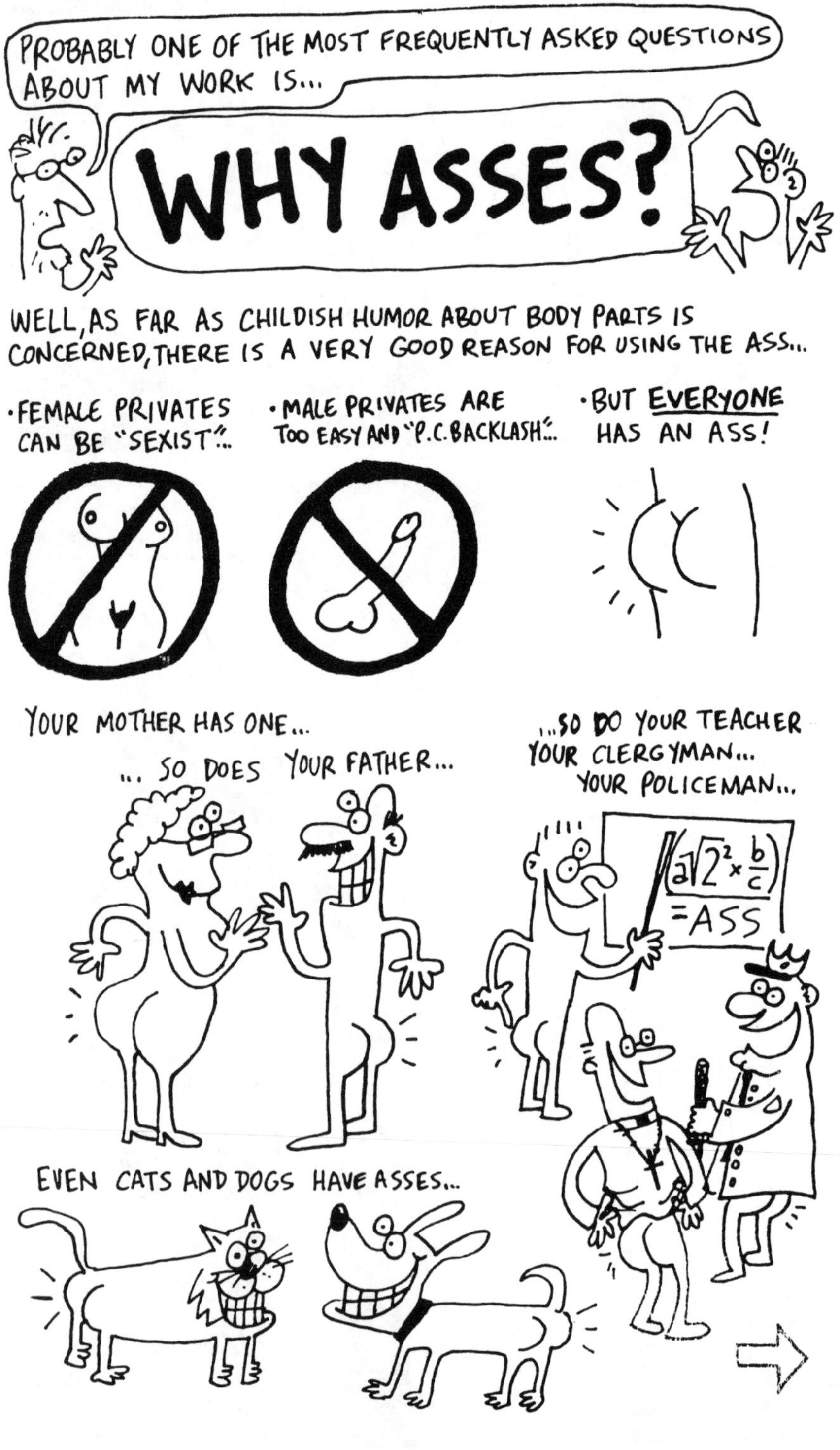
PROBABLY ONE OF THE MOST FREQUENTLY ASKED QUESTIONS ABOUT MY WORK IS...
WHY ASSES?
WELL, AS FAR AS CHILDISH HUMOR ABOUT BODY PARTS IS CONCERNED, THERE IS A VERY GOOD REASON FOR USING THE ASS...
• FEMALE PRIVATES CAN BE "SEXIST"...
• MALE PRIVATES ARE TOO EASY AND "P.C. BACKLASH"...
• BUT EVERYONE HAS AN ASS!
YOUR MOTHER HAS ONE...
... SO DOES YOUR FATHER...
...SO DO YOUR TEACHER
YOUR CLERGYMAN...
YOUR POLICEMAN...
$(a\sqrt{2}^2 \times \frac{b}{c})$
$=$ASS
EVEN CATS AND DOGS HAVE ASSES...

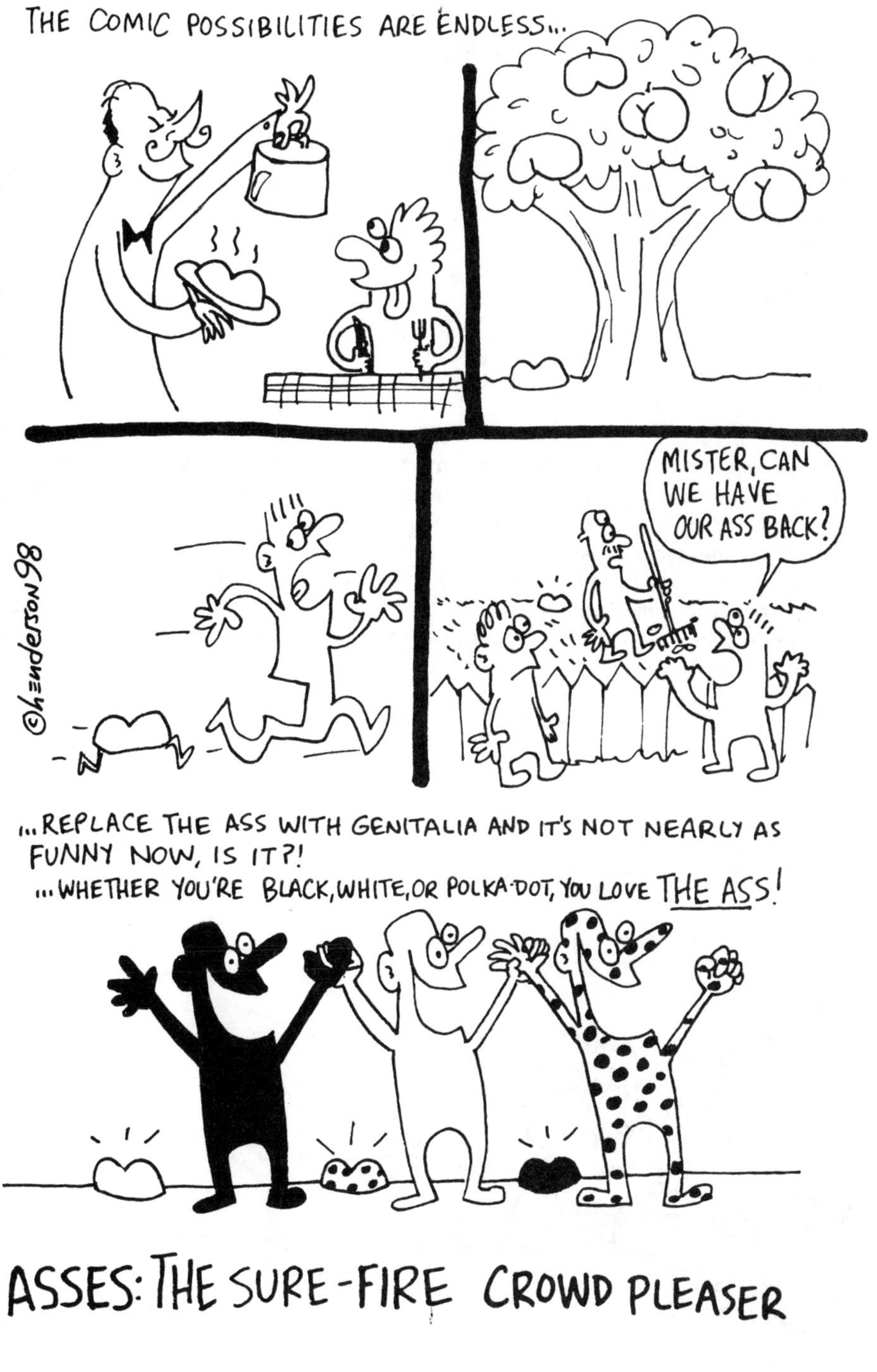
THE COMIC POSSIBILITIES ARE ENDLESS...
©henderson98
MISTER, CAN WE HAVE OUR ASS BACK?
...REPLACE THE ASS WITH GENITALIA AND IT'S NOT NEARLY AS FUNNY NOW, IS IT?!
...WHETHER YOU'RE BLACK, WHITE, OR POLKA-DOT, YOU LOVE THE ASS!
ASSES: THE SURE-FIRE CROWD PLEASER

RECIPE FOR FUN #2

ingredients:

1 Boss
1 Beautiful Movie Actress
1 Always-reliable Neighbor (male)
1 Wig and Dress
1 Candle
3 TV Dinners

directions:

Lie to boss and tell him you are married to beautiful actress. When he invites himself over for dinner, call beautiful actress and ask her to pretend to be your wife. When she refuses, ask neighbor to play the role. Dress him up in wig and dress from thrift store, and teach him to talk and walk like lady. (Shaving optional). Cook TV dinners for time specified on package and wait for boss. As boss compliments on "wife" and "her cooking", allow friend's wig to accidentally catch fire from candle on table, forcing him to remove it and scream in real male voice. Apologize to boss for acting like bigshot, and allow him to chew you out for a minute until he decides to manufacture fireproof wigs and split royalties with you and friend.

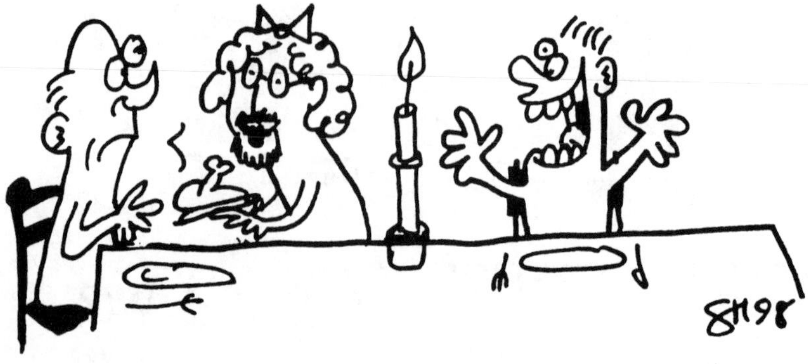
SH98

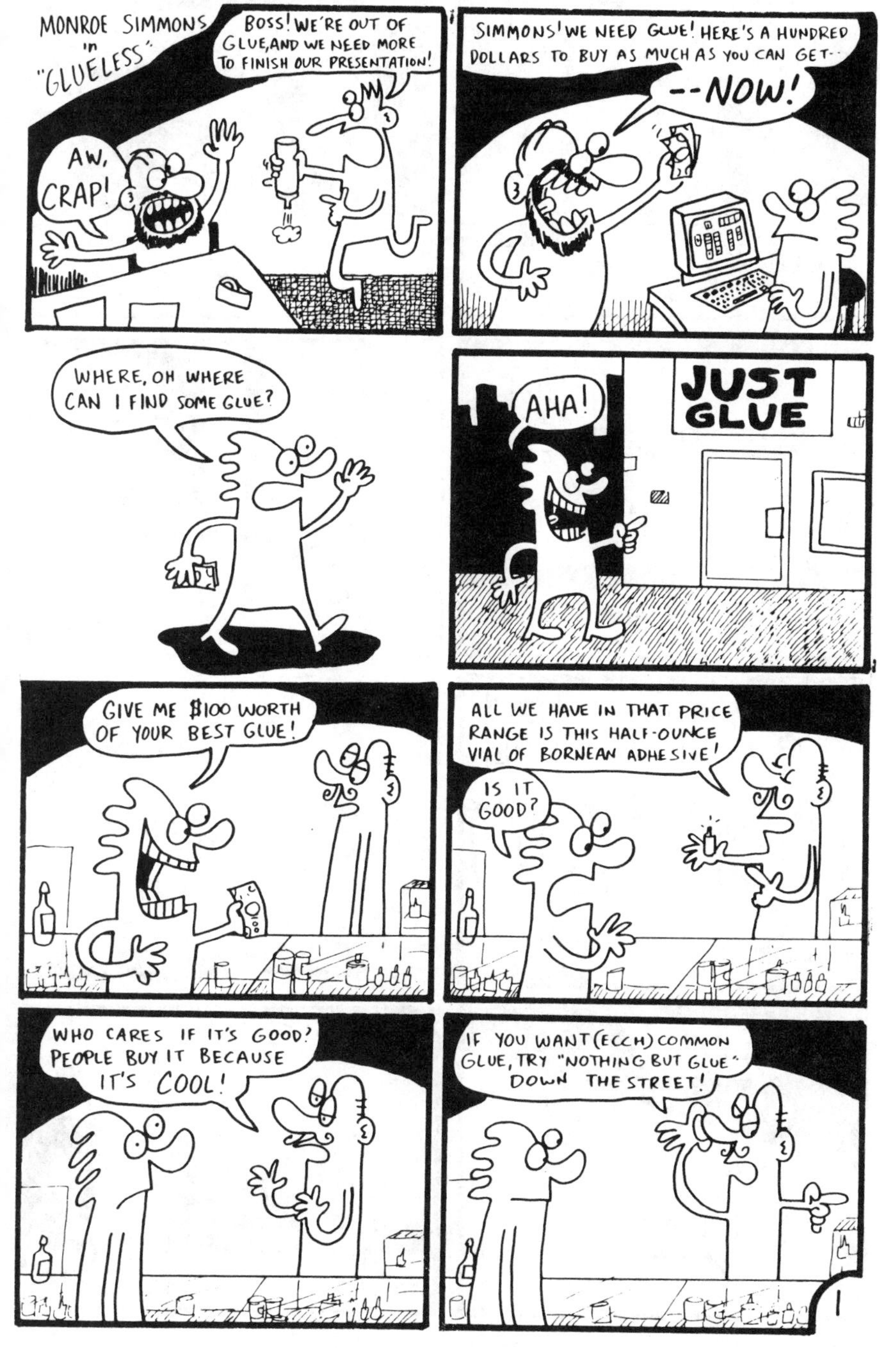
MONROE SIMMONS in "GLUELESS"
BOSS! WE'RE OUT OF GLUE, AND WE NEED MORE TO FINISH OUR PRESENTATION!
AW, CRAP!
SIMMONS! WE NEED GLUE! HERE'S A HUNDRED DOLLARS TO BUY AS MUCH AS YOU CAN GET--
--NOW!
WHERE, OH WHERE CAN I FIND SOME GLUE?
AHA!
JUST GLUE
GIVE ME $100 WORTH OF YOUR BEST GLUE!
ALL WE HAVE IN THAT PRICE RANGE IS THIS HALF-OUNCE VIAL OF BORNEAN ADHESIVE!
IS IT GOOD?
WHO CARES IF IT'S GOOD? PEOPLE BUY IT BECAUSE IT'S COOL!
IF YOU WANT (ECCH) COMMON GLUE, TRY "NOTHING BUT GLUE" DOWN THE STREET!

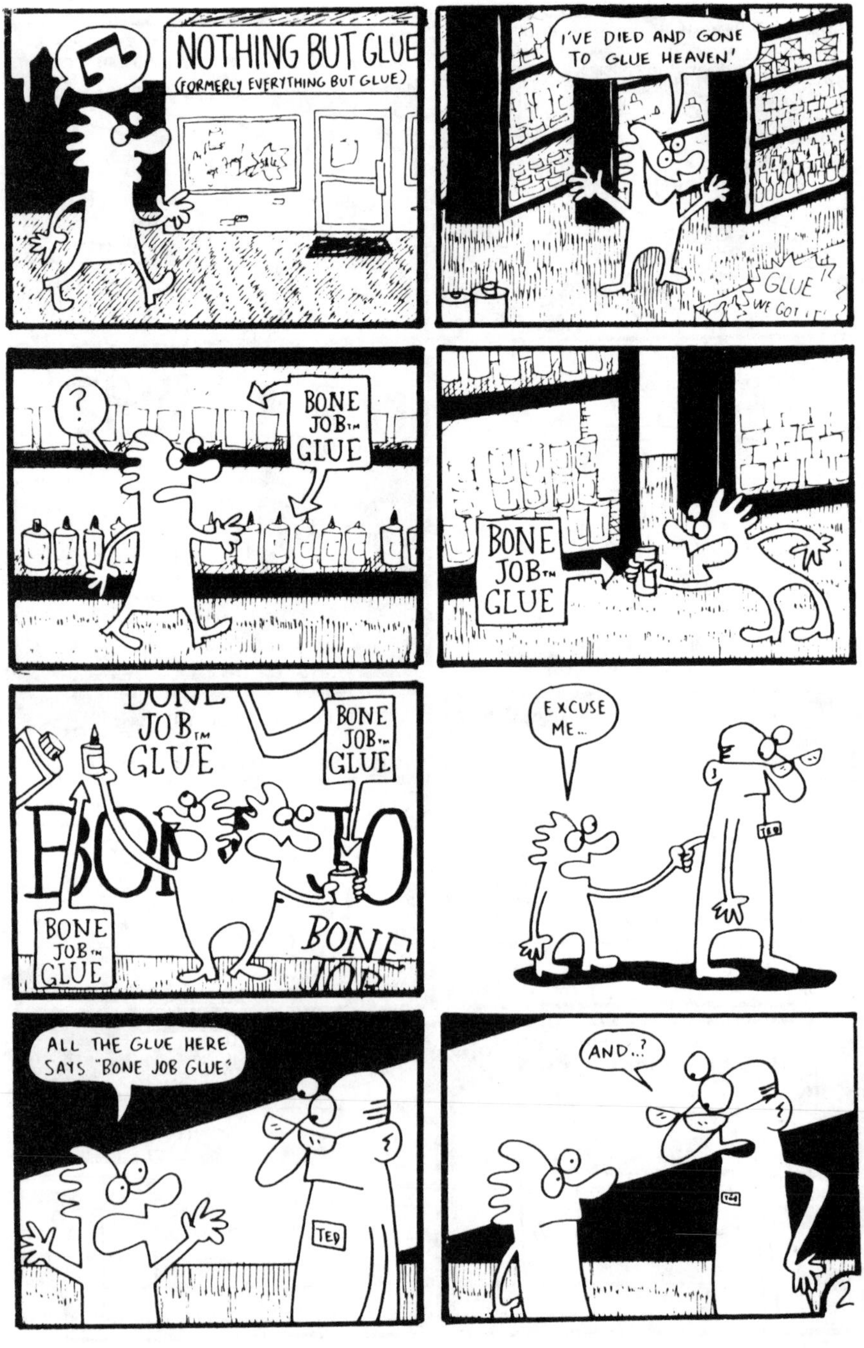
NOTHING BUT GLUE
(FORMERLY EVERYTHING BUT GLUE)
I'VE DIED AND GONE TO GLUE HEAVEN!
GLUE WE GOT
?
BONE JOB™ GLUE
BONE JOB™ GLUE
BONE JOB™ GLUE
BONE JOB™ GLUE
BONE JOB™ GLUE
EXCUSE ME...
TED
ALL THE GLUE HERE SAYS "BONE JOB GLUE"
TED
AND...?
TED

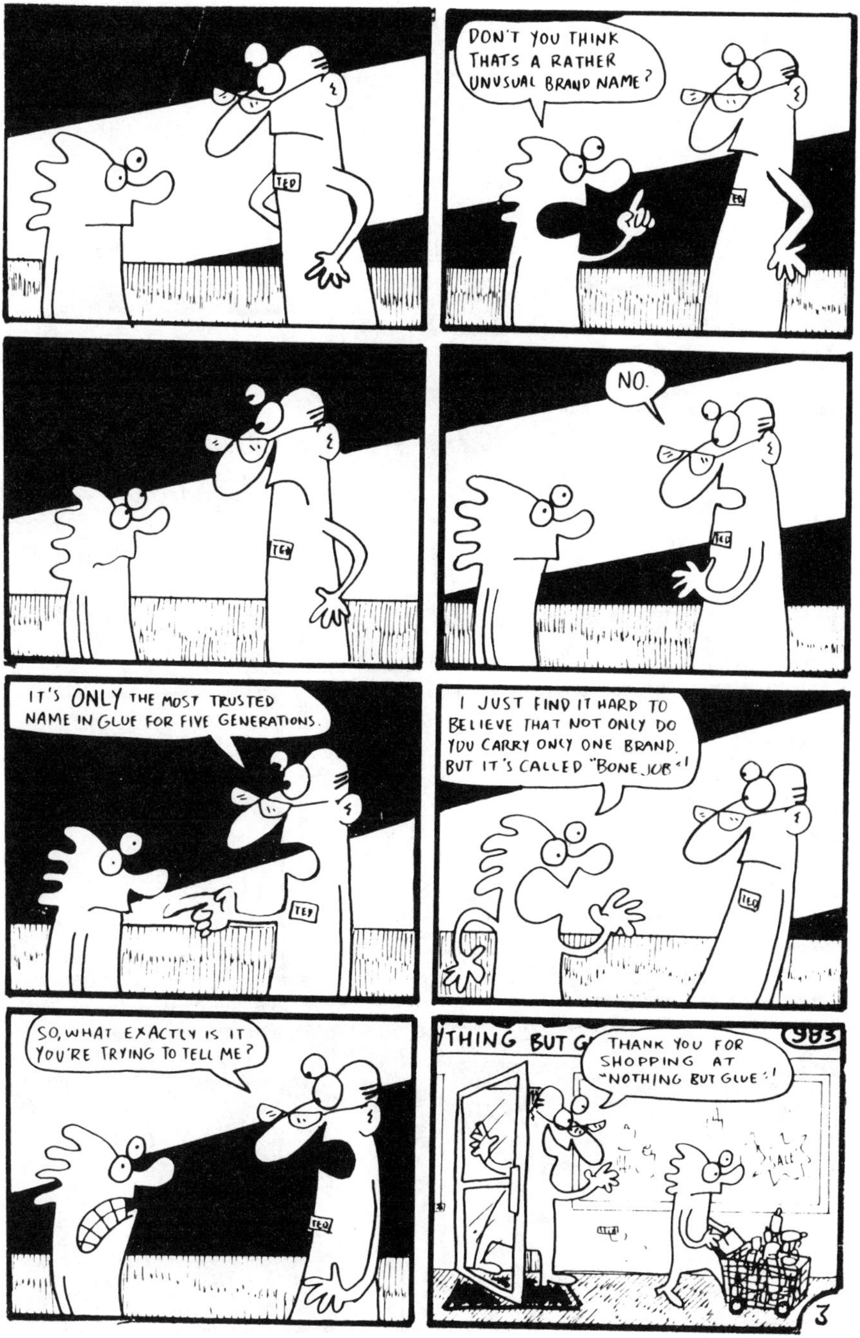
TED
DON'T YOU THINK THATS A RATHER UNUSUAL BRAND NAME?
NO.
IT'S ONLY THE MOST TRUSTED NAME IN GLUE FOR FIVE GENERATIONS.
I JUST FIND IT HARD TO BELIEVE THAT NOT ONLY DO YOU CARRY ONLY ONE BRAND, BUT IT'S CALLED "BONE JOB"!
SO, WHAT EXACTLY IS IT YOU'RE TRYING TO TELL ME?
THING BUT G
THANK YOU FOR SHOPPING AT "NOTHING BUT GLUE"!

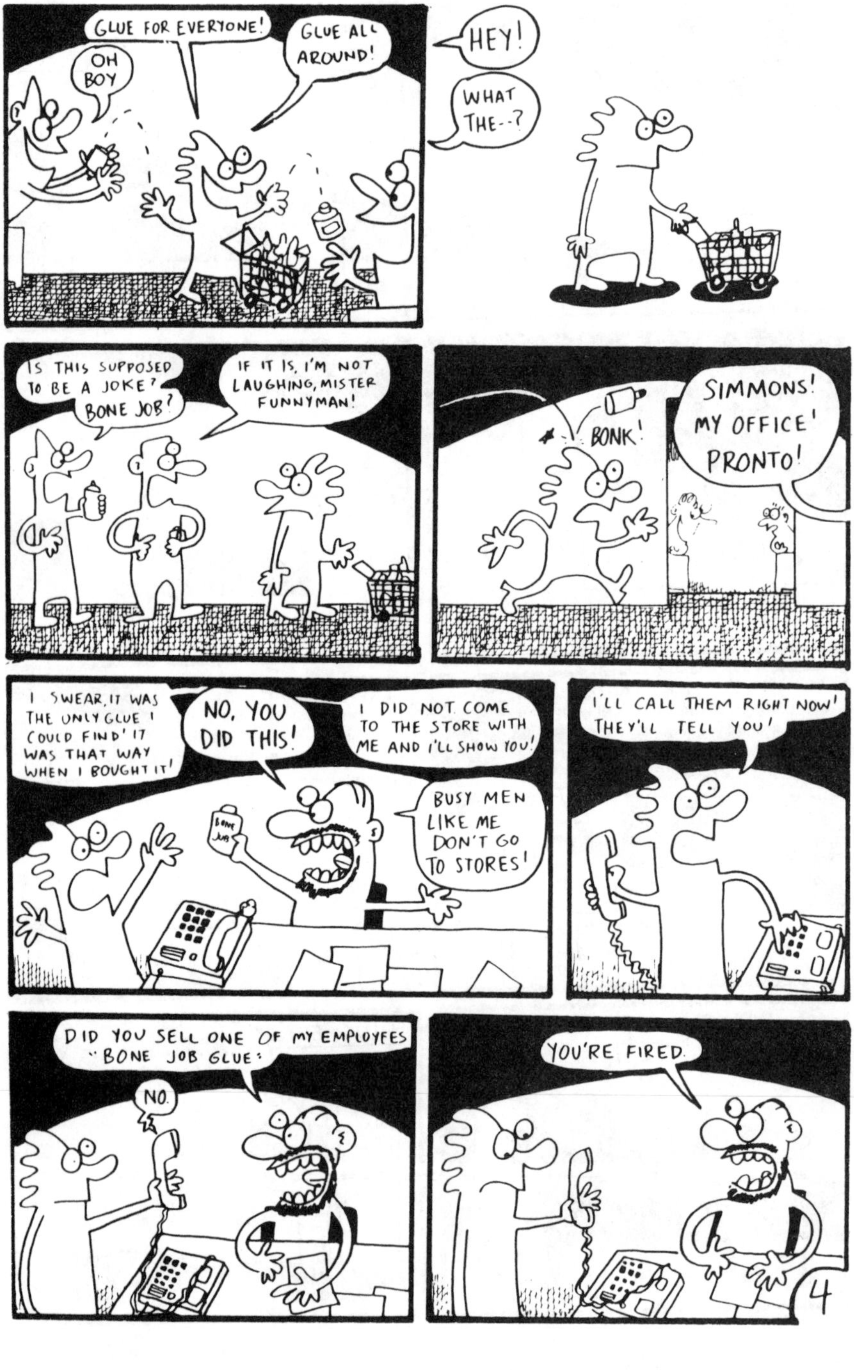
GLUE FOR EVERYONE!
OH BOY
GLUE ALL AROUND!
HEY!
WHAT THE--?
IS THIS SUPPOSED TO BE A JOKE? BONE JOB?
IF IT IS, I'M NOT LAUGHING, MISTER FUNNYMAN!
BONK!
SIMMONS! MY OFFICE! PRONTO!
I SWEAR, IT WAS THE ONLY GLUE I COULD FIND! IT WAS THAT WAY WHEN I BOUGHT IT!
NO, YOU DID THIS!
I DID NOT. COME TO THE STORE WITH ME AND I'LL SHOW YOU!
BONE JOB
BUSY MEN LIKE ME DON'T GO TO STORES!
I'LL CALL THEM RIGHT NOW! THEY'LL TELL YOU!
DID YOU SELL ONE OF MY EMPLOYEES "BONE JOB GLUE"
NO.
YOU'RE FIRED.
4

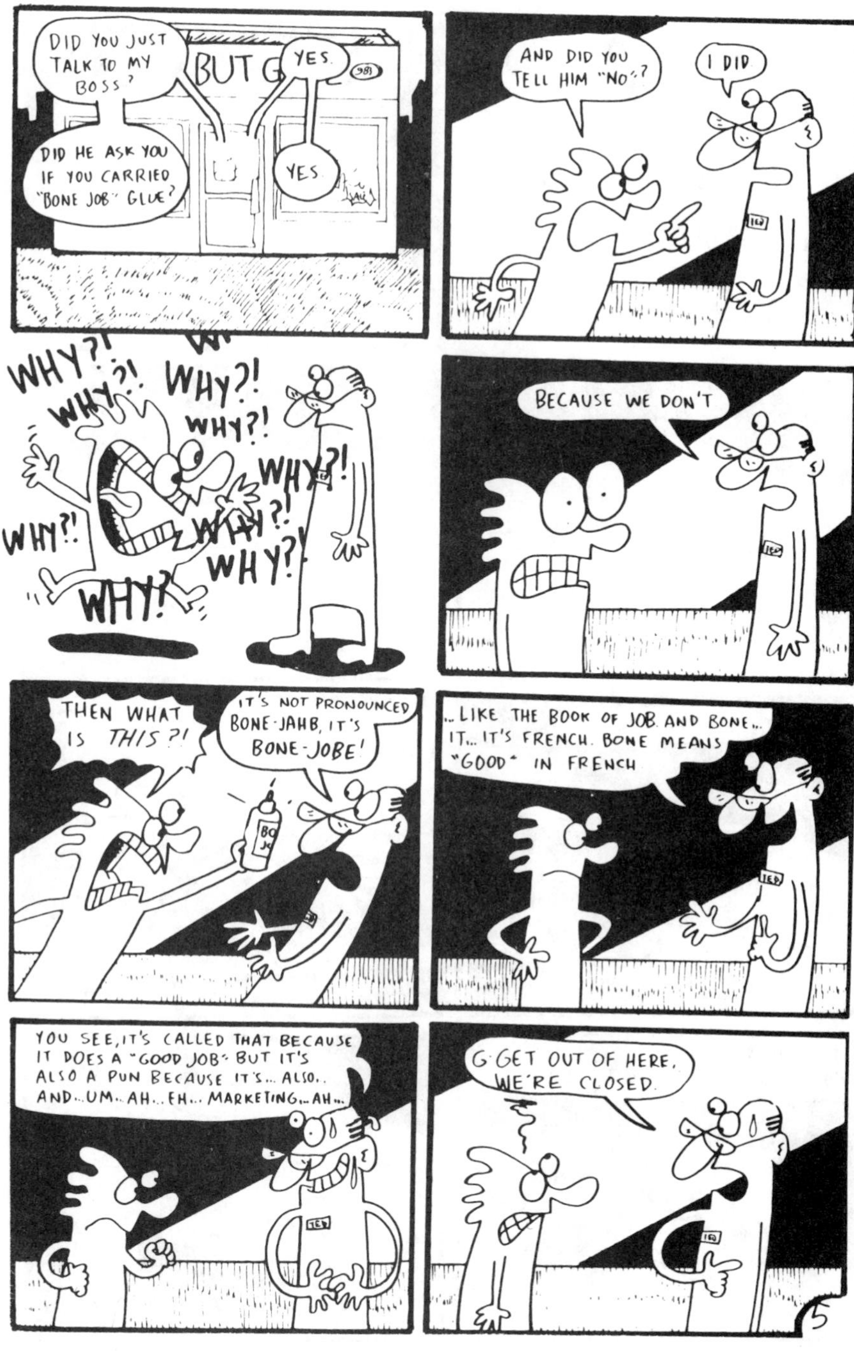
DID YOU JUST TALK TO MY BOSS?
YES.
DID HE ASK YOU IF YOU CARRIED "BONE JOB" GLUE?
YES.
BUT G
AND DID YOU TELL HIM "NO"?
I DID.
WHY?! WHY?! WHY?! WHY?! WHY?! WHY?! WHY?! WHY?! WHY?!
BECAUSE WE DON'T
THEN WHAT IS THIS?!
IT'S NOT PRONOUNCED BONE-JAHB, IT'S BONE-JOBE!
..LIKE THE BOOK OF JOB. AND BONE... IT... IT'S FRENCH. BONE MEANS "GOOD" IN FRENCH.
YOU SEE, IT'S CALLED THAT BECAUSE IT DOES A "GOOD JOB" BUT IT'S ALSO A PUN BECAUSE IT'S... ALSO.. AND...UM...AH...EH... MARKETING...AH...
G-GET OUT OF HERE, WE'RE CLOSED.

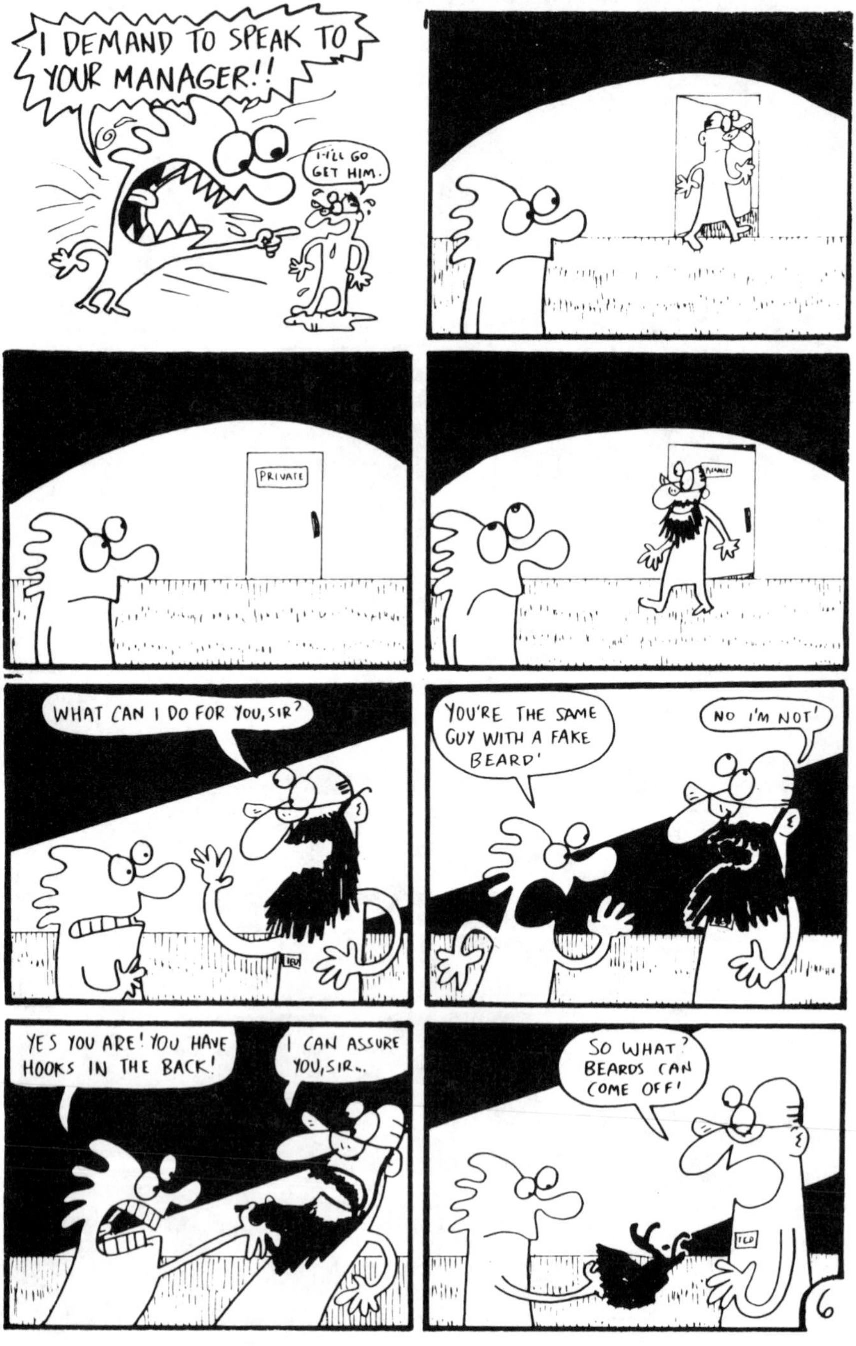
I DEMAND TO SPEAK TO YOUR MANAGER!!
I-I'LL GO GET HIM.
PRIVATE
WHAT CAN I DO FOR YOU, SIR?
YOU'RE THE SAME GUY WITH A FAKE BEARD!
NO I'M NOT!
YES YOU ARE! YOU HAVE HOOKS IN THE BACK!
I CAN ASSURE YOU, SIR..
SO WHAT? BEARDS CAN COME OFF!

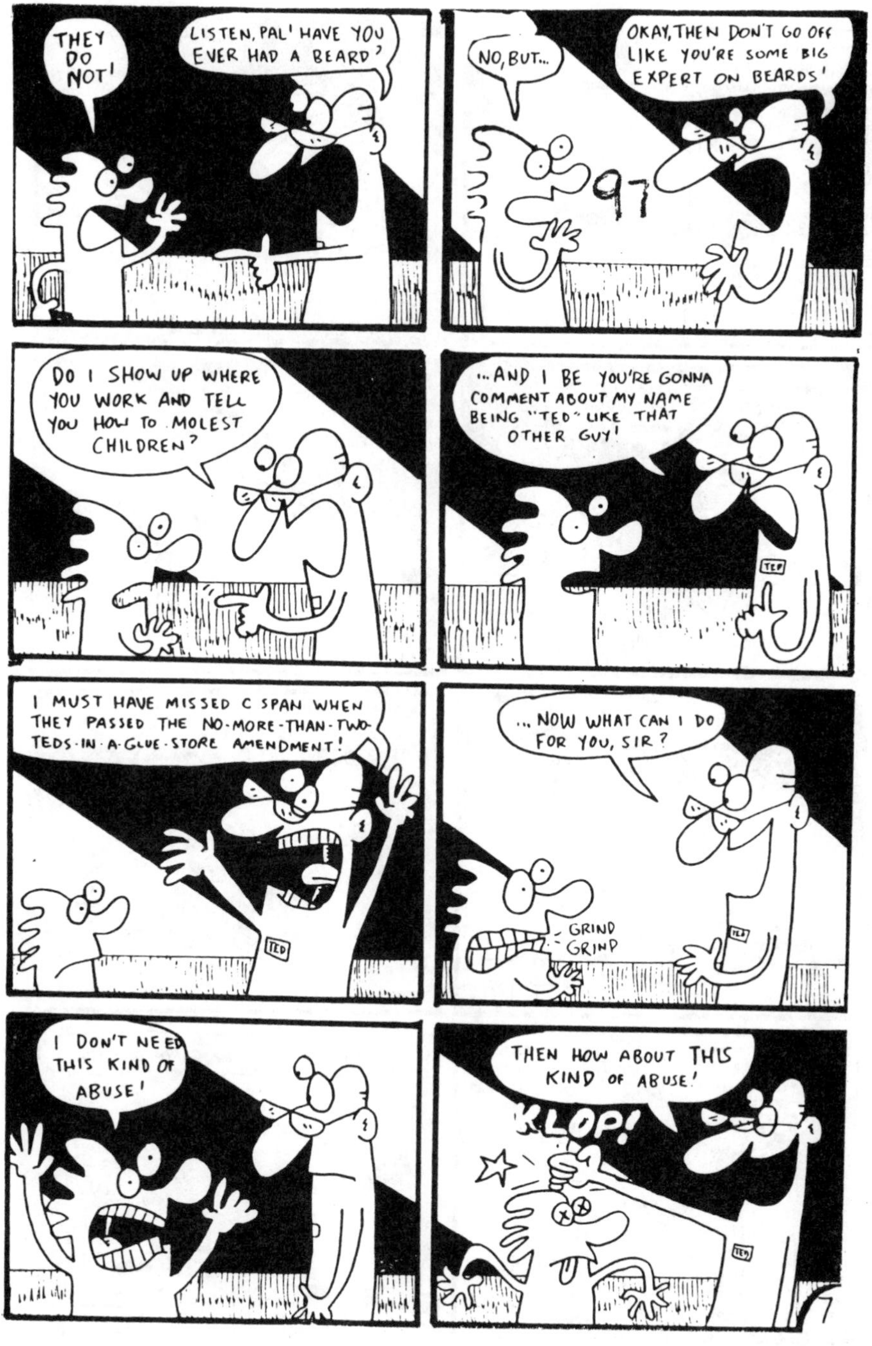
THEY DO NOT!
LISTEN, PAL! HAVE YOU EVER HAD A BEARD?
NO, BUT...
OKAY, THEN DON'T GO OFF LIKE YOU'RE SOME BIG EXPERT ON BEARDS!
DO I SHOW UP WHERE YOU WORK AND TELL YOU HOW TO MOLEST CHILDREN?
...AND I BE YOU'RE GONNA COMMENT ABOUT MY NAME BEING "TED" LIKE THAT OTHER GUY!
TED
I MUST HAVE MISSED C SPAN WHEN THEY PASSED THE NO-MORE-THAN-TWO-TEDS-IN-A-GLUE-STORE AMENDMENT!
TED
...NOW WHAT CAN I DO FOR YOU, SIR?
GRIND GRIND
TED
I DON'T NEED THIS KIND OF ABUSE!
THEN HOW ABOUT THIS KIND OF ABUSE!
KLOP!
TED

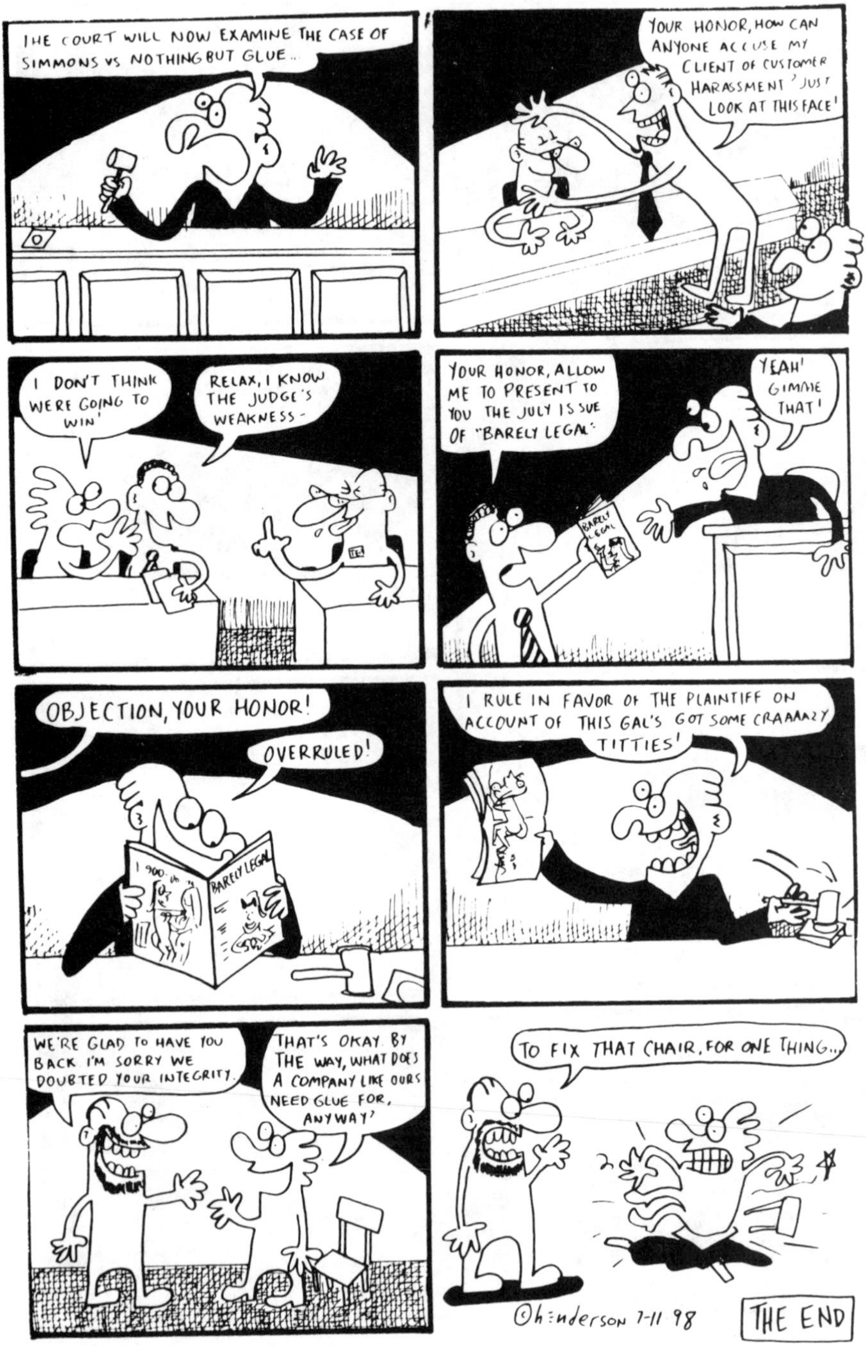
THE COURT WILL NOW EXAMINE THE CASE OF SIMMONS VS NOTHING BUT GLUE..
YOUR HONOR, HOW CAN ANYONE ACCUSE MY CLIENT OF CUSTOMER HARASSMENT? JUST LOOK AT THIS FACE!
I DON'T THINK WE'RE GOING TO WIN!
RELAX, I KNOW THE JUDGE'S WEAKNESS-
YOUR HONOR, ALLOW ME TO PRESENT TO YOU THE JULY ISSUE OF "BARELY LEGAL".
YEAH! GIMME THAT!
BARELY LEGAL
OBJECTION, YOUR HONOR!
OVERRULED!
BARELY LEGAL
I RULE IN FAVOR OF THE PLAINTIFF ON ACCOUNT OF THIS GAL'S GOT SOME CRAAAAZY TITTIES!
WE'RE GLAD TO HAVE YOU BACK. I'M SORRY WE DOUBTED YOUR INTEGRITY.
THAT'S OKAY. BY THE WAY, WHAT DOES A COMPANY LIKE OURS NEED GLUE FOR, ANYWAY?
TO FIX THAT CHAIR, FOR ONE THING..
©henderson 7-11-98
THE END

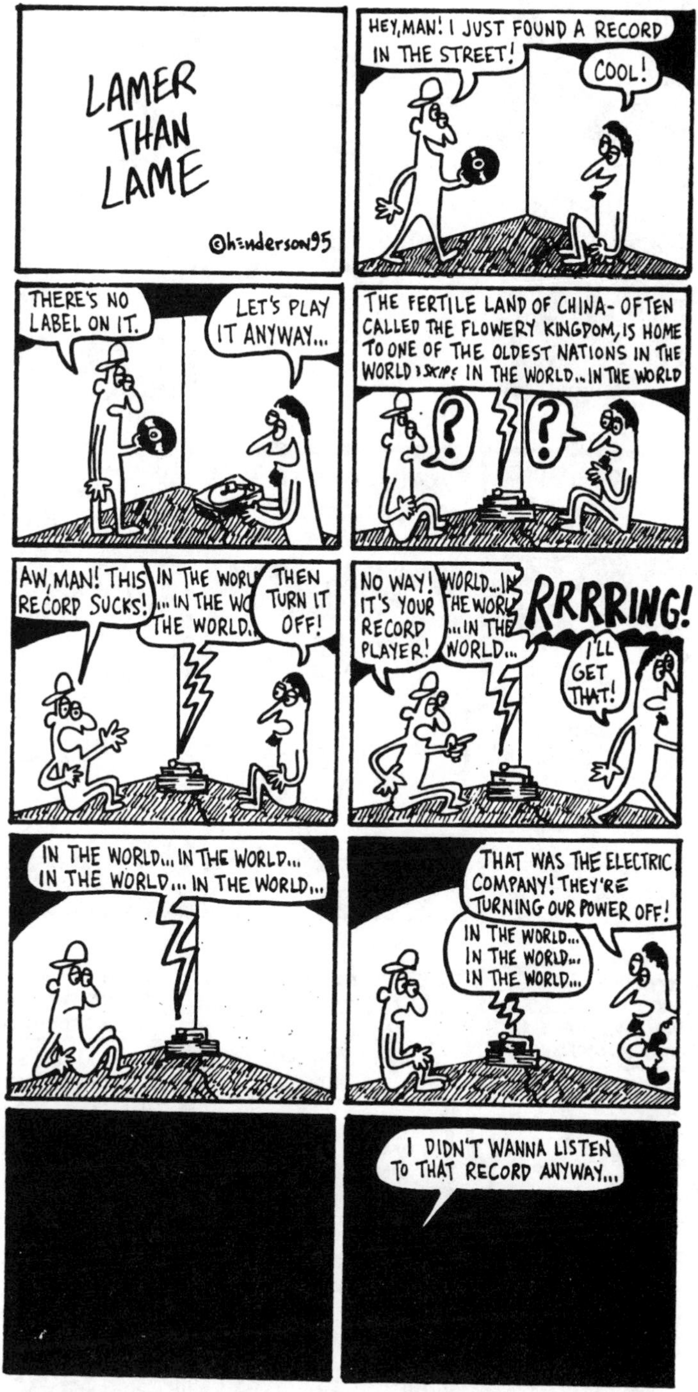
LAMER THAN LAME
©henderson95
HEY, MAN! I JUST FOUND A RECORD IN THE STREET!
COOL!
THERE'S NO LABEL ON IT.
LET'S PLAY IT ANYWAY...
THE FERTILE LAND OF CHINA- OFTEN CALLED THE FLOWERY KINGDOM, IS HOME TO ONE OF THE OLDEST NATIONS IN THE WORLD SKIP IN THE WORLD.. IN THE WORLD
?
?
AW, MAN! THIS RECORD SUCKS!
IN THE WORL ... IN THE WO THE WORLD..
THEN TURN IT OFF!
NO WAY! IT'S YOUR RECORD PLAYER!
WORLD...IN THE WORL ...IN THE WORLD...
RRRRING!
I'LL GET THAT!
IN THE WORLD... IN THE WORLD... IN THE WORLD... IN THE WORLD...
THAT WAS THE ELECTRIC COMPANY! THEY'RE TURNING OUR POWER OFF!
IN THE WORLD... IN THE WORLD... IN THE WORLD...
I DIDN'T WANNA LISTEN TO THAT RECORD ANYWAY...

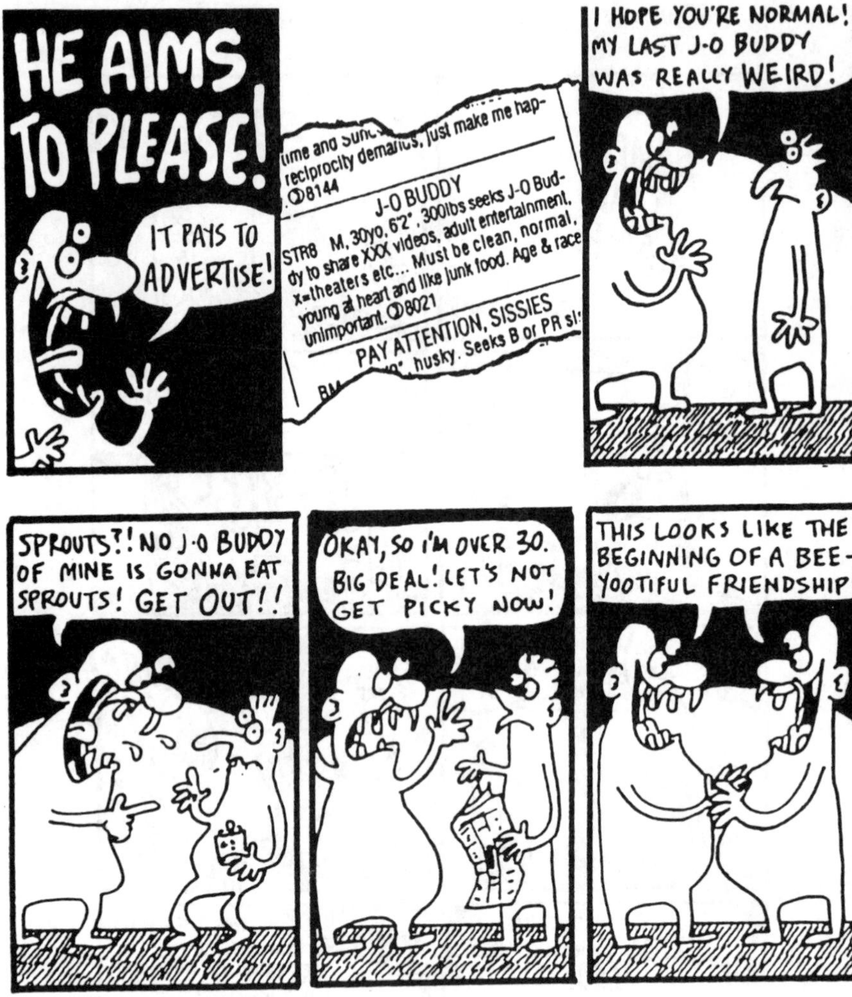
HE AIMS TO PLEASE!
IT PAYS TO ADVERTISE!
time and Sunc... reciprocity demands, just make me hap- . 8144
J-O BUDDY
STR8 M, 30yo, 6'2", 300lbs seeks J-O Buddy to share XXX videos, adult entertainment, x-theaters etc... Must be clean, normal, young at heart and like junk food. Age & race unimportant. 8021
PAY ATTENTION, SISSIES
husky. Seeks B or PR s
I HOPE YOU'RE NORMAL! MY LAST J-O BUDDY WAS REALLY WEIRD!
SPROUTS?! NO J-O BUDDY OF MINE IS GONNA EAT SPROUTS! GET OUT!!
OKAY, SO I'M OVER 30. BIG DEAL! LET'S NOT GET PICKY NOW!
THIS LOOKS LIKE THE BEGINNING OF A BEE-YOOTIFUL FRIENDSHIP!

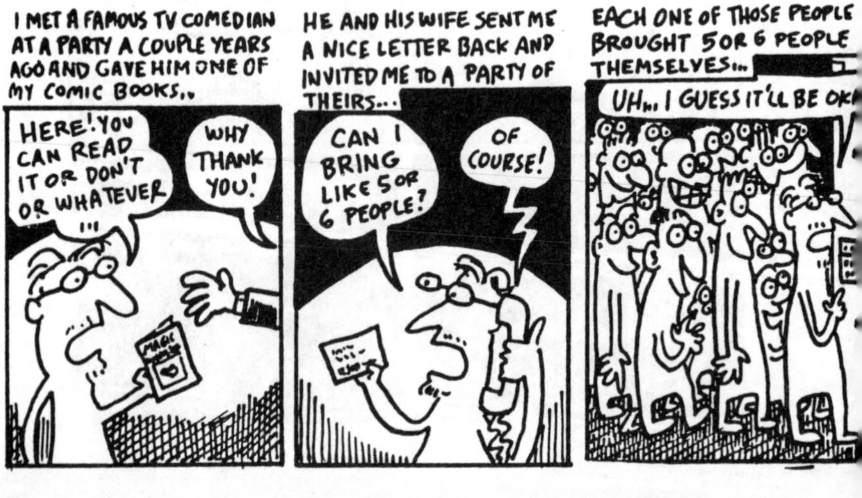
I MET A FAMOUS TV COMEDIAN AT A PARTY A COUPLE YEARS AGO AND GAVE HIM ONE OF MY COMIC BOOKS..
HERE! YOU CAN READ IT OR DON'T OR WHATEVER ...
WHY THANK YOU!
HE AND HIS WIFE SENT ME A NICE LETTER BACK AND INVITED ME TO A PARTY OF THEIRS...
CAN I BRING LIKE 5 OR 6 PEOPLE?
OF COURSE!
EACH ONE OF THOSE PEOPLE BROUGHT 5 OR 6 PEOPLE THEMSELVES..
UH.. I GUESS IT'LL BE OK

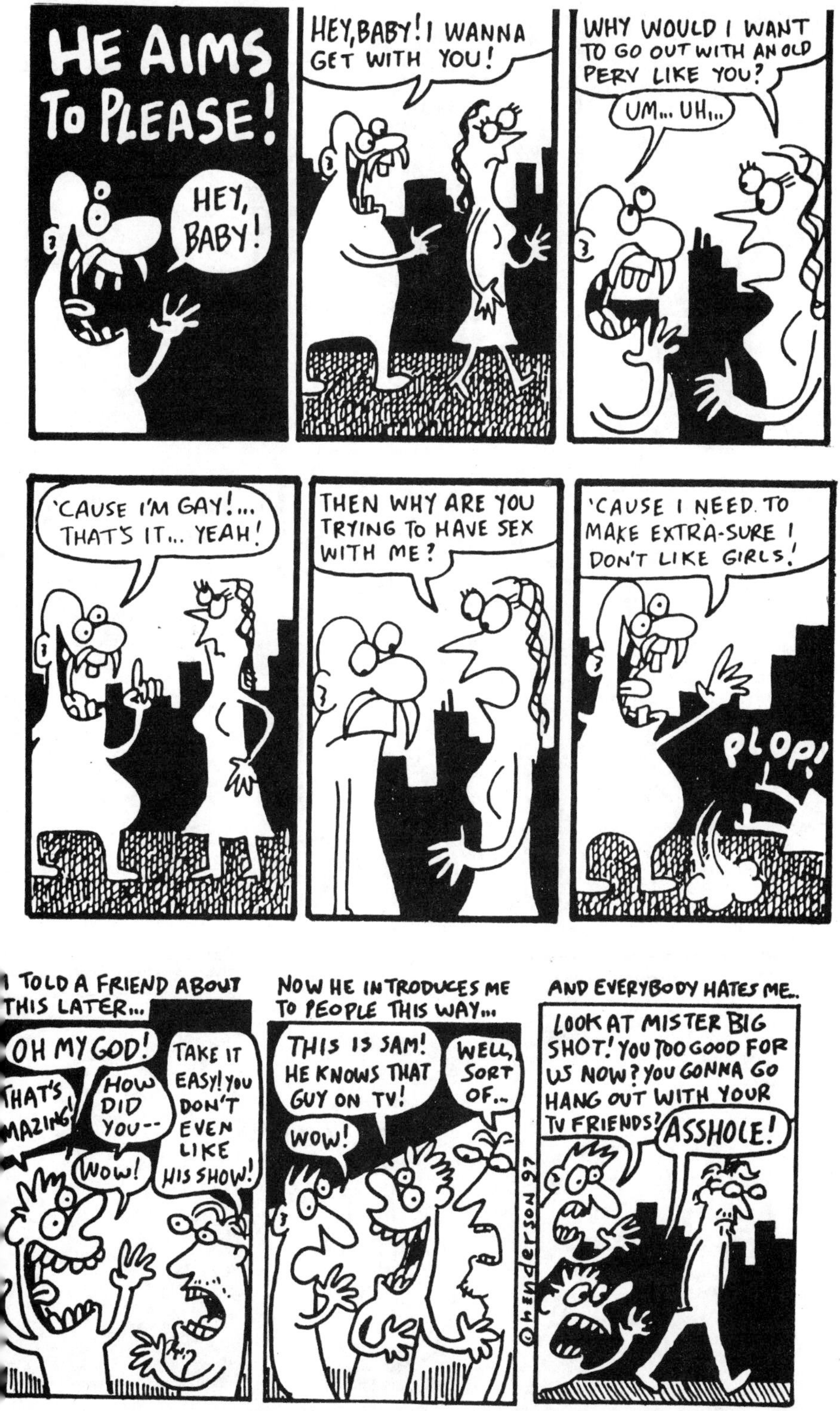
HE AIMS TO PLEASE!
HEY, BABY!
HEY, BABY! I WANNA GET WITH YOU!
WHY WOULD I WANT TO GO OUT WITH AN OLD PERV LIKE YOU?
UM... UH...
'CAUSE I'M GAY!... THAT'S IT... YEAH!
THEN WHY ARE YOU TRYING TO HAVE SEX WITH ME?
'CAUSE I NEED TO MAKE EXTRA-SURE I DON'T LIKE GIRLS!
PLOP!
I TOLD A FRIEND ABOUT THIS LATER...
OH MY GOD!
THAT'S MAZING!
HOW DID YOU--
WOW!
TAKE IT EASY! YOU DON'T EVEN LIKE HIS SHOW!
NOW HE INTRODUCES ME TO PEOPLE THIS WAY...
THIS IS SAM! HE KNOWS THAT GUY ON TV!
WELL, SORT OF...
WOW!
©HENDERSON 97
AND EVERYBODY HATES ME..
LOOK AT MISTER BIG SHOT! YOU TOO GOOD FOR US NOW? YOU GONNA GO HANG OUT WITH YOUR TV FRIENDS?
ASSHOLE!

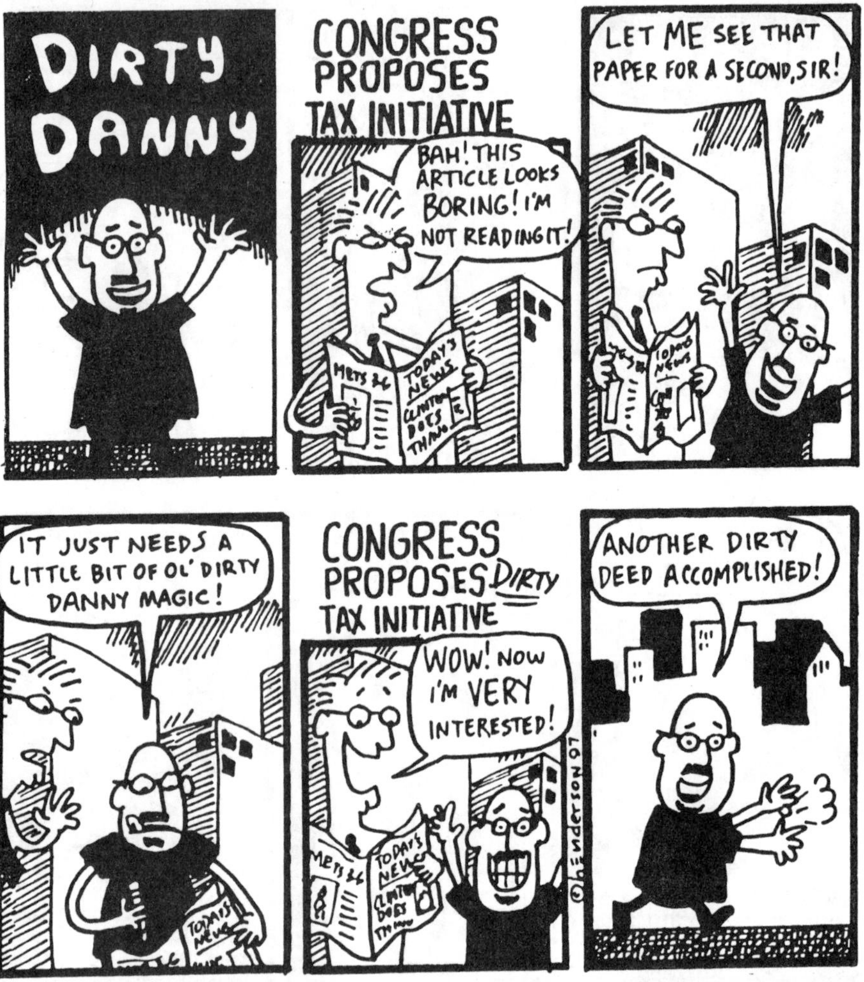
DIRTY DANNY
CONGRESS PROPOSES TAX INITIATIVE
BAH! THIS ARTICLE LOOKS BORING! I'M NOT READING IT!
TODAY'S NEWS
CLINTON DOES THING
LET ME SEE THAT PAPER FOR A SECOND, SIR!
IT JUST NEEDS A LITTLE BIT OF OL' DIRTY DANNY MAGIC!
CONGRESS PROPOSES DIRTY TAX INITIATIVE
WOW! NOW I'M VERY INTERESTED!
©henderson 97
ANOTHER DIRTY DEED ACCOMPLISHED!

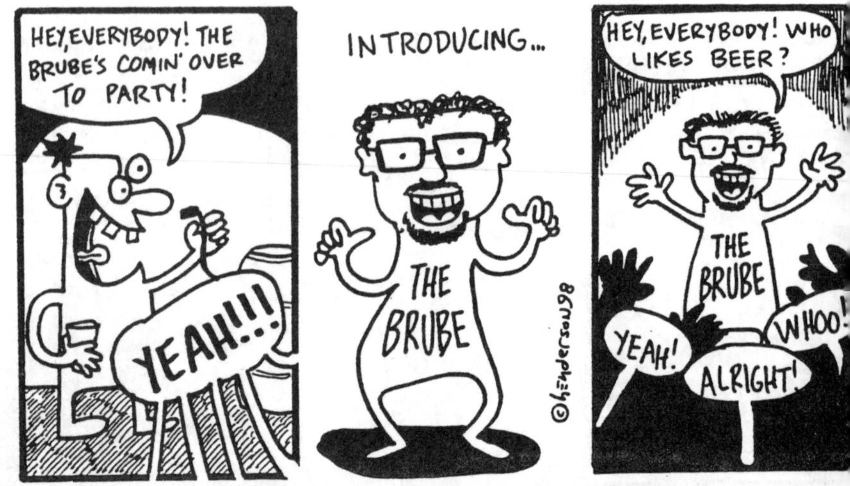
HEY, EVERYBODY! THE BRUBE'S COMIN' OVER TO PARTY!
YEAH!!!
INTRODUCING...
THE BRUBE
©henderson98
HEY, EVERYBODY! WHO LIKES BEER?
THE BRUBE
YEAH!
ALRIGHT!
WHOO!

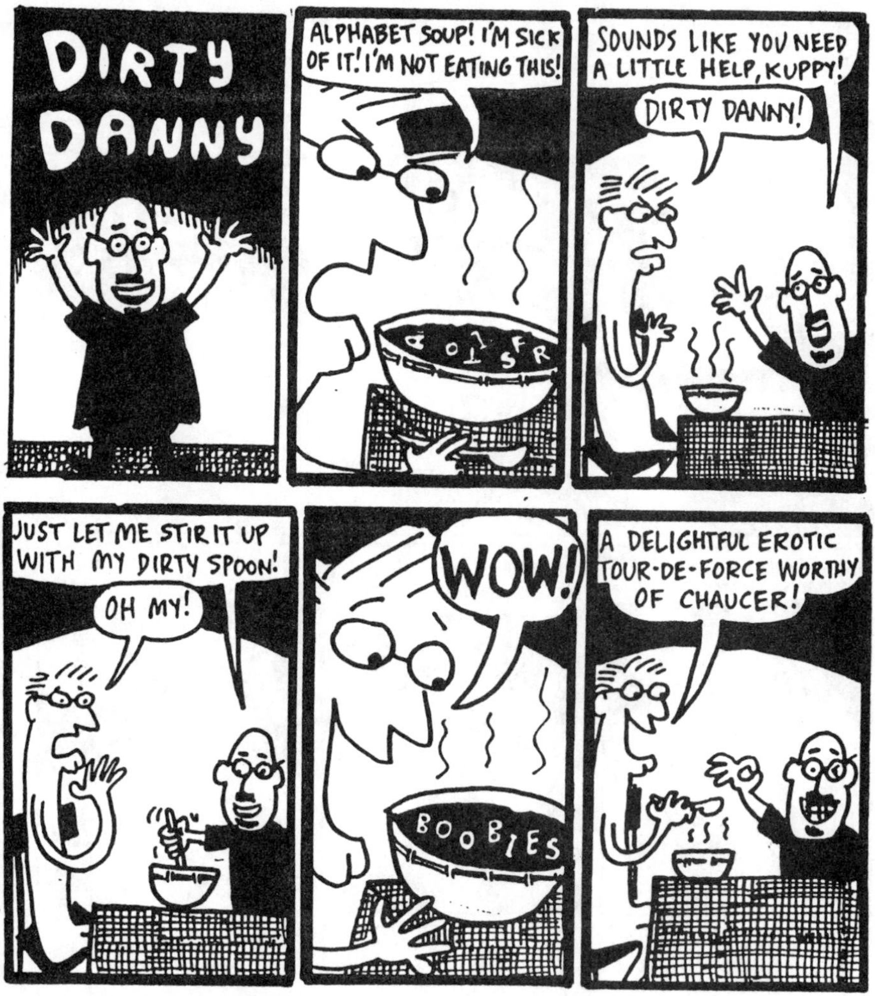
DIRTY DANNY
ALPHABET SOUP! I'M SICK OF IT! I'M NOT EATING THIS!
SOUNDS LIKE YOU NEED A LITTLE HELP, KUPPY!
DIRTY DANNY!
JUST LET ME STIR IT UP WITH MY DIRTY SPOON!
OH MY!
WOW!
BOOBIES
A DELIGHTFUL EROTIC TOUR-DE-FORCE WORTHY OF CHAUCER!

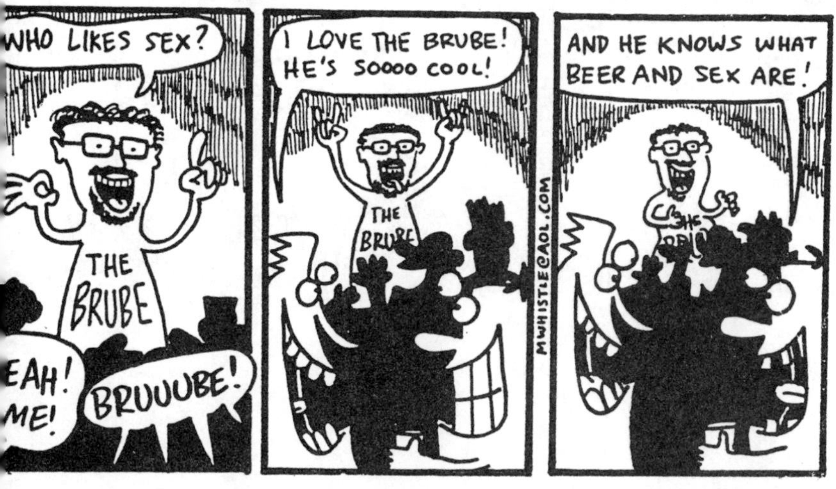
WHO LIKES SEX?
THE BRUBE
EAH!
ME!
BRUUUBE!
I LOVE THE BRUBE! HE'S SOOOO COOL!
THE BRUBE
AND HE KNOWS WHAT BEER AND SEX ARE!
MWHISTLE@AOL.COM

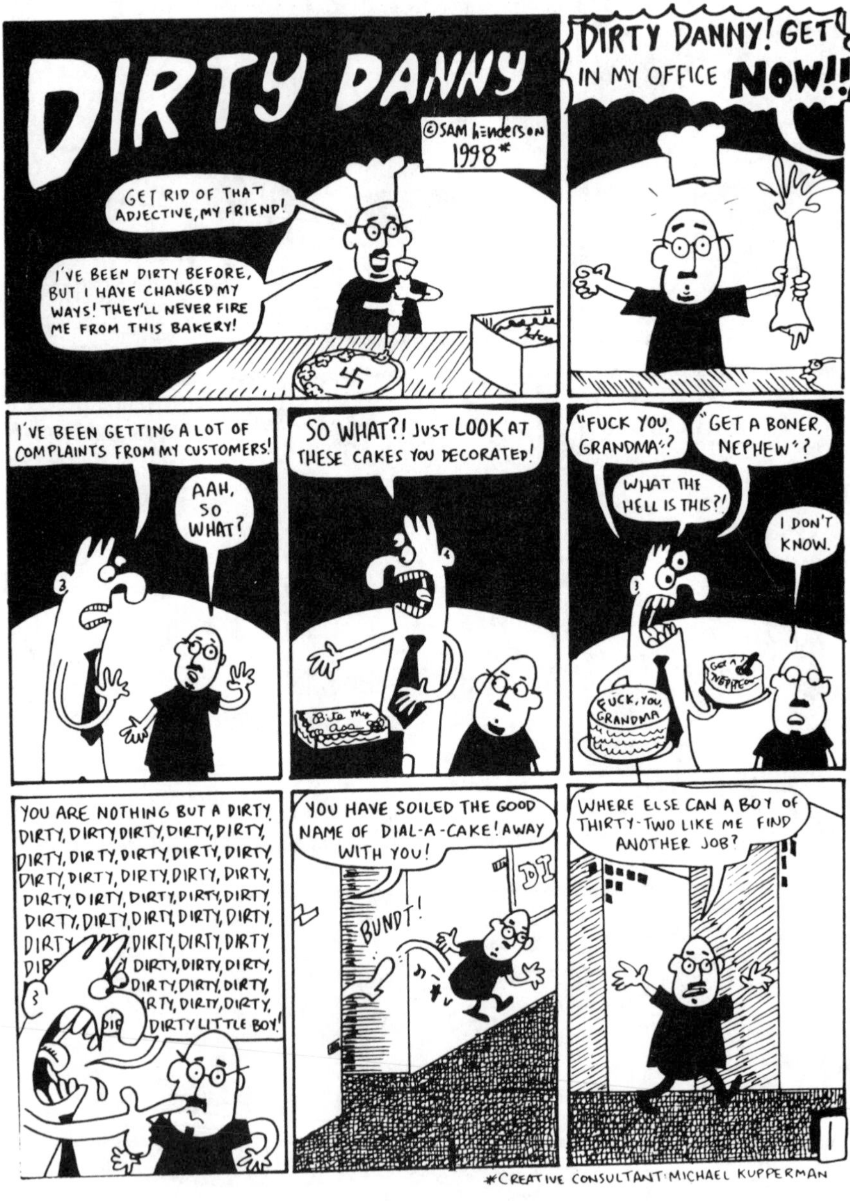
DIRTY DANNY
©SAM henderson 1998*
GET RID OF THAT ADJECTIVE, MY FRIEND!
I'VE BEEN DIRTY BEFORE, BUT I HAVE CHANGED MY WAYS! THEY'LL NEVER FIRE ME FROM THIS BAKERY!
DIRTY DANNY! GET IN MY OFFICE NOW!!
I'VE BEEN GETTING A LOT OF COMPLAINTS FROM MY CUSTOMERS!
AAH, SO WHAT?
SO WHAT?! JUST LOOK AT THESE CAKES YOU DECORATED!
Bite My Ass
"FUCK YOU, GRANDMA"?
"GET A BONER, NEPHEW"?
WHAT THE HELL IS THIS?!
I DON'T KNOW.
FUCK, YOU, GRANDMA
YOU ARE NOTHING BUT A DIRTY, DIRTY DIRTY, DIRTY, DIRTY DIRTY, DIRTY, DIRTY, DIRTY, DIRTY, DIRTY LITTLE BOY!
YOU HAVE SOILED THE GOOD NAME OF DIAL-A-CAKE! AWAY WITH YOU!
BUNDT!
WHERE ELSE CAN A BOY OF THIRTY-TWO LIKE ME FIND ANOTHER JOB?
1

*CREATIVE CONSULTANT: MICHAEL KUPPERMAN

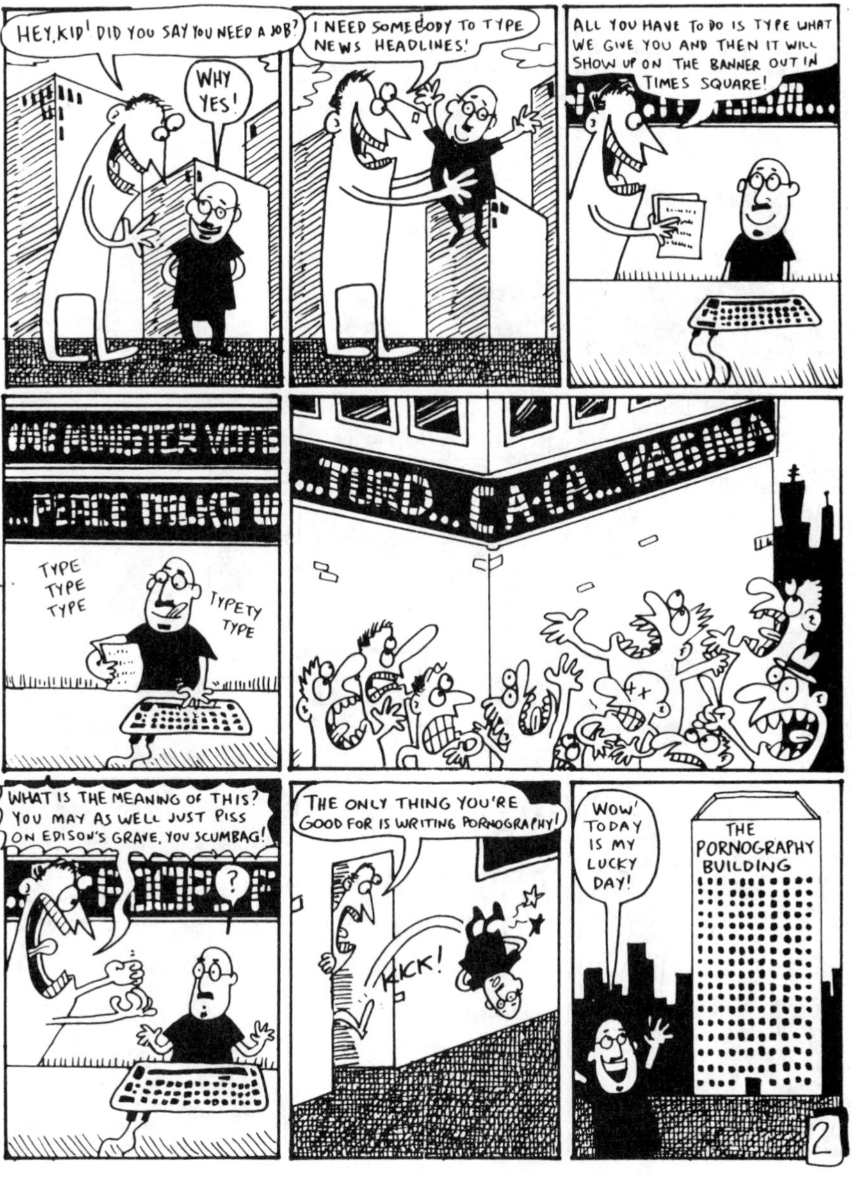
HEY, KID! DID YOU SAY YOU NEED A JOB?
WHY YES!
I NEED SOMEBODY TO TYPE NEWS HEADLINES!
ALL YOU HAVE TO DO IS TYPE WHAT WE GIVE YOU AND THEN IT WILL SHOW UP ON THE BANNER OUT IN TIMES SQUARE!
...PEACE TALKS
TYPE TYPE TYPE
TYPETY TYPE
...TURD... CA-CA... VAGINA
WHAT IS THE MEANING OF THIS? YOU MAY AS WELL JUST PISS ON EDISON'S GRAVE, YOU SCUMBAG!
?
THE ONLY THING YOU'RE GOOD FOR IS WRITING PORNOGRAPHY!
KICK!
WOW! TODAY IS MY LUCKY DAY!
THE PORNOGRAPHY BUILDING

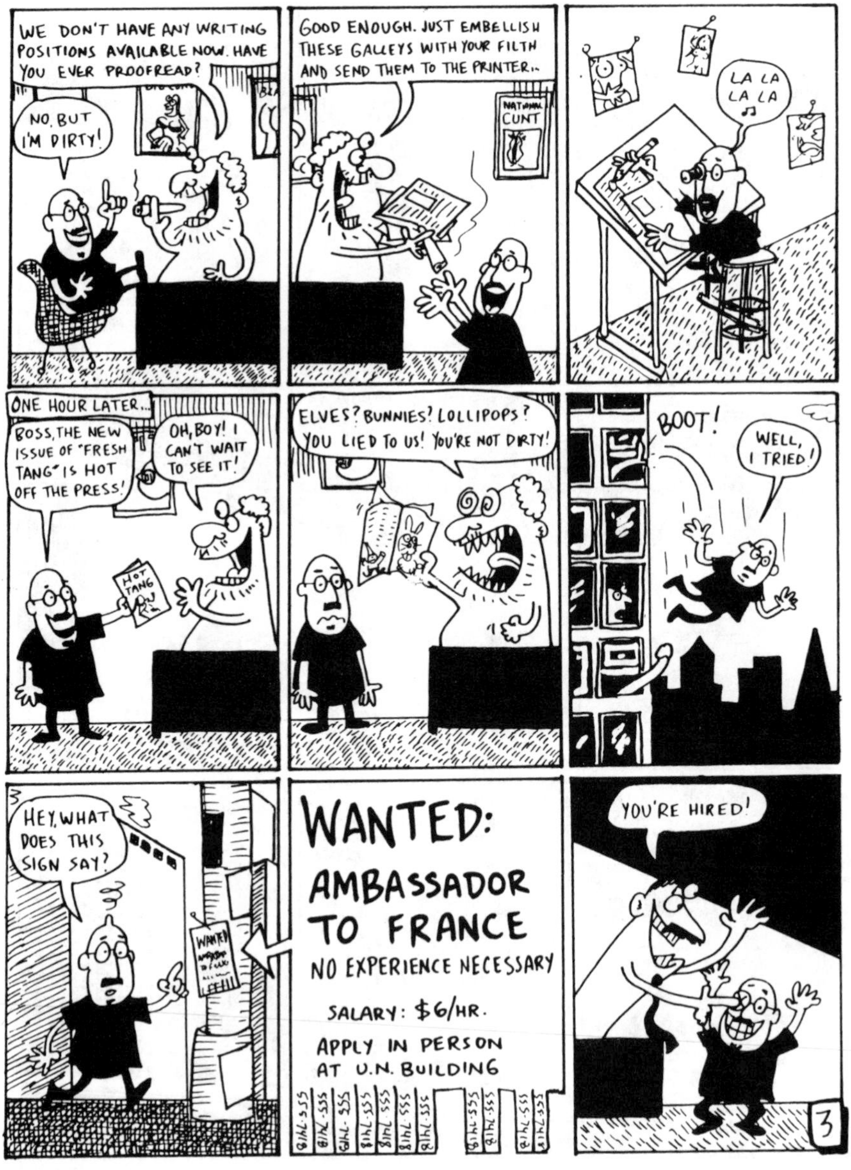
WE DON'T HAVE ANY WRITING POSITIONS AVAILABLE NOW. HAVE YOU EVER PROOFREAD?
NO, BUT I'M DIRTY!
GOOD ENOUGH. JUST EMBELLISH THESE GALLEYS WITH YOUR FILTH AND SEND THEM TO THE PRINTER..
NATIONAL CUNT
LA LA LA LA ♫
ONE HOUR LATER...
BOSS, THE NEW ISSUE OF "FRESH TANG" IS HOT OFF THE PRESS!
OH, BOY! I CAN'T WAIT TO SEE IT!
HOT TANG
ELVES? BUNNIES? LOLLIPOPS? YOU LIED TO US! YOU'RE NOT DIRTY!
BOOT!
WELL, I TRIED!
HEY, WHAT DOES THIS SIGN SAY?
WANTED
WANTED:
AMBASSADOR TO FRANCE
NO EXPERIENCE NECESSARY
SALARY: $6/HR.
APPLY IN PERSON AT U.N. BUILDING
YOU'RE HIRED!

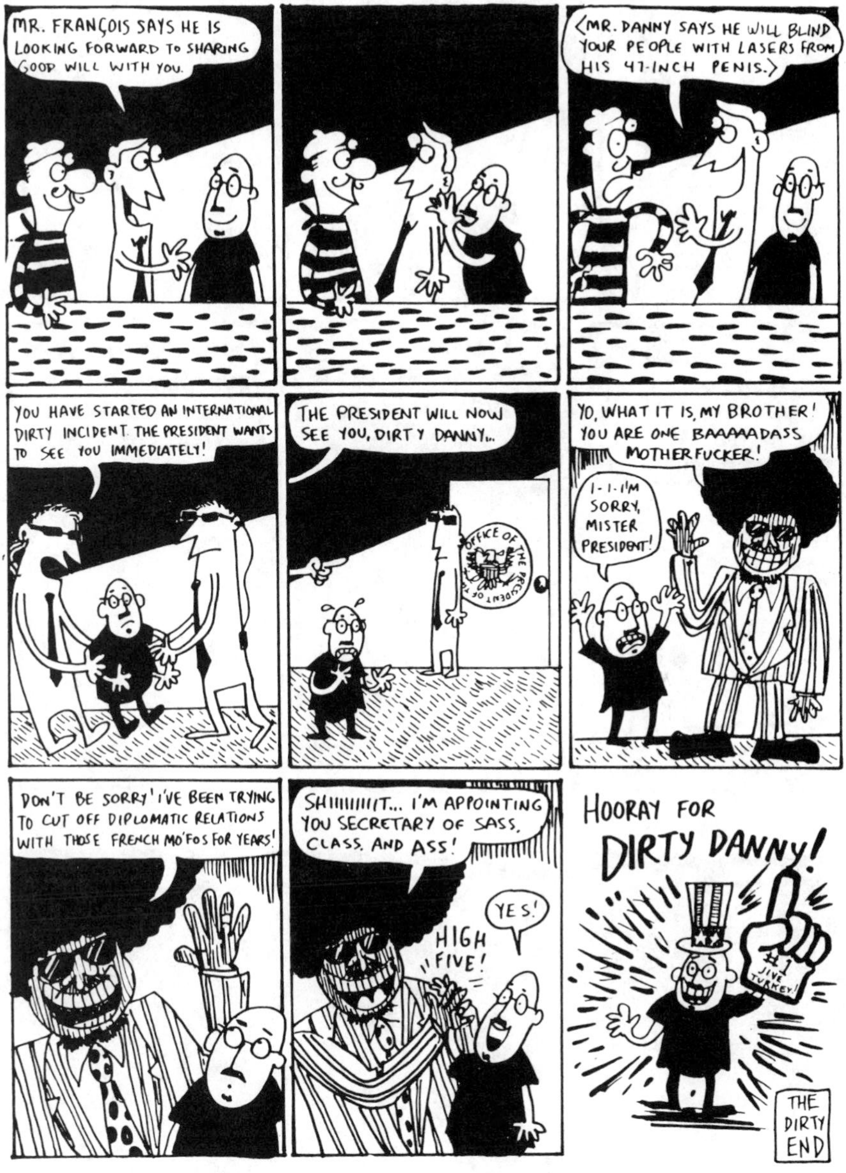
MR. FRANÇOIS SAYS HE IS LOOKING FORWARD TO SHARING GOOD WILL WITH YOU.
<MR. DANNY SAYS HE WILL BLIND YOUR PEOPLE WITH LASERS FROM HIS 47-INCH PENIS.>
YOU HAVE STARTED AN INTERNATIONAL DIRTY INCIDENT. THE PRESIDENT WANTS TO SEE YOU IMMEDIATELY!
THE PRESIDENT WILL NOW SEE YOU, DIRTY DANNY...
OFFICE OF THE PRESIDENT OF THE
YO, WHAT IT IS, MY BROTHER! YOU ARE ONE BAAAAADASS MOTHERFUCKER!
I-I-I'M SORRY, MISTER PRESIDENT!
DON'T BE SORRY! I'VE BEEN TRYING TO CUT OFF DIPLOMATIC RELATIONS WITH THOSE FRENCH MO'FOS FOR YEARS!
SHIIIIIIIIT... I'M APPOINTING YOU SECRETARY OF SASS, CLASS, AND ASS!
YES!
HIGH FIVE!
HOORAY FOR DIRTY DANNY!
#1 JIVE TURKEY!
THE DIRTY END

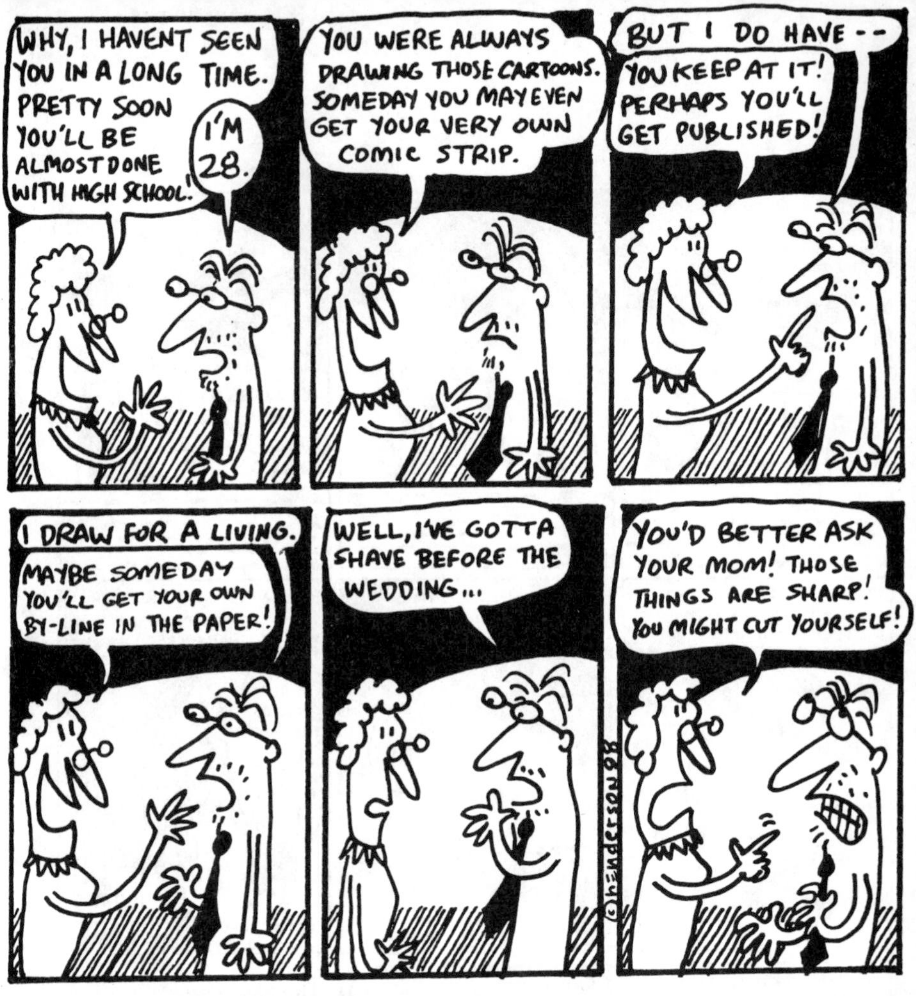
WHY, I HAVENT SEEN YOU IN A LONG TIME. PRETTY SOON YOU'LL BE ALMOST DONE WITH HIGH SCHOOL!
I'M 28.
YOU WERE ALWAYS DRAWING THOSE CARTOONS. SOMEDAY YOU MAY EVEN GET YOUR VERY OWN COMIC STRIP.
BUT I DO HAVE --
YOU KEEP AT IT! PERHAPS YOU'LL GET PUBLISHED!
I DRAW FOR A LIVING.
MAYBE SOMEDAY YOU'LL GET YOUR OWN BY-LINE IN THE PAPER!
WELL, I'VE GOTTA SHAVE BEFORE THE WEDDING...
YOU'D BETTER ASK YOUR MOM! THOSE THINGS ARE SHARP! YOU MIGHT CUT YOURSELF!
©henderson 98

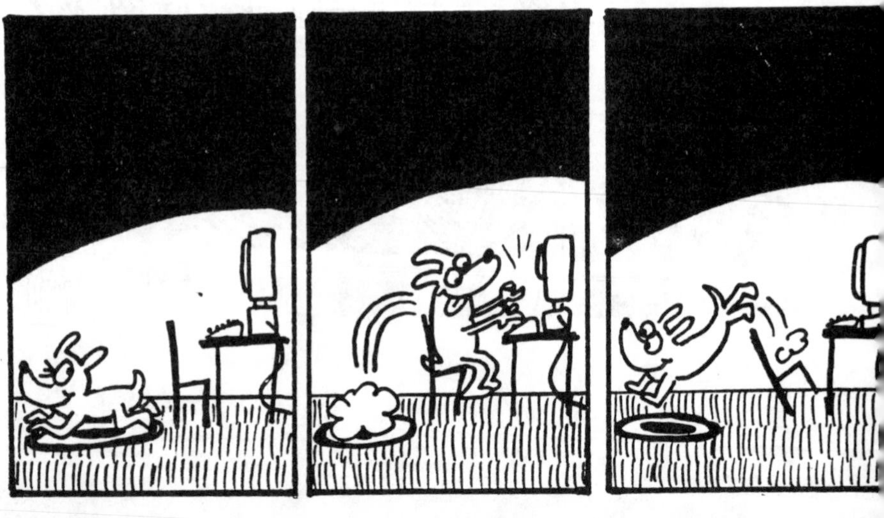

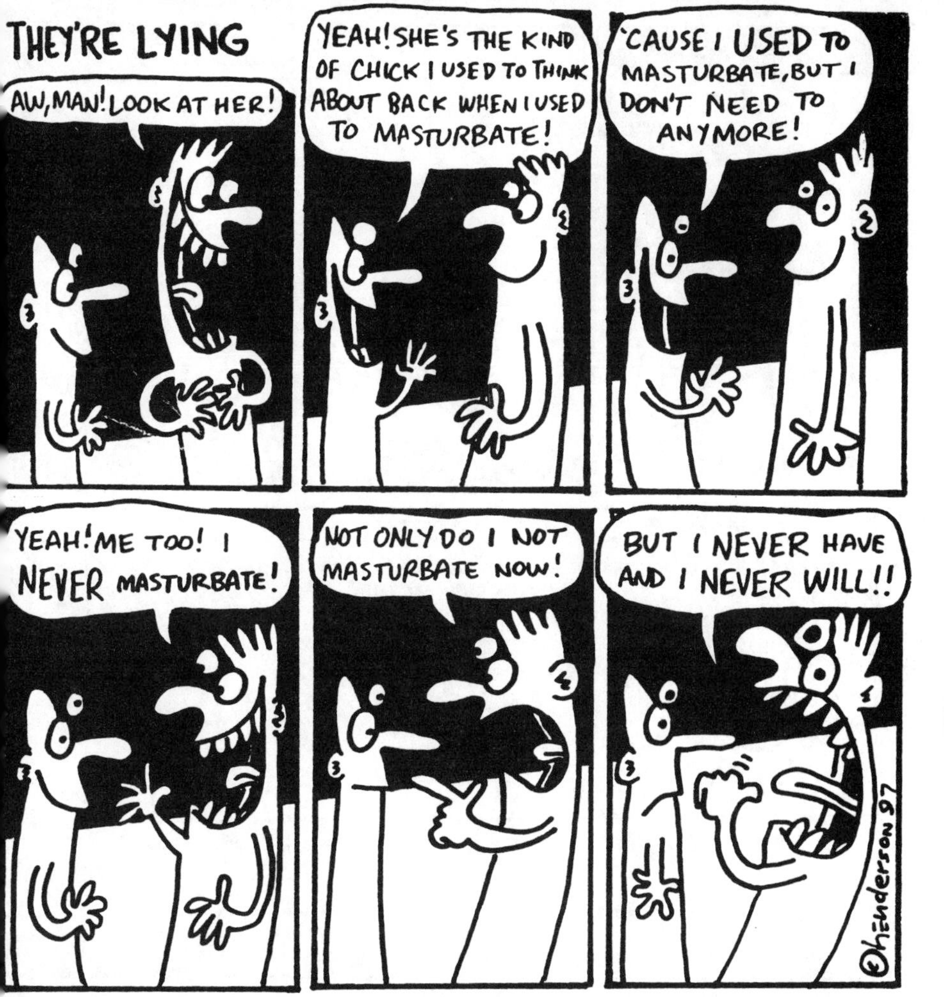
THEY'RE LYING
AW, MAN! LOOK AT HER!
YEAH! SHE'S THE KIND OF CHICK I USED TO THINK ABOUT BACK WHEN I USED TO MASTURBATE!
'CAUSE I USED TO MASTURBATE, BUT I DON'T NEED TO ANYMORE!
YEAH! ME TOO! I NEVER MASTURBATE!
NOT ONLY DO I NOT MASTURBATE NOW!
BUT I NEVER HAVE AND I NEVER WILL!!
©henderson 97

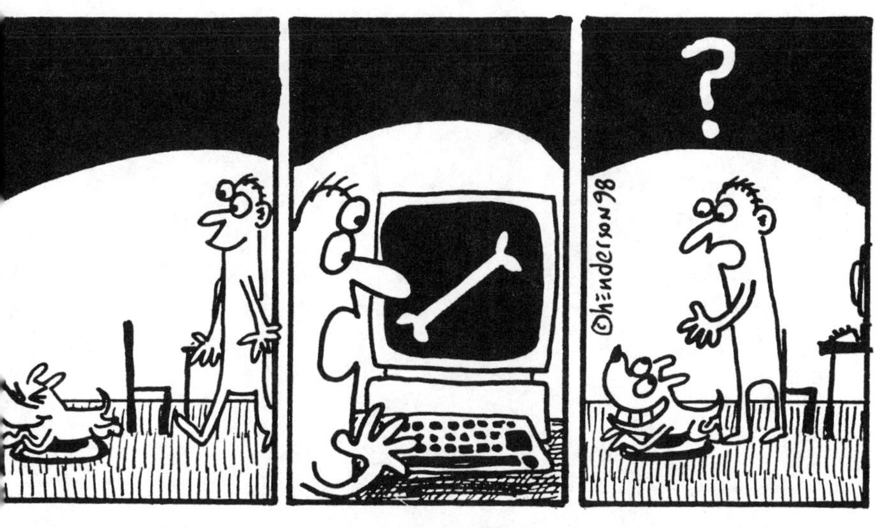
©henderson 98
?

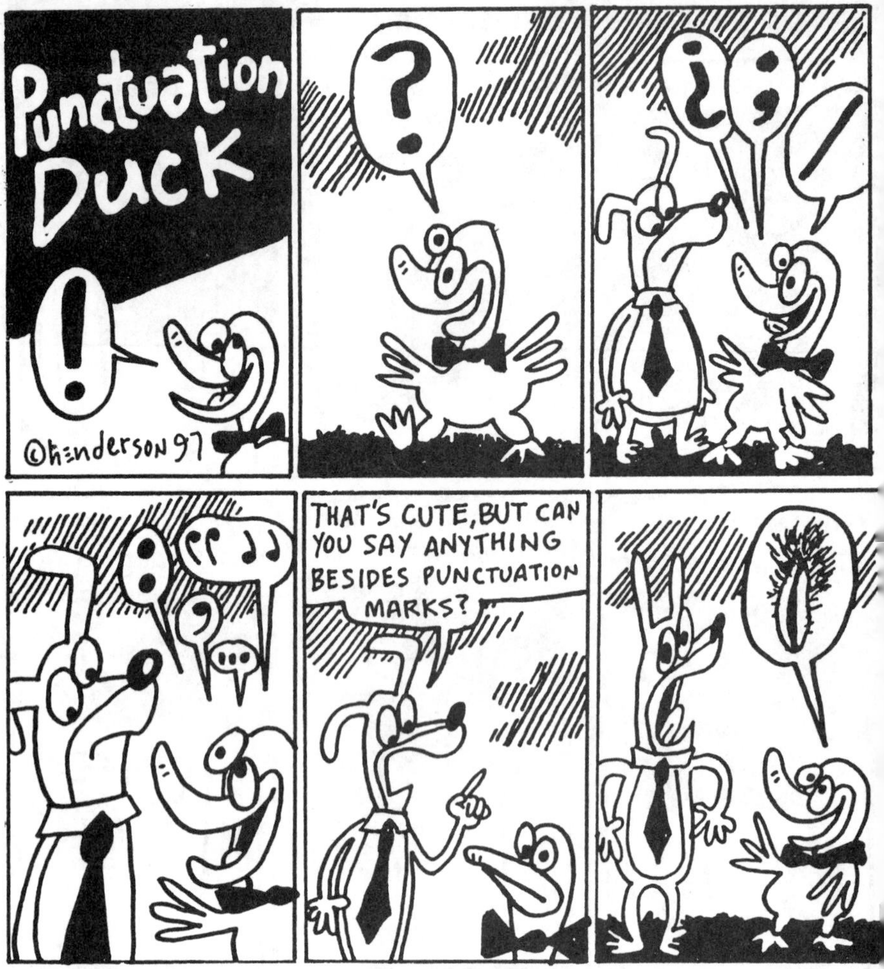
Punctuation Duck
!
©henderson 97
?
¿
;
/
THAT'S CUTE, BUT CAN YOU SAY ANYTHING BESIDES PUNCTUATION MARKS?

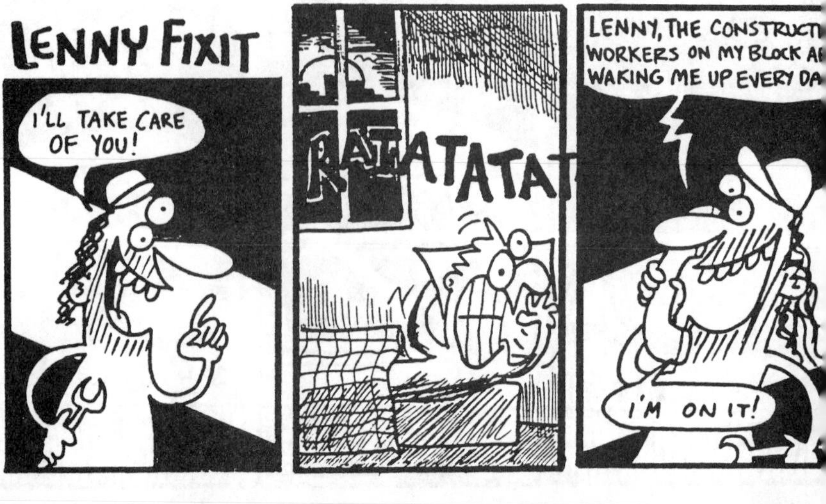
LENNY FIXIT
I'LL TAKE CARE OF YOU!
RATATATATAT
LENNY, THE CONSTRUCTI
WORKERS ON MY BLOCK A
WAKING ME UP EVERY DA
I'M ON IT!

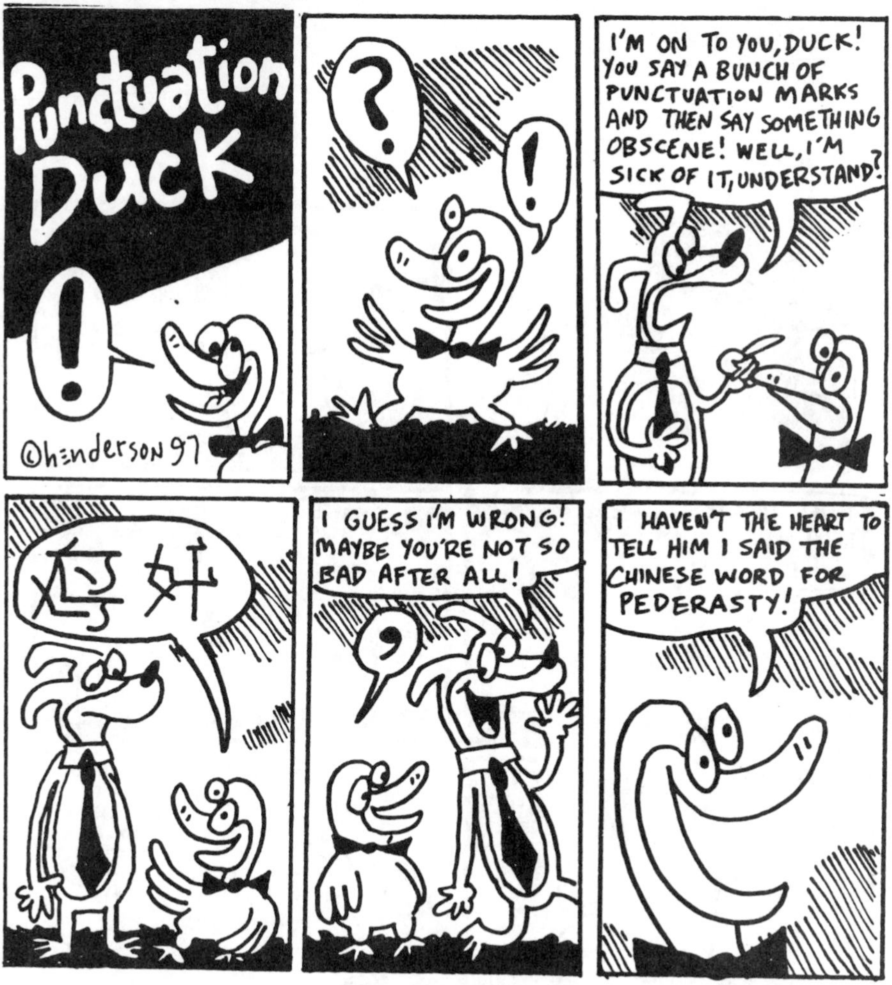
Punctuation Duck
!
©henderson 97
?
!
I'M ON TO YOU, DUCK! YOU SAY A BUNCH OF PUNCTUATION MARKS AND THEN SAY SOMETHING OBSCENE! WELL, I'M SICK OF IT, UNDERSTAND?
I GUESS I'M WRONG! MAYBE YOU'RE NOT SO BAD AFTER ALL!
,
I HAVEN'T THE HEART TO TELL HIM I SAID THE CHINESE WORD FOR PEDERASTY!

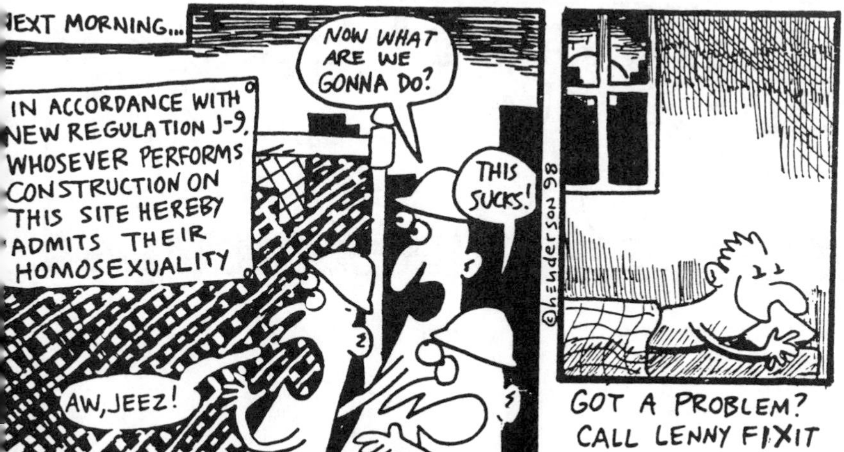
NEXT MORNING...
IN ACCORDANCE WITH NEW REGULATION J-9, WHOSEVER PERFORMS CONSTRUCTION ON THIS SITE HEREBY ADMITS THEIR HOMOSEXUALITY
NOW WHAT ARE WE GONNA DO?
THIS SUCKS!
AW, JEEZ!
©henderson 98
GOT A PROBLEM? CALL LENNY FIXIT

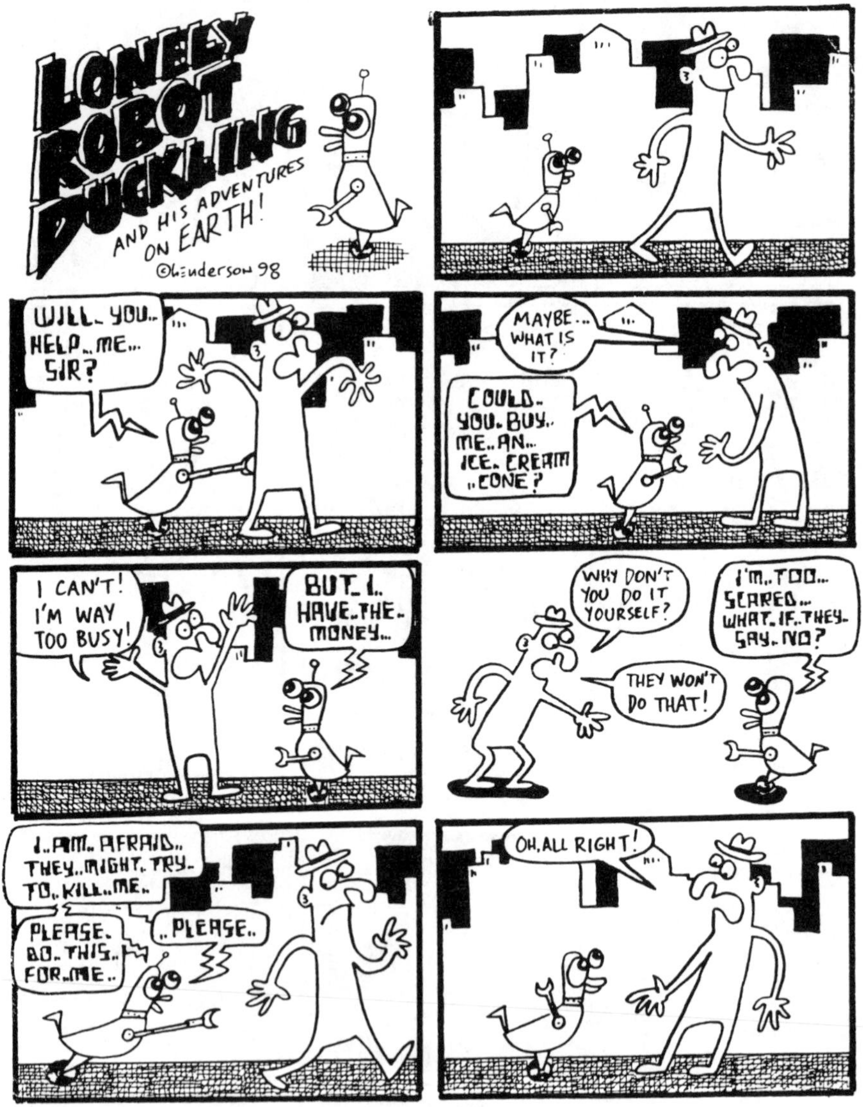
LONELY ROBOT DUCKLING
AND HIS ADVENTURES ON EARTH!
©Henderson 98
WILL.. YOU.. HELP.. ME... SIR?
MAYBE... WHAT IS IT?
COULD.. YOU.. BUY.. ME.. AN... ICE.. CREAM ..CONE?
I CAN'T! I'M WAY TOO BUSY!
BUT.. I.. HAVE..THE.. MONEY...
WHY DON'T YOU DO IT YOURSELF?
I'M.. TOO... SCARED... WHAT..IF..THEY.. SAY..NO?
THEY WON'T DO THAT!
I..AM.. AFRAID.. THEY..MIGHT..TRY.. TO..KILL..ME..
PLEASE.. DO..THIS.. FOR..ME..
..PLEASE..
OH, ALL RIGHT!

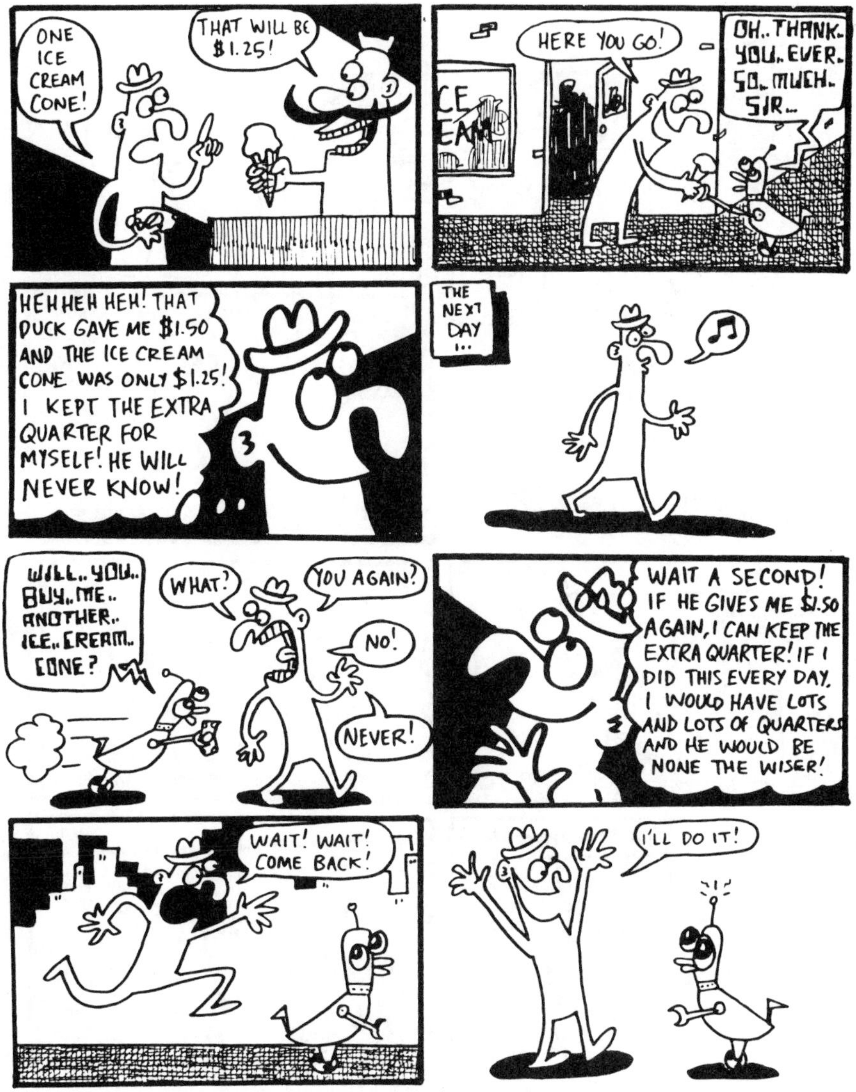
ONE ICE CREAM CONE!
THAT WILL BE $1.25!
HERE YOU GO!
OH.. THANK-YOU.. EVER-SO.. MUCH. SIR...
HEH HEH HEH! THAT DUCK GAVE ME $1.50 AND THE ICE CREAM CONE WAS ONLY $1.25! I KEPT THE EXTRA QUARTER FOR MYSELF! HE WILL NEVER KNOW!
THE NEXT DAY...
WILL.. YOU.. BUY.. ME.. ANOTHER.. ICE.. CREAM.. CONE?
WHAT?
YOU AGAIN?
NO!
NEVER!
WAIT A SECOND! IF HE GIVES ME $1.50 AGAIN, I CAN KEEP THE EXTRA QUARTER! IF I DID THIS EVERY DAY, I WOULD HAVE LOTS AND LOTS OF QUARTERS AND HE WOULD BE NONE THE WISER!
WAIT! WAIT! COME BACK!
I'LL DO IT!

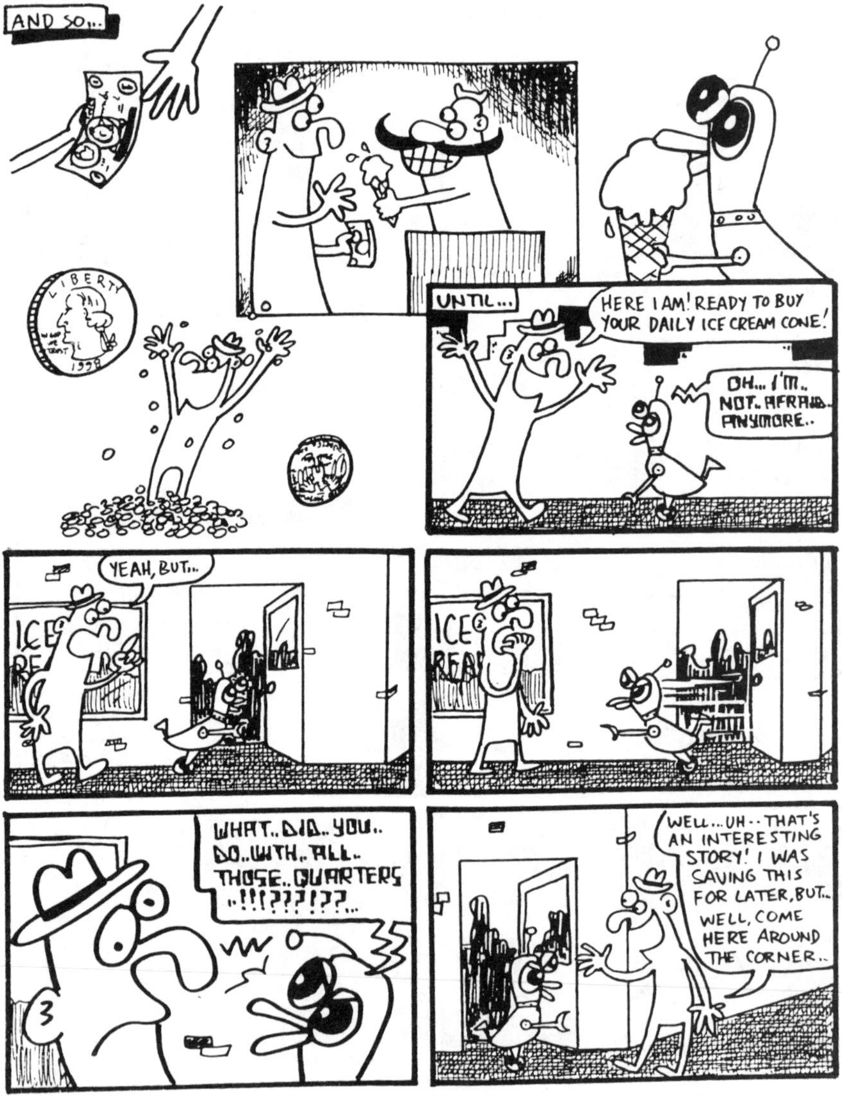
AND SO...
LIBERTY
IN GOD WE TRUST
1998
UNTIL...
HERE I AM! READY TO BUY YOUR DAILY ICE CREAM CONE!
OH... I'M.. NOT.. AFRAID.. ANYMORE..
YEAH, BUT..
WHAT.. DID.. YOU.. DO.. WITH.. ALL.. THOSE.. QUARTERS ..!!!???!??...
WELL... UH.. THAT'S AN INTERESTING STORY! I WAS SAVING THIS FOR LATER, BUT.. WELL, COME HERE AROUND THE CORNER..

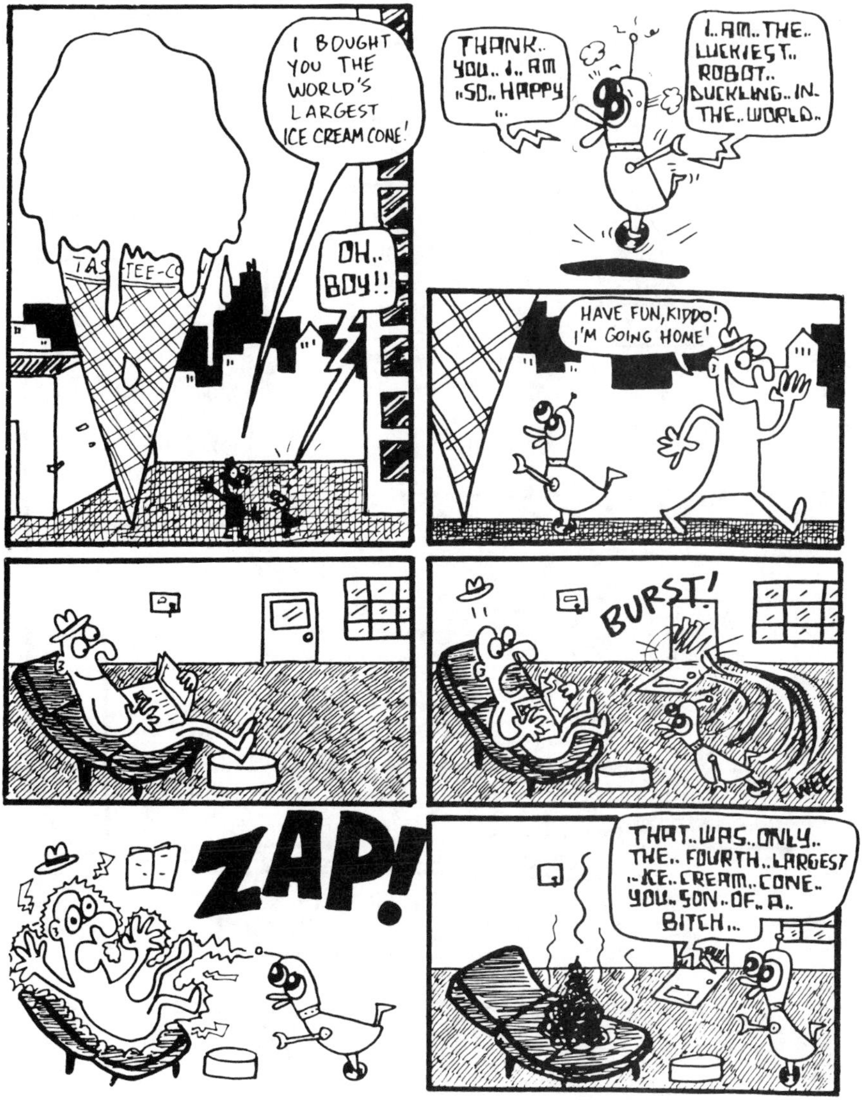
I BOUGHT YOU THE WORLD'S LARGEST ICE CREAM CONE!
OH.. BOY!!
THANK.. YOU.. I.. AM ..SO.. HAPPY ..
I.. AM.. THE.. LUCKIEST.. ROBOT.. DUCKLING.. IN. THE.. WORLD..
HAVE FUN, KIDDO! I'M GOING HOME!
BURST!
ZAP!
THAT.. WAS.. ONLY.. THE.. FOURTH.. LARGEST ..ICE.. CREAM.. CONE.. YOU.. SON.. OF.. A.. BITCH...

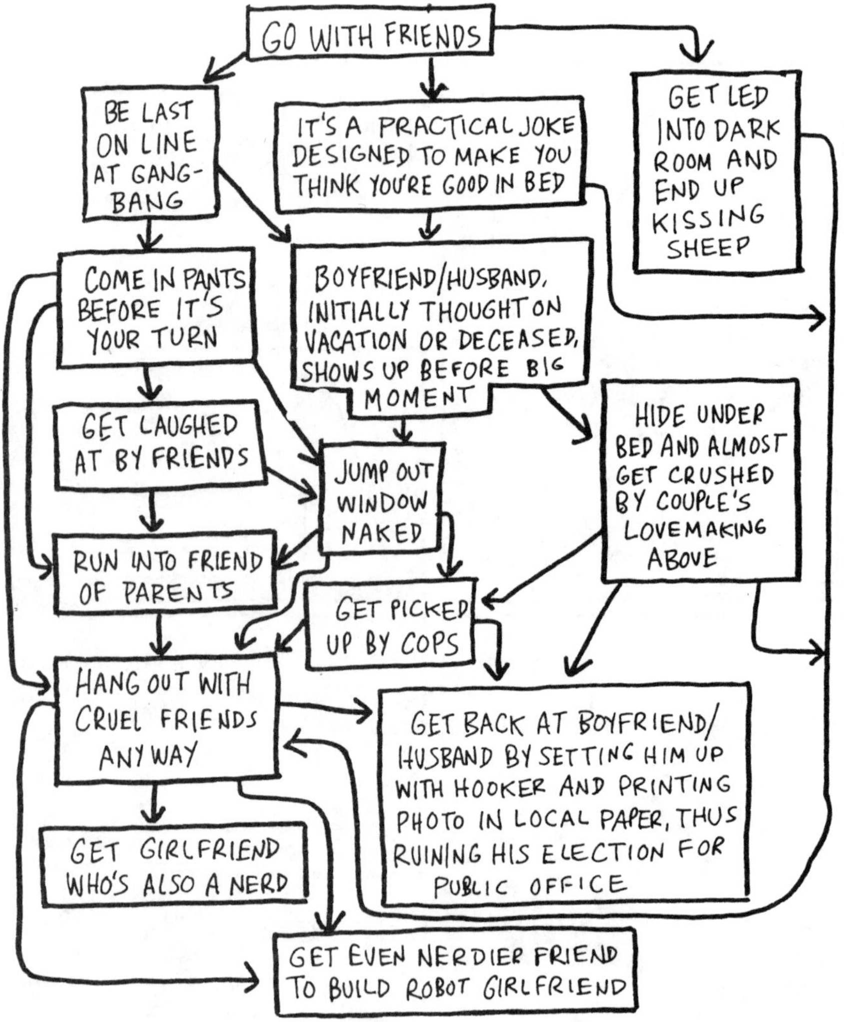
GO WITH FRIENDS
BE LAST ON LINE AT GANG-BANG
IT'S A PRACTICAL JOKE DESIGNED TO MAKE YOU THINK YOU'RE GOOD IN BED
GET LED INTO DARK ROOM AND END UP KISSING SHEEP
COME IN PANTS BEFORE IT'S YOUR TURN
BOYFRIEND/HUSBAND, INITIALLY THOUGHT ON VACATION OR DECEASED, SHOWS UP BEFORE BIG MOMENT
GET LAUGHED AT BY FRIENDS
JUMP OUT WINDOW NAKED
HIDE UNDER BED AND ALMOST GET CRUSHED BY COUPLE'S LOVEMAKING ABOVE
RUN INTO FRIEND OF PARENTS
GET PICKED UP BY COPS
HANG OUT WITH CRUEL FRIENDS ANYWAY
GET BACK AT BOYFRIEND/HUSBAND BY SETTING HIM UP WITH HOOKER AND PRINTING PHOTO IN LOCAL PAPER, THUS RUINING HIS ELECTION FOR PUBLIC OFFICE
GET GIRLFRIEND WHO'S ALSO A NERD
GET EVEN NERDIER FRIEND TO BUILD ROBOT GIRLFRIEND

HOW TO GET LAID IN A TEEN MOVIE

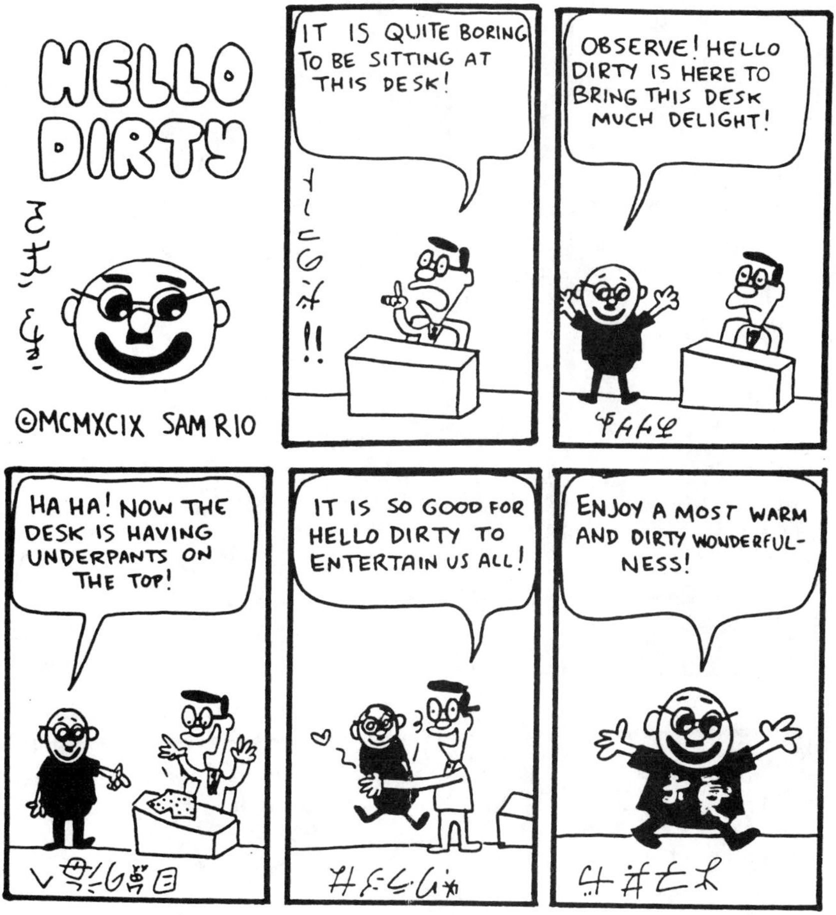
HELLO DIRTY
©MCMXCIX SAM RIO
IT IS QUITE BORING TO BE SITTING AT THIS DESK!
OBSERVE! HELLO DIRTY IS HERE TO BRING THIS DESK MUCH DELIGHT!
HA HA! NOW THE DESK IS HAVING UNDERPANTS ON THE TOP!
IT IS SO GOOD FOR HELLO DIRTY TO ENTERTAIN US ALL!
ENJOY A MOST WARM AND DIRTY WONDERFUL-NESS!

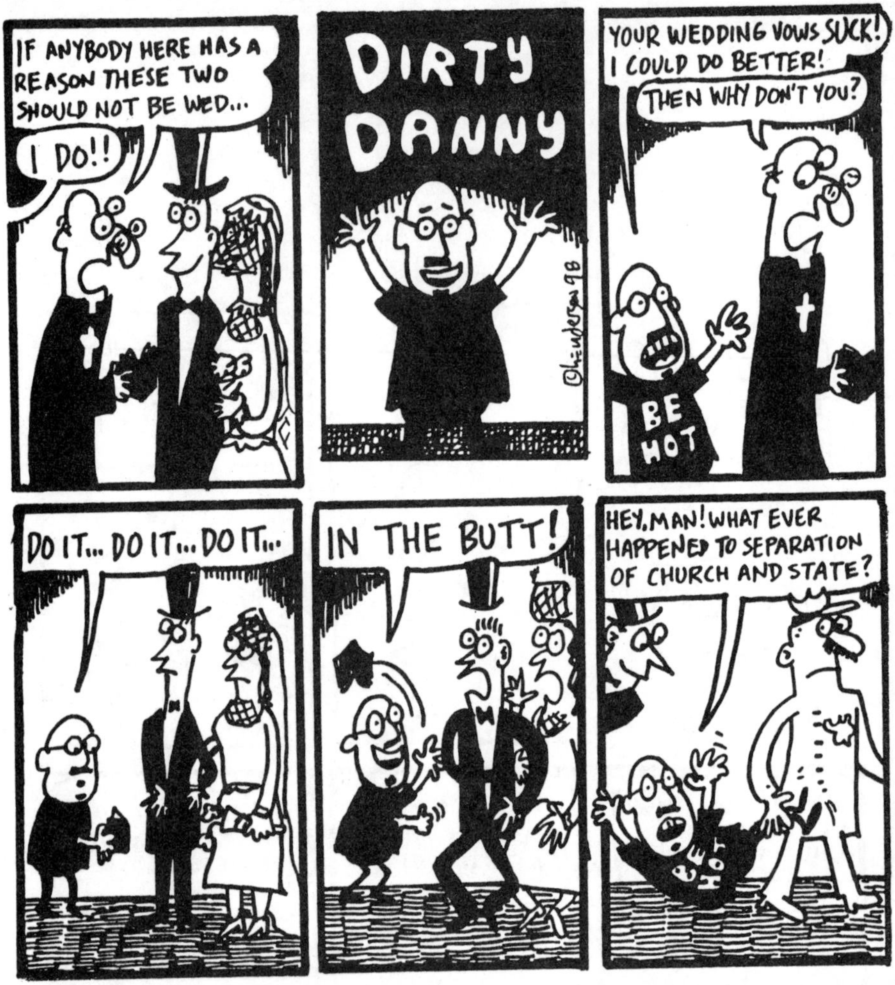
IF ANYBODY HERE HAS A REASON THESE TWO SHOULD NOT BE WED...
I DO!!
DIRTY DANNY
YOUR WEDDING VOWS SUCK! I COULD DO BETTER!
THEN WHY DON'T YOU?
BE HOT
DO IT... DO IT... DO IT...
IN THE BUTT!
HEY, MAN! WHAT EVER HAPPENED TO SEPARATION OF CHURCH AND STATE?

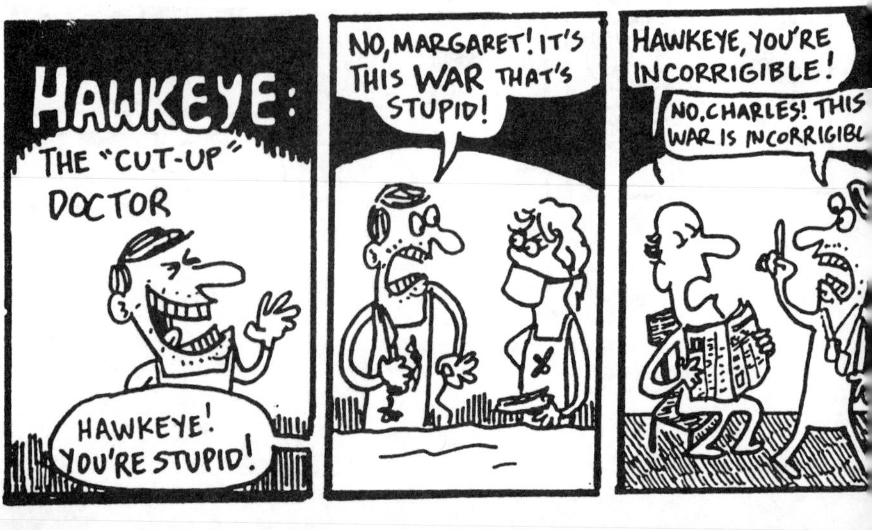
HAWKEYE:
THE "CUT-UP" DOCTOR
HAWKEYE! YOU'RE STUPID!
NO, MARGARET! IT'S THIS WAR THAT'S STUPID!
HAWKEYE, YOU'RE INCORRIGIBLE!
NO, CHARLES! THIS WAR IS INCORRIGIBL

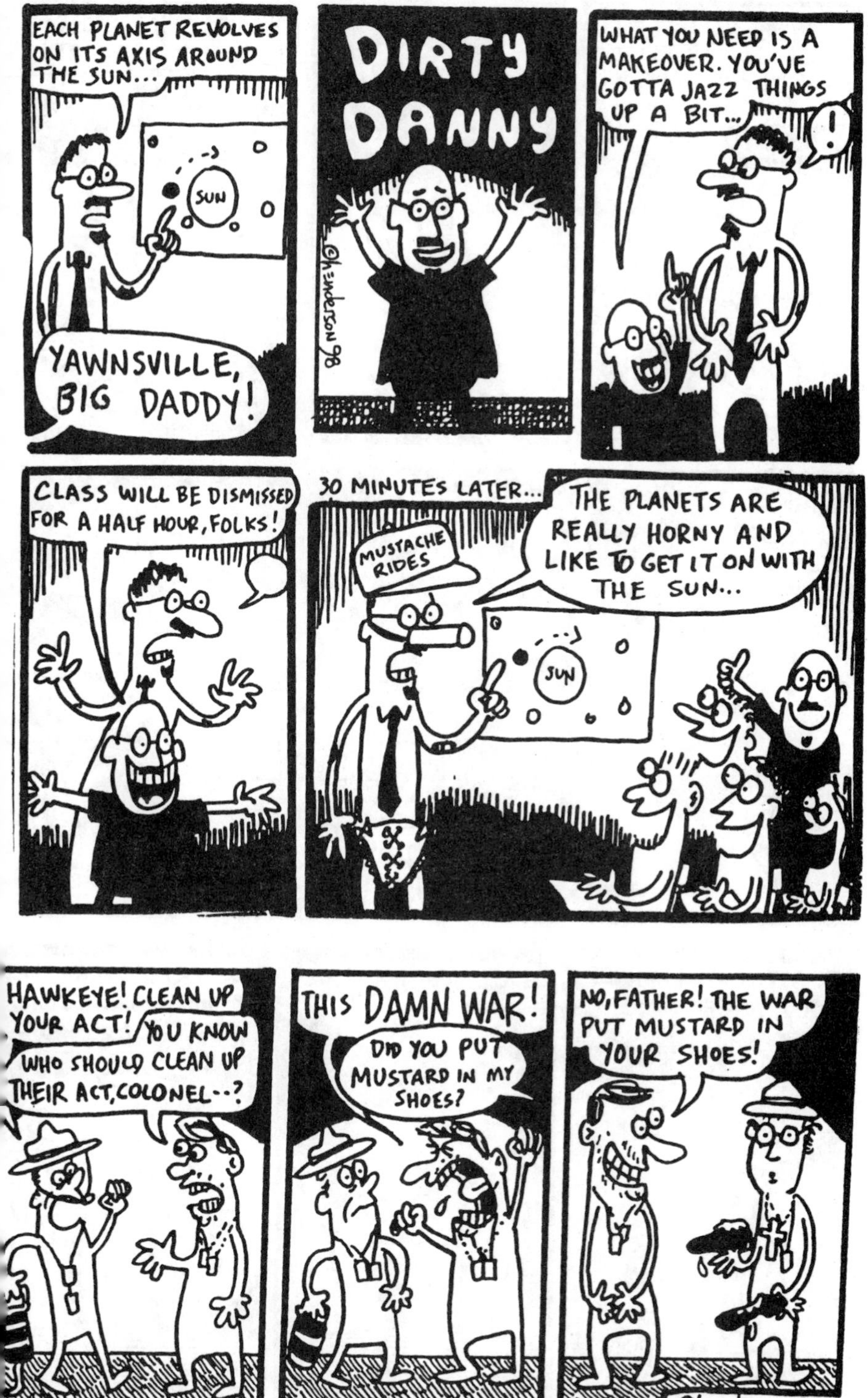
EACH PLANET REVOLVES ON ITS AXIS AROUND THE SUN...
SUN
YAWNSVILLE, BIG DADDY!
DIRTY DANNY
©henderson98
WHAT YOU NEED IS A MAKEOVER. YOU'VE GOTTA JAZZ THINGS UP A BIT...
!
CLASS WILL BE DISMISSED FOR A HALF HOUR, FOLKS!
30 MINUTES LATER...
MUSTACHE RIDES
THE PLANETS ARE REALLY HORNY AND LIKE TO GET IT ON WITH THE SUN...
SUN
HAWKEYE! CLEAN UP YOUR ACT!
YOU KNOW WHO SHOULD CLEAN UP THEIR ACT, COLONEL--?
THIS DAMN WAR!
DID YOU PUT MUSTARD IN MY SHOES?
NO, FATHER! THE WAR PUT MUSTARD IN YOUR SHOES!
©henderson98

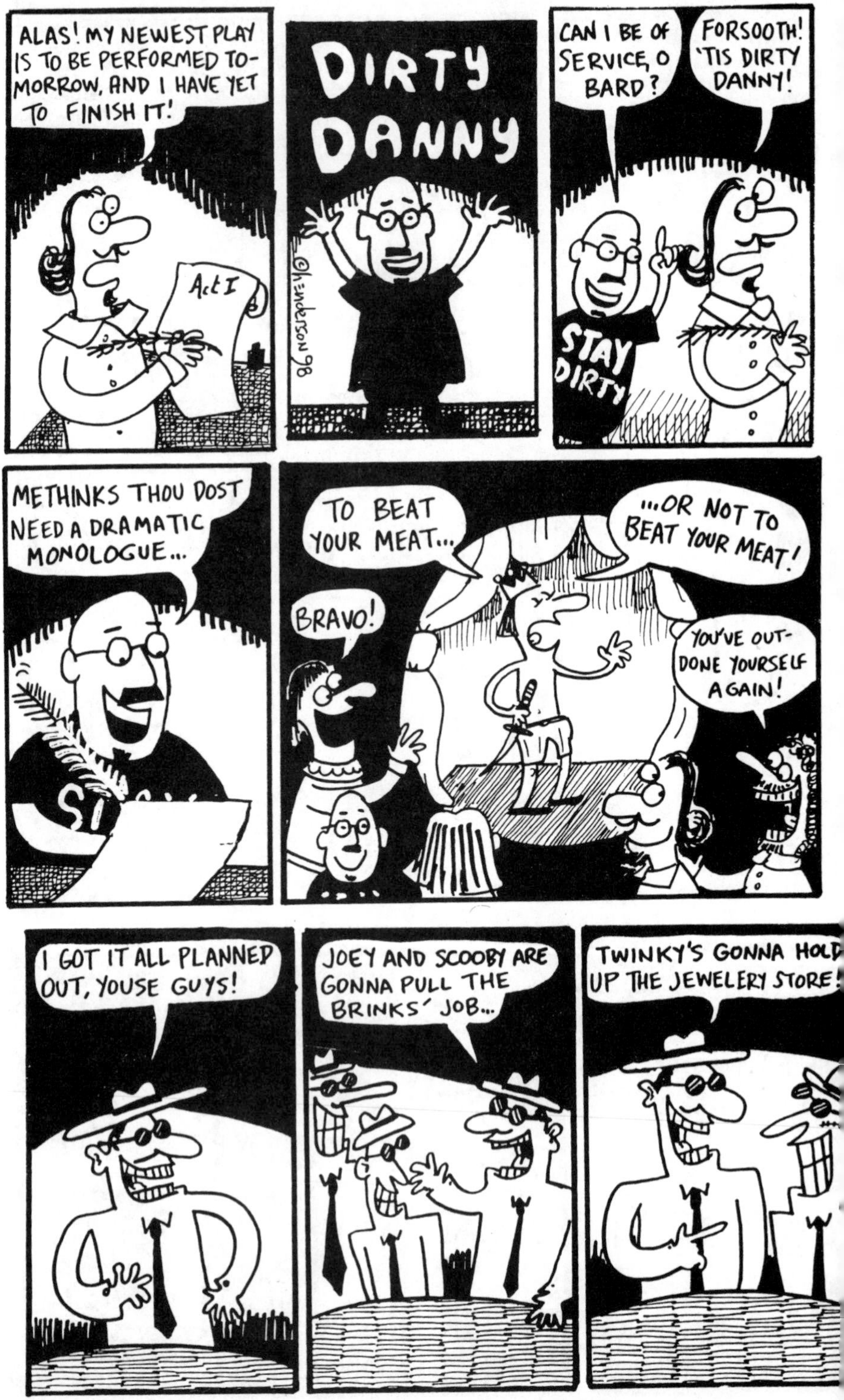

ALAS! MY NEWEST PLAY IS TO BE PERFORMED TO-MORROW, AND I HAVE YET TO FINISH IT!
Act I
DIRTY DANNY
©henderson 98
CAN I BE OF SERVICE, O BARD?
FORSOOTH! 'TIS DIRTY DANNY!
STAY DIRTY
METHINKS THOU DOST NEED A DRAMATIC MONOLOGUE...
TO BEAT YOUR MEAT...
...OR NOT TO BEAT YOUR MEAT!
BRAVO!
YOU'VE OUT-DONE YOURSELF AGAIN!
I GOT IT ALL PLANNED OUT, YOUSE GUYS!
JOEY AND SCOOBY ARE GONNA PULL THE BRINKS' JOB...
TWINKY'S GONNA HOLD UP THE JEWELERY STORE!

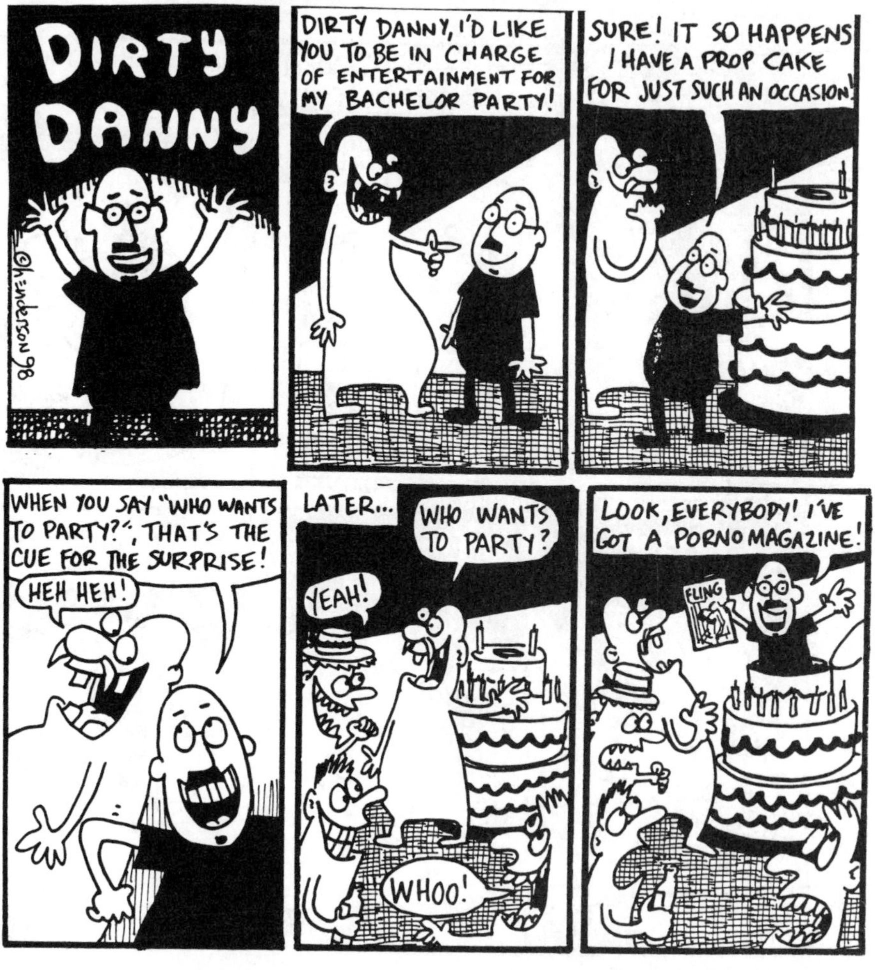
DIRTY DANNY
©henderson 98
DIRTY DANNY, I'D LIKE YOU TO BE IN CHARGE OF ENTERTAINMENT FOR MY BACHELOR PARTY!
SURE! IT SO HAPPENS I HAVE A PROP CAKE FOR JUST SUCH AN OCCASION!
WHEN YOU SAY "WHO WANTS TO PARTY?", THAT'S THE CUE FOR THE SURPRISE!
HEH HEH!
LATER...
WHO WANTS TO PARTY?
YEAH!
WHOO!
LOOK, EVERYBODY! I'VE GOT A PORNO MAGAZINE!
FLING

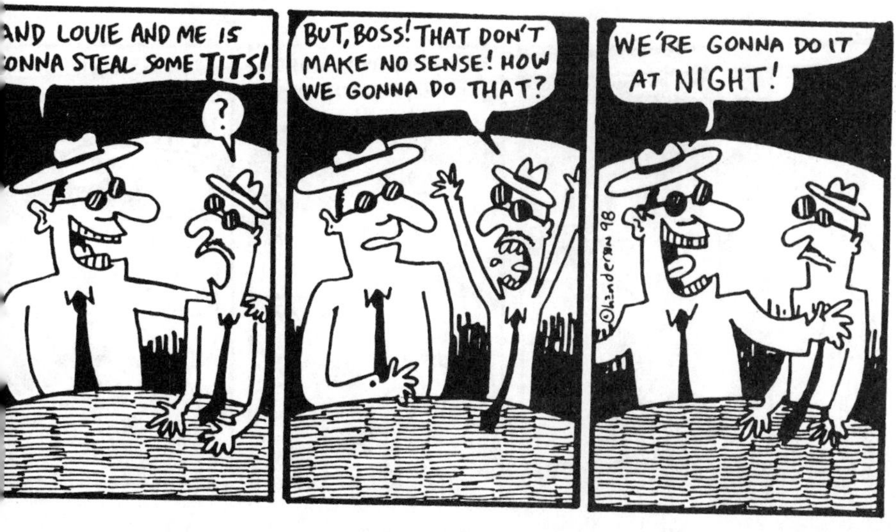
AND LOUIE AND ME IS GONNA STEAL SOME TITS!
?
BUT, BOSS! THAT DON'T MAKE NO SENSE! HOW WE GONNA DO THAT?
WE'RE GONNA DO IT AT NIGHT!
©henderson 98

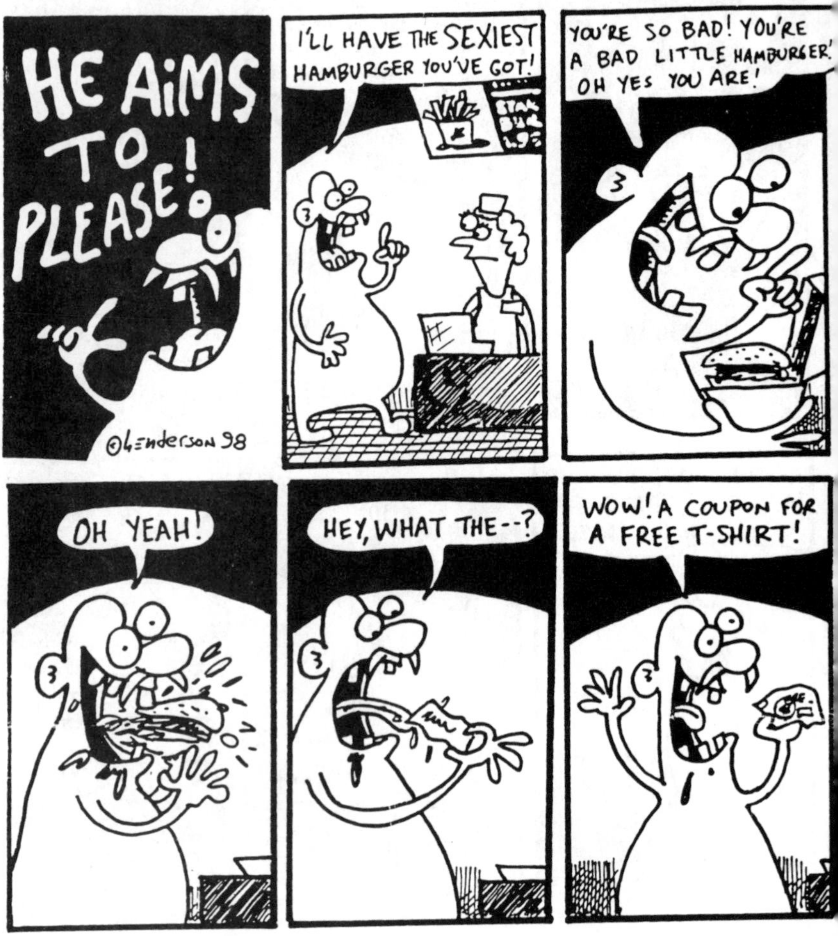
HE AiMS TO PLEASE!
©Henderson 98
I'LL HAVE THE SEXIEST HAMBURGER YOU'VE GOT!
YOU'RE SO BAD! YOU'RE A BAD LITTLE HAMBURGER! OH YES YOU ARE!
OH YEAH!
HEY, WHAT THE--?
WOW! A COUPON FOR A FREE T-SHIRT!

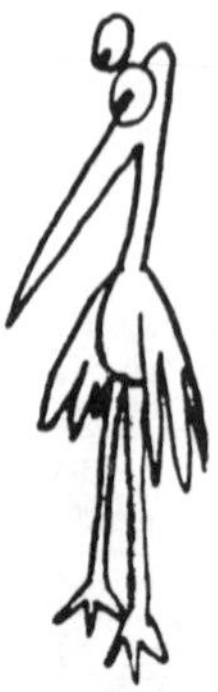

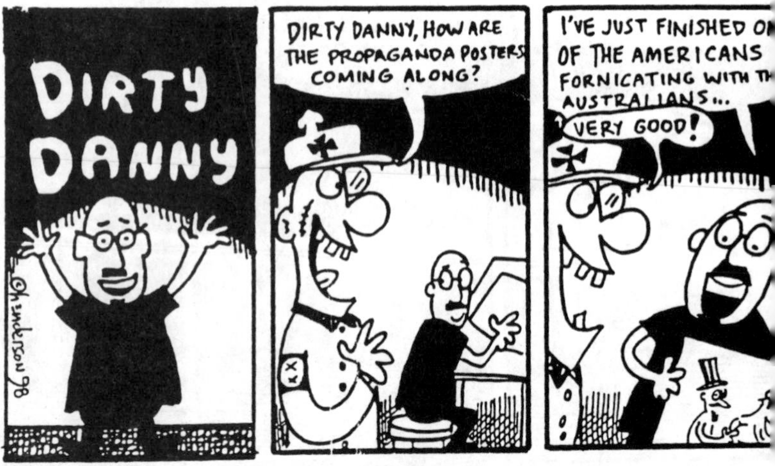
DIRTY DANNY
©Henderson 98
DIRTY DANNY, HOW ARE THE PROPAGANDA POSTERS COMING ALONG?
I'VE JUST FINISHED O
OF THE AMERICANS
FORNICATING WITH TH
AUSTRALIANS...
VERY GOOD!

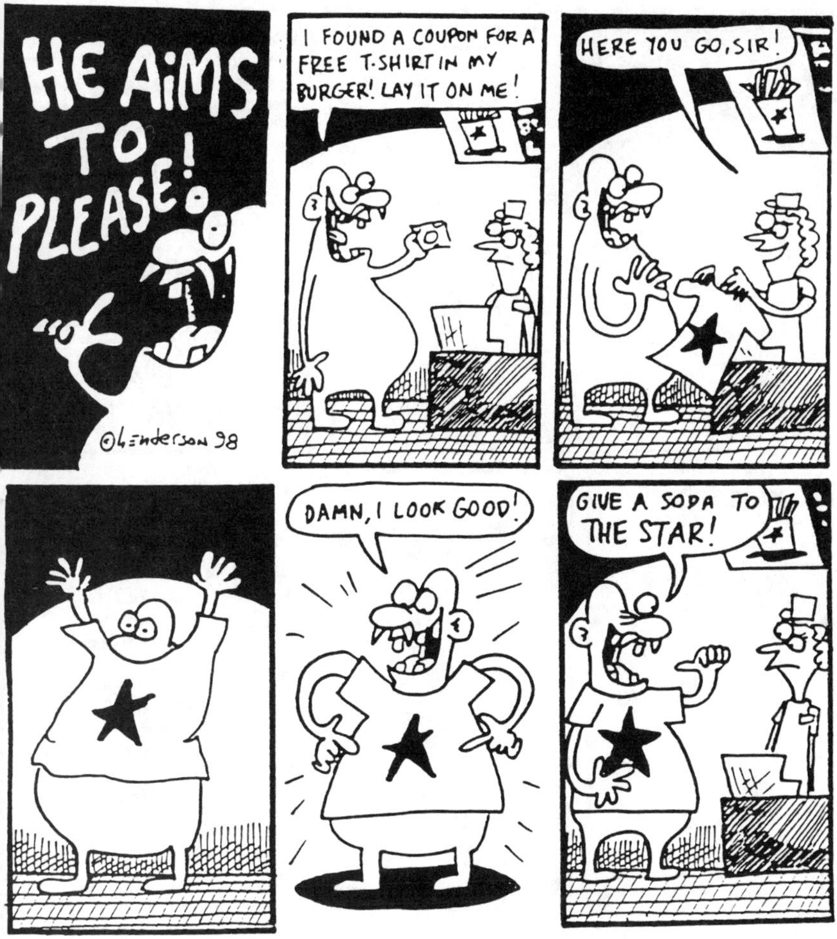
HE AiMS TO PLEASE!
©Henderson 98
I FOUND A COUPON FOR A FREE T-SHIRT IN MY BURGER! LAY IT ON ME!
HERE YOU GO, SIR!
DAMN, I LOOK GOOD!
GIVE A SODA TO THE STAR!

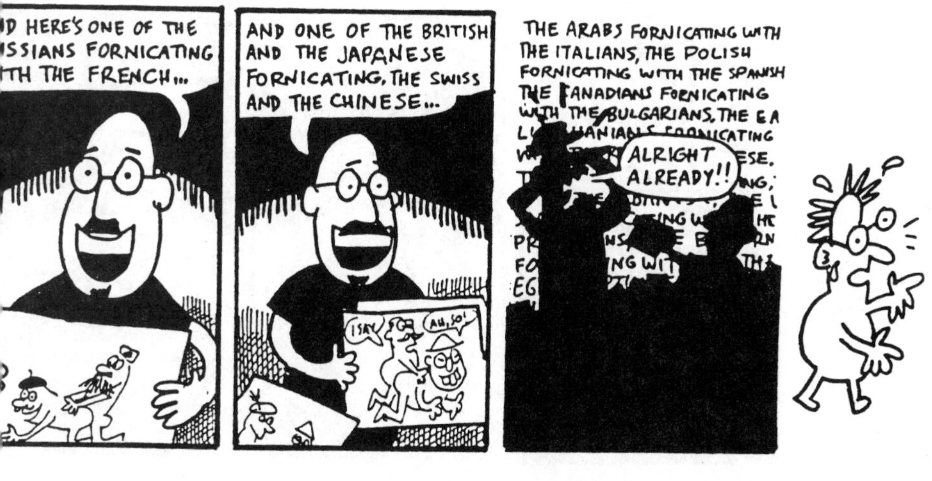
D HERE'S ONE OF THE SSIANS FORNICATING TH THE FRENCH...
AND ONE OF THE BRITISH AND THE JAPANESE FORNICATING, THE SWISS AND THE CHINESE...
I SAY
AH, SO!
THE ARABS FORNICATING WITH THE ITALIANS, THE POLISH FORNICATING WITH THE SPANISH THE CANADIANS FORNICATING WITH THE BULGARIANS, THE EA
ALRIGHT ALREADY!!

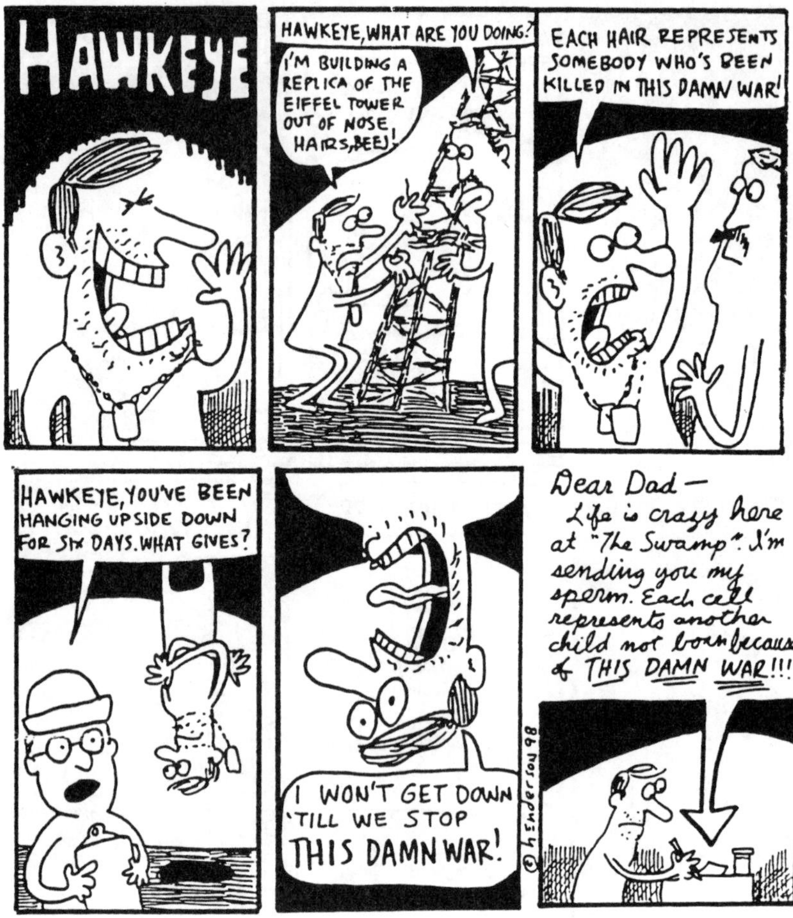
HAWKEYE
HAWKEYE, WHAT ARE YOU DOING?
I'M BUILDING A REPLICA OF THE EIFFEL TOWER OUT OF NOSE HAIRS, BEEJ!
EACH HAIR REPRESENTS SOMEBODY WHO'S BEEN KILLED IN THIS DAMN WAR!
HAWKEYE, YOU'VE BEEN HANGING UPSIDE DOWN FOR SIX DAYS. WHAT GIVES?
I WON'T GET DOWN 'TILL WE STOP THIS DAMN WAR!
© henderson 98
Dear Dad—
Life is crazy here at "The Swamp". I'm sending you my sperm. Each cell represents another child not born because of THIS DAMN WAR!!!

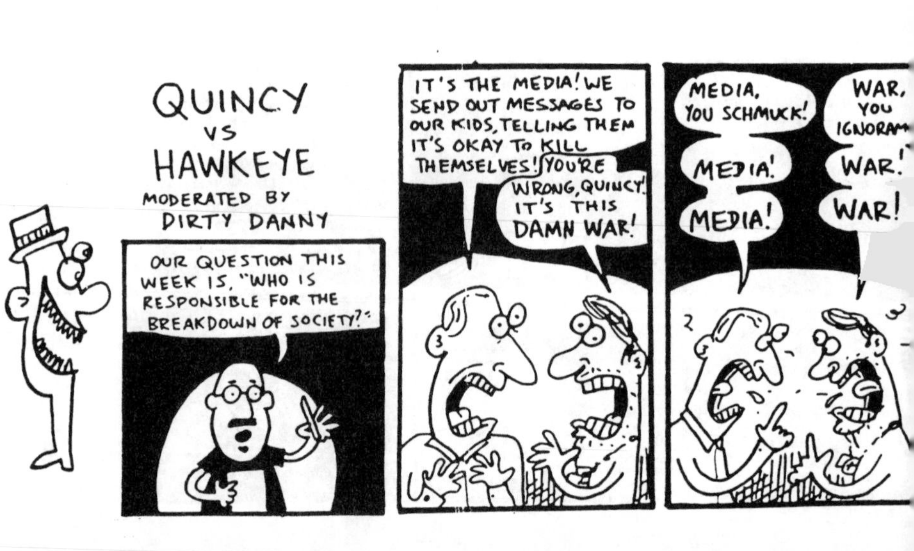
QUINCY VS HAWKEYE
MODERATED BY DIRTY DANNY
OUR QUESTION THIS WEEK IS, "WHO IS RESPONSIBLE FOR THE BREAKDOWN OF SOCIETY?"
IT'S THE MEDIA! WE SEND OUT MESSAGES TO OUR KIDS, TELLING THEM IT'S OKAY TO KILL THEMSELVES!
YOU'RE WRONG, QUINCY! IT'S THIS DAMN WAR!
MEDIA, YOU SCHMUCK!
WAR, YOU
MEDIA!
WAR!
MEDIA!
WAR!

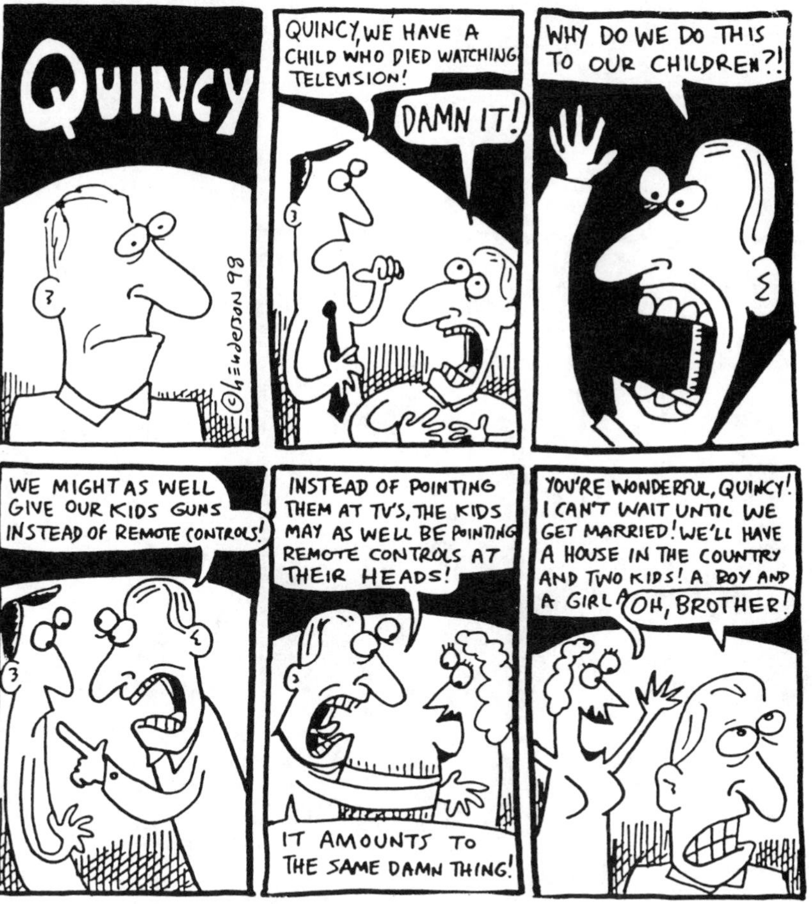
QUINCY
©henderson 98
QUINCY, WE HAVE A CHILD WHO DIED WATCHING TELEVISION!
DAMN IT!
WHY DO WE DO THIS TO OUR CHILDREN?!
WE MIGHT AS WELL GIVE OUR KIDS GUNS INSTEAD OF REMOTE CONTROLS!
INSTEAD OF POINTING THEM AT TV'S, THE KIDS MAY AS WELL BE POINTING REMOTE CONTROLS AT THEIR HEADS!
IT AMOUNTS TO THE SAME DAMN THING!
YOU'RE WONDERFUL, QUINCY! I CAN'T WAIT UNTIL WE GET MARRIED! WE'LL HAVE A HOUSE IN THE COUNTRY AND TWO KIDS! A BOY AND A GIRL
OH, BROTHER!

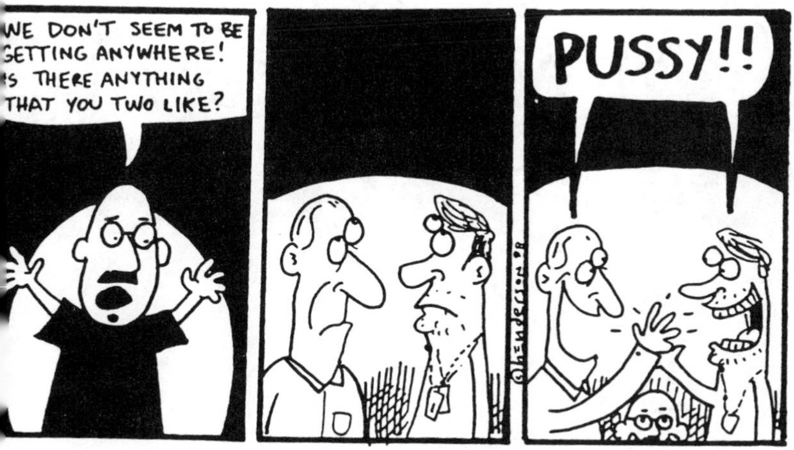
WE DON'T SEEM TO BE GETTING ANYWHERE! IS THERE ANYTHING THAT YOU TWO LIKE?
©henderson 98
PUSSY!!

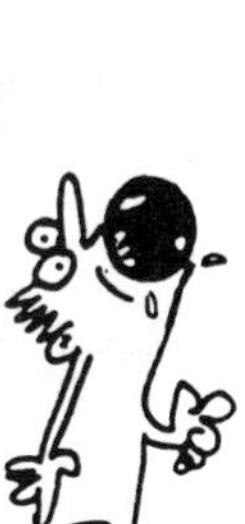

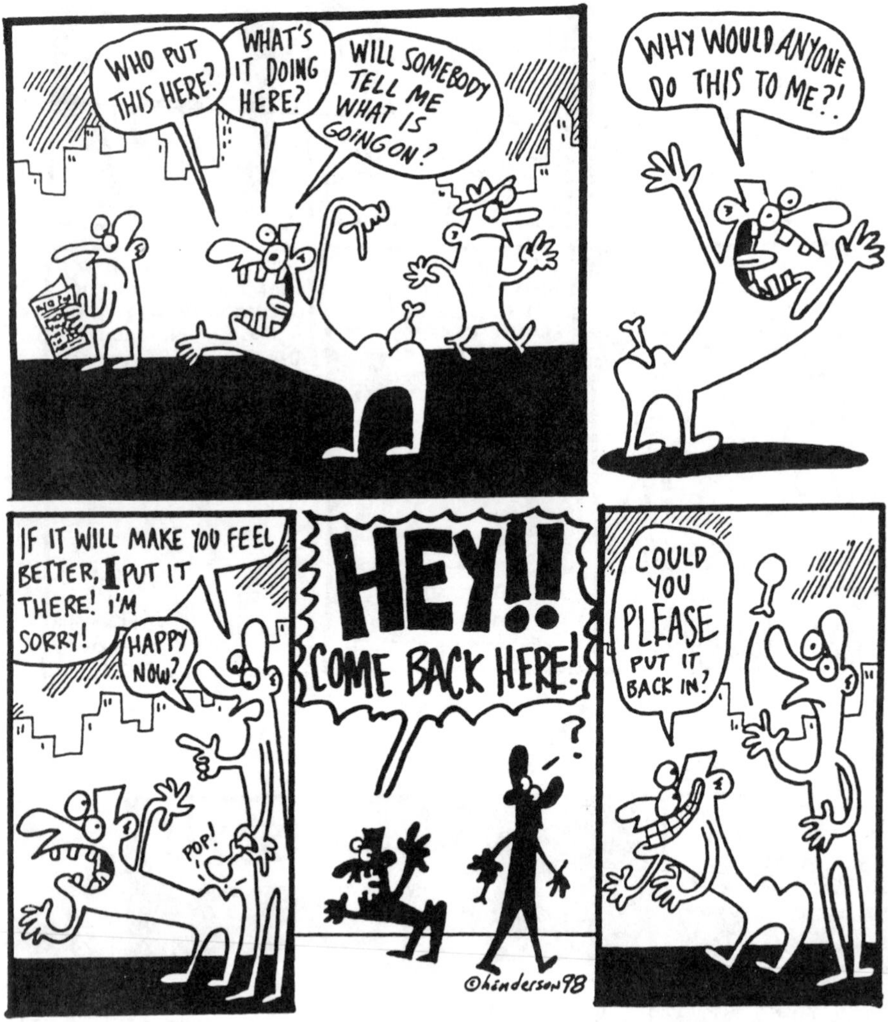
WHO PUT THIS HERE?
WHAT'S IT DOING HERE?
WILL SOMEBODY TELL ME WHAT IS GOINGON?
WHY WOULD ANYONE DO THIS TO ME?!
IF IT WILL MAKE YOU FEEL BETTER, I PUT IT THERE! I'M SORRY!
HAPPY NOW?
POP!
HEY!!
COME BACK HERE!
?
COULD YOU PLEASE PUT IT BACK IN?
©henderson98